24. —

Titles available from boyd & fraser

BASIC Programming

Applesoft BASIC Fundamentals and Style
BASIC Fundamentals and Style
Complete BASIC for the Short Course
Structured BASIC Fundamentals and Style for the IBM® PC and Compatibles
Structured Microsoft BASIC: Essentials for Business
Structuring Programs in Microsoft BASIC

COBOL Programming

Advanced Structured COBOL: Batch and Interactive
COBOL: Structured Programming Techniques for Solving Problems
Comprehensive Structured COBOL
Fundamentals of Structured COBOL

Database

A Guide to SQL
Database Systems: Management and Design

Computer Information Systems

Applications Software Programming with Fourth-Generation Languages
Business Data Communications and Networks
Expert Systems for Business: Concepts and Applications
Fundamentals of Systems Analysis with Application Design
Investment Management: Decision Support and Expert Systems
Learning Computer Programming: Structured Logic Algorithms, and Flowcharting
Office Automation: An Information Systems Approach

Microcomputer Applications

An Introduction to Desktop Publishing
dBASE III PLUS® Programming
DOS: Complete and Simplified
Introduction to Computers and Microcomputer Applications
Macintosh Productivity Tools
Mastering and Using Lotus 1-2-3®, Release 3
Mastering and Using Lotus 1-2-3®, Version 2.2
Mastering and Using WordPerfect® 5.0 and 5.1
Mastering Lotus 1-2-3®
Microcomputer Applications: A Practical Approach
Microcomputer Applications: Using Small Systems Software, Second Edition
Microcomputer Database Management Using dBASE III PLUS®
Microcomputer Database Management Using dBASE IV®
Microcomputer Database Management Using R:BASE System V®
Microcomputer Productivity Tools
Microcomputer Systems Management and Applications
PC-DOS®/MS-DOS® Simplified, Second Edition
Using Enable®: An Introduction to Integrated Software

Shelly and Cashman Titles

Computer Concepts with Microcomputer Applications (Lotus 1-2-3® and VP-Planner Plus® versions)
Computer Concepts
Essential Computer Concepts
Learning to Use WordPerfect®, Lotus 1-2-3®, and dBASE III PLUS®
Learning to Use WordPerfect®, VP-Planner Plus®, and dBASE III PLUS®
Learning to Use WordPerfect®
Learning to Use Lotus 1-2-3®
Learning to Use VP-Planner Plus®
Learning to Use dBASE III PLUS®
Computer Fundamentals with Application Software
Learning to Use SuperCalc®3, dBASE III®, and WordStar® 3.3: An Introduction
Learning to Use SuperCalc®3: An Introduction
Learning to Use dBASE III®: An Introduction
Learning to Use WordStar® 3.3: An Introduction
BASIC Programming for the IBM Personal Computer
Structured COBOL: Pseudocode Edition
Structured COBOL: Flowchart Edition
RPG II, RPG III, & RPG/400

Order information on page vi.

An Introduction to Desktop Publishing

Kenneth S. Hulme

boyd & fraser publishing company

Credits:

Publisher: Tom Walker

Editor: Pat Donegan

Director of Manufacturing: Dean Sherman

Cover Design: Becky L. Herrington

Cover Graphics: Huntington & Black Typography

Colophon

This book was desktop published on a Macintosh SE computer using Microsoft Word versions 3.01 and 4.0 for the initial composition and ReadySetGo! version 4.5 to create the page layouts. Electronic artwork was accomplished with MacDraw version 1.9.5, MacDraw II version 1.0, and MacPaint versions 1.9 and 2.0.

The body copy is set in 10/12 Palatino, with varying sizes of Palatino Bold for heads. Chapter head quotations and illustration descriptions are set in 8 pt. Palatino Italic. Folios are in 12 pt. Palatino, and headers are in 10 pt. Palatino Bold type.

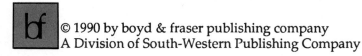 © 1990 by boyd & fraser publishing company
A Division of South-Western Publishing Company

Manufactured in the United States of America

Library of Congress Cataloging-in-Publication Data

```
Hulme, Kenneth S.
    An introduction to desktop publishing / by Kenneth S. Hulme.
        p.   cm.
    ISBN 0-87835-448-4
    1. Desktop publishing.   I. Title.
  Z286.D47H84   1990
  686.2'2544--dc20                                          89-22278
                                                               CIP
```

2 3 4 5 6 7 8 9 10 D 4 3 2 1 0

Dedication

To
Marjorie, who had the idea;
Bill, who got me into this;
Pat, who put up with me;
H. Bruce Linn, who made me a writer.

ORDER INFORMATION AND FACULTY SUPPORT INFORMATION

For the quickest service, refer to the map below for the South-Western Regional Office serving your area.

1 ORDER INFORMATION
5101 Madison Road
Cincinnati, OH 45227-1490
General Telephone–513-527-6945
Telephone: 1-800-543-8440
FAX: 513-527-6979
Telex: 214371

FACULTY SUPPORT INFORMATION
5101 Madison Road
Cincinnati, OH 45227-1490
General Telephone–513-527-6950
Telephone: 1-800-543-8444

Alabama	Massachusetts	Ohio
Connecticut	Michigan	Pennsylvania
Delaware	Minnesota	Rhode Island
Florida	Mississippi	South Carolina
Georgia	Missouri	South Dakota
Illinois	Nebraska	Tennessee
Indiana	New Hampshire	Vermont
Iowa	New Jersey	Virginia
Kentucky	New York	West Virginia
Maine	North Dakota	Wisconsin
Maryland	North Carolina	District of Columbia

2 ORDER INFORMATION
13800 Senlac Drive
Suite 100
Dallas, TX 75234
General Telephone–214-241-8541
Telephone: 1-800-543-7972

FACULTY SUPPORT INFORMATION
5101 Madison Road
Cincinnati, OH 45227-1490
General Telephone–513-527-6950
Telephone: 1-800-543-8444

Arkansas	Louisiana	Texas
Colorado	New Mexico	Wyoming
Kansas	Oklahoma	

3 ORDER INFORMATION and FACULTY SUPPORT INFORMATION
6185 Industrial Way
Livermore, CA 94550
General Telephone–415-449-2280
Telephone: 1-800-543-7972

Alaska	Idaho	Oregon
Arizona	Montana	Utah
California	Nevada	Washington
Hawaii		

Table Of Contents

Preface

Although desktop publishing is a relatively new concept, it is already in widespread use in business and industry. There are numerous "how-to" books that provide instruction on the use of various desktop publishing software packages, but few books contain the information necessary to take full advantage of the capabilities of desktop publishing. This text provides students with a comprehensive introduction to the field, but also includes thorough coverage of the principles of page layout and design. *An Introduction to Desktop Publishing* is the first textbook to provide users with this vital knowledge.

Special Features

A Comprehensive Introduction to Desktop Publishing

Rather than a "how-to" presentation featuring one software package or one machine, *An Introduction to Desktop Publishing* provides users with a solid base from which they can build their desktop publishing knowledge relative to their own needs. The text focuses on principles of layout and design rather than on the use of specific software packages or machines. Concepts presented in the text can be applied to *any* desktop publishing system.

Flexible and Readable

The text is suited to a variety of teaching environments, course lengths, and teaching techniques. It is useful for college courses, training classes, individual learning, and as a reference manual. The presentation of material makes it suitable for both lecture and classroom discussion. It can also be used in a laboratory environment where students can practice concepts as they learn them. The author's informal style enhances both readability and comprehension.

An Ideal Resource

An Introduction to Desktop Publishing is an ideal primary or supplemental text for any course on desktop publishing.

It presents the information users need to know in one volume rather than the many, many volumes the author had to wade through to compile the material.

Review Questions

Each chapter has a number of review questions that reinforce learning of the material presented in the chapters. These questions can be used to stimulate classroom discussion or as student assignments.

Exercises

End-of-chapter exercises present the student with real world situations, requiring them to apply the knowledge they have gained. These integrated exercises take students from simple text and graphic creation in early chapters to integrating these elements into complex publication designs in later chapters. For example, in Chapter 2, students write an article. In Chapter 3 they illustrate it. In Chapters 5, 6, 7, and 8, students use the same text and graphics to design a brochure, magazine, book, and newsletter.

Instructor's Manual

A comprehensive instructor's manual is available free of charge to adopters of *An Introduction to Desktop Publishing*. It includes lecture outlines, teaching tips, and additional exercises. It is available from boyd & fraser through South-Western Publishing Company. See page vi for ordering information.

Organization of the Textbook

The text begins with a historical look at technological developments in both the printing and computer fields. Three core chapters discuss key facets of desktop publishing: typography, graphics, and techniques for combining them on the printed page. The remaining chapters detail the principles of publication design and layout for the major categories of publishing projects: small publications, magazines, books, and newsletters and newspapers. Four appendices present both technical specifications and discussion of state-of-the-art hardware, software, printers, and peripherals for desktop publishing.

Acknowledgements

I would like to thank several individuals for their contributions to the preparation of this book.

Thanks to Dill Salmon for hours of campfire and office bull sessions and for being an example. Thanks too, to Ed Sharp and the staff of the University of Utah Computer Center, without whom I wouldn't have been in a position to write this book, and with whom I've shared many pleasant years.

And, to all my friends and loved ones, thanks for the support you've given me in this project and through the years.

I greatly appreciate the efforts of the following individuals who reviewed the textbook and made many helpful suggestions: Gary Gehman, Temple University; Walter Norris, Rappahannock Community College; Jeff Trevas, Chaparral Career College; and Jean Vining, Houston Community College.

Special thanks to Arthur Weisbach for the fantastic editing job he did on the final manuscript. This text wouldn't be what it is without his help.

The efforts of the following members of the boyd and fraser staff have been invaluable: Tom Walker, vice president and publisher; Pat Donegan, editor; and Becky Herrington, Mike Broussard, and Ken Russo, photography.

Ken Hulme
December 1989

Graphics Credits

The following companies and individuals provided photographs and computer art for use in this textbook and we thank them:

Figure 1.12, IBM Corporation; Figure 1.14, IBM Corporation; Figure 3.5, Shauna Buchanan; Figure 5.2, Michael P. George; Figure B.1, Apple Computer, Inc.; Figure B.2, Apple Computer, Inc.; Figure B.3, Apple Computer, Inc.; Figure B.4, Apple Computer, Inc.; Figure B.5, Apple Computer, Inc.; Figure B.6, Apple Computer, Inc.; Figure B.7, IBM Corporation; Figure B.8, IBM Corporation; Figure B.9, IBM Corporation; Figure B.10, IBM Corporation; Figure C.2, Apple Computer, Inc.; Figure C.3, Apple Computer, Inc.; Figure C.4, Apple Computer, Inc.; Figure C.5, Apple Computer, Inc.; Figure C.6, Hewlett-Packard; Figure D.1, Apple Computer, Inc.; Figure D.2, ThunderWare; Figure D.3, Apple Computer, Inc.; Figure D.4, Apple Computer, Inc.; and Figure D.5, IBM Corporation.

Chapter 1: In the Beginning...

The advent of printing...was one of the crucial events in the history of mankind.
Printing first and foremost made it easy to transmit information without personal
contact, and in this sense it revolutionized the spread of knowledge, and craft tech-
nique in particular.

– *James Burke*, Connections

Since the evolution of the printing press in Europe, its
possession and use have been subject to great con-
troversy, fines and taxes, and other governmental
constraints, praised as the voice and spokesman of
the people, and condemned as the instigator of rebellions.
In the First Amendment to the Constitution of the United
States, the rights of the press are encapsuled with the rights
of other major influences on mankind – religion, free speech,
and peaceable assembly. America was first of the modern
nations to guarantee a free press, a right which is still not
found in many countries, and taken somewhat for granted
by those living in free press nations.

Why all the furor over printing? Knowledge is power.
Those in the know can and have controlled those who don't
know, simply by misinformation or no information at all.
By looking at the history of printing, we will see not only
how what we have today came about, but also some of the
effects printing has had on the societies of the world.

It all started with rags and bark. The earliest reference we
have to papermaking comes from court records of ancient
China. In the year 105 AD by the Christian calendar, a government official called Ts'ai Lun officially reported to the
Emperor of the time the invention of paper. Ts'ai Lun gets
the credit for inventing paper, but chances are he had very
little to do with the actual invention. Paper was undoubtedly the evolutionary product of a number of people, perhaps
over generations. Ts'ai Lun may have wanted credit for
bringing a local product to the attention of the Emperor, or
may have in fact been reporting a new process for making it.

From two thousand years away and translations from a foreign language, it is difficult to tell. At any rate, the materials he reports using are tree bark, hemp stalks, rags, and old fishnets. These and similar materials are still used in papermaking today.

The basic techniques of papermaking are very simple. Organic vegetable materials such as leaves, bark, and stalks are soaked and beaten to a very fine pulp, so that they break down into their natural fibers. The fiber pulp may or may not have chemicals (natural or artificial) added to improve the color and other attributes of the finished product. The resultant fiber soup is spread in a thin layer over a porous surface and the majority of the water drained off. The damp sheet is then removed from the mold by "couching" or pressing it onto a layer of felt, so that a new sheet of paper could be dipped up from the vat. The couched sheets are stacked, pressed, and hung to dry. They are then "sized" by dipping them into a solution of starch or animal glue, to make them less absorbent, and again pressed and dried.

Fig. 1.1 An old Japanese print showing a papermaker at work dipping up a new sheet of paper.

Since the processes of making paper and making felt cloth are so similar (the only real difference is that felt is made from animal fur fibers while paper is vegetable fiber) that there is a great possibility that papermaking evolved from feltmaking, a much older process.

At first, cloth was used as the porous surface of the wood-framed mold which dipped up the pulp. Then later, thin strips of split bamboo were arranged in a grid to retain the pulp and let the water drain off. Later still, various kinds and shapes of wire were employed for the mold. These strips or wires left a barely discernable pattern in the structure of the paper, called a watermark. As technology got better, additional wires were added to the screen to form patterns that acted as a manufacturer's or personal logo.

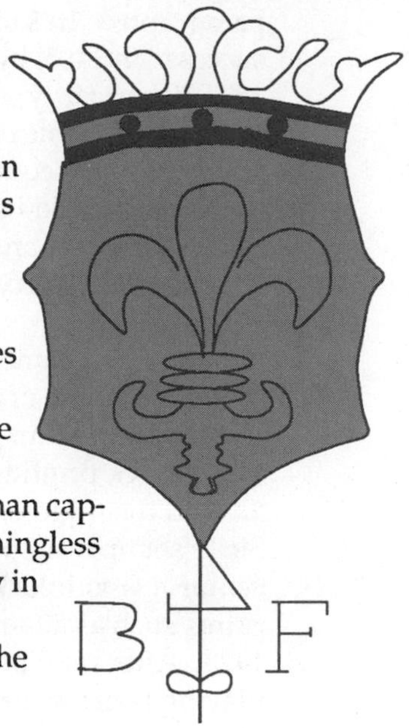

The year 114 AD is the first notable year in the European connection to printing. This is the accepted date for the inscription at the base of Trajan's Column in Rome. This lettering is not only the finest extant example of Roman lettering, but continues to be a source of inspiration to type designers today. The prolific American type designer Frederic W. Goudy said about Roman lettering, "The great merit of Roman capitals is simplicity; every useless and meaningless line has been eliminated. The letters vary in shape and proportion; to bring out their beauty requires a nice discrimination in the spacing and combining of their irregular forms."

Fig. 1.2 A computer sketch of Ben Franklin's personal watermark.

The very first books were undoubtedly hand written, but the earliest known printed book is the Chinese *Diamond Sutra*, a scroll book bearing the inscription which translates as "printed on the 11th of May 868, by Wang Chieh." The book was found in 1907. It is sixteen feet long, made of seven sheets of paper pasted together, and was printed with carved wooden blocks. The quality of printing is so good that it seems obvious that the technique was not a new one, but so far, no earlier printed books have been found. Wood block book printing did spread beyond China, though; there exists a book of Korean manufacture dated 1361.

Sometime between 1040 and 1048, printing from moveable type was invented in China. The "official inventor" is Pi Sheng, of the Northern Sung Dynasty, who made the types from hard baked clay. Like Ts'ai Lun, however, Pi Sheng may not be the actual inventor. Although moveable type was invented over a thousand years ago, it never really caught on in China due to the additive pictographic nature of the Chinese written language. Rather than sounds, Chinese ideograms represent words, concepts, sometimes whole paragraphs. In Korea, however, moveable type had better success. In 1403, by the command of the king, a set of 100,000 copper types were cast; they were used for many books over the next 140 years. Had printing caught on in China, the subsequent history of printing (and other things) in Europe would have been radically different. Imagine if Marco Polo had brought back a printing press and set up shop in mid-14th century Venice!

Papermaking came to Europe, probably via the Moors, around the time of the Norman Conquest. In 1085, there was a papermill in Játiva, Spain, making linen rag paper. Woodblock printing technology appeared in Palermo, Italy around the middle of the twelfth century, when Roger of Sicily set up a shop for printing on fabric. By the fourteenth century, woodblocks were being used to make devotional prints such as a famous illustration of St. Christopher dated 1423. After religion, printing turned to recreation. Card playing became popular in the late fourteenth century, and playing cards were mass produced from woodblock masters.

When paper arrived in Europe, it was looked upon as a cheap imitation of the *real* writing material, parchment, and its high quality cousin, vellum. Both materials were made from the skins of animals, vellum being made from the skins of newborn calves, kids, or lambs. For centuries, parchment and vellum were the writing materials of choice. In the second century B.C., the Greek city of Pergamum, in what is now Turkey, became the most famous site for the laborious and time-consuming preparation of these skins, and from the word *pergamena* we derive "parchment." It took over two hundred years for paper to become popular in Europe. Some rulers disliked this newfangled imitation so much that they declared that all official documents had to be inscribed on parchment. This prejudice toward writing official documents on animal skins still exists today, although it is seldom practiced. Why else would your college diploma be called a "sheepskin"? Papermakers weren't slow in adopting the terms "parchment" and "vellum" for their finest grades of papers, and they worked hard to create pulp mixtures that, when dried, would have similar inking qualities, texture, and feel similar to the real thing.

By the early to mid fifteenth century, European society was changing drastically. To boil a lot of social upheaval, wars, and strife down into a few words, feudalism was, for all intents and purposes, dead. A new social order was taking over – the bourgeoisie or middle class: merchants, tradesmen, and the like. They had a lot of money and were willing to spend it on objects such as art, architecture, and their new playtoy, education. More people were starting to read. There were lots of records which needed keeping, and a wide variety of information which needed to be passed around in multiple identical copies, without scribes having to handwrite each copy laboriously. People also wanted (and needed) to send and receive news and information about their various goings on quickly and easily.

Once people found an inexpensive medium to write on, the problems of mass printed communications were still several-fold. First, there were vested interests trying to keep the status quo. Organized guilds of calligraphers and and illuminators brought great political pressure to bear to restrict the methods and materials of reproduction. Second, carving woodblocks for printing flyers, or more importantly, books like the Bible, took an enormous amount of time and skill, and thus were *very* expensive. Carved woodblocks also tended to wear down quickly, producing poorer and poorer prints as time went on.

Having a thirty- or fifty-page book printed might cost the fifteenth century equivalent of a house and automobile! So there was a need for a cheap method of creating the letters to print with. The stage was set for another world-shattering invention. The Law of Necessity was operating. This law says that when social and economic pressures combine to produce conditions whereby society will be benefitted by some technological solution to those social and economic problems, a solution, *of necessity*, will be found.

For over four thousand years, man had been able to write. The alphabets of Europe were suitable for moveable type. Paper, a suitably cheap printing medium, had been invented over five hundred years before, and had been available for several generations. The idea of putting letters in a reusable

form had been around for an equally long time. The social
and economic conditions were right. Enter...

Johann zum Gansfleisch

Born sometime around the turn of the fifteenth century (we
aren't sure when). He never cared for his last name (it
means "gooseflesh") so he decided to use the name of the
town where his mother was born – Gutenberg.

We really know very little about Johann, such as whether he
really invented moveable type and the printing press, or just
"improved" on some ideas he "borrowed" from a Dutchman
named Laurens Janszoons Coster, to whom he may or may
not have been apprenticed at one time. As Hendrik Willem
van Loon says in his *Observations on the Mystery of Print and
the Work of Johann Gutenberg*:

> "He was a crochety old fellow. There is no doubt about his
> ability. He must have been a first-rate craftsman, full of
> imagination and with a highly developed sense of the
> practical. But his fellow townsmen knew him best as an
> eternal litigant–a man to whom a contract meant a lawsuit
> and a partnership, a case in chancery [business court]."

Although we speak of the Gutenberg Bible, he didn't print it.
To get the project underway, he took out several loans, and
when they came due, he couldn't pay.   He sold his business
to his partners. They printed the Gutenberg Bible, also
called the 42-line Bible. Not one book exists with his name
on it as printer. He didn't "invent" the printing press, but he
did come up with modifications of existing mechanical
presses that a cabinetmaker named Konrad Saspoch built for
him.

Most of what we do know about Gutenberg comes from
court records and other legal documents. He was born
sometime around 1397, the son of a member of the gentry,
Friele zum Gensfleisch. Friele had been an official in the
bishop's mint in Mainz, and taught his son how to handle
soft metals. Guttenberg worked under the goldsmith Hans
Duenne, and apparently began experimenting with type as

early as 1436. In connection with a lawsuit, Duenne stated to a Strasburg court in 1439 that Gutenberg had been working for three years on a project having to do with printing. In 1438 a press was made to his specifications, and he was buying lead.

Regardless of the actual series of events, to most of us (except the Dutch), Johann Gutenberg is the "official inventor" of moveable type and the printing press. His most significant invention is the adjustable metal mold which holds the matrix from which individual letters are cast. Keeping this in mind, let's move on to a discussion of the type iteself.

Fig. 1.3 The steps involved in hand cutting type. First, a letter punch is carved out of a steel rod. Then, the letter punch is used to stamp the letter into a copper matrix. Finally, the matrix is inserted into the adjustable mold and the mold filled with molten metal. Removed from the mold, the pieces of type are trimmed and ready for use.

Handmade type is created as follows: First, the shapes of the letters and symbols are drawn and approved. The typecutter then takes a small square rod of steel and, using files, gravers and punches, carves the shape of a letter onto the tip of the rod. Characters must be cut so that they are raised mirror images of the final printed character. The process is then repeated for each character until the entire font has

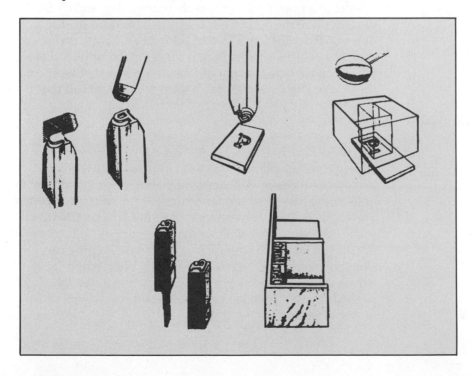

been made as a set of steel punches.

The steel letter punches are then used to stamp a depressed but correct left-to-right version of each character into small blocks of copper called **matrices**. A matrix is placed in one end of the two-part mold in which the actual type will be cast. The interior of the mold is carved to form the nick, feet, pin mark and groove which are used to help align the type when it it time to assemble letters for printing. By using individual matrices for each character, the typemaker needs only one mold to cast an entire font.

Molten type metal, a mixture of lead with a small amounts of antimony for hardening and tin for meltability, is then poured into the mold. When it cools, the piece of type is taken out of the mold and then trimmed, smoothed, and squared. The type has a raised mirror image of the letter so that, when printed, the letters read correctly on the paper.

Once the type is cast, words are assembled into lines of type, a letter at a time, on an adjustable "composing stick." Since the letters are mirror images, they are assembled upside down so that new letters can be added to the right end of the stick (the same way we add new letters to the right end of a line when we type something). Lines (or sticks) of type are then racked up in an adjustable form which holds all the type for printing one or more pages of text on a single piece of paper.

The press Konrad Saspoch built was a modification of the widely common platen press used in making olive oil, felt, and other products. A heavy iron platen is cranked down onto a base plate (bed) under controlled pressure. The bed is moveable to allow easy removal of printed pages. Clamped to the bed is the form, with the type face up. Atop the form is a hinged lid called a **tympan** which takes the pressure from the platen, and on which the paper is stretched. Pressure is applied by turning a lever attached to a steeply pitched screw. The steep pitch delivers the most pressure for the least effort.

Operation of the hand press went something like this: Use whole body to swing lever to raise the platen. Pull bed out from under platen; fasten form onto bed. Paint the form with just enough, but not too much, ink. Attach sheet of paper to tympan and lower into place just above the form. Slide bed under platen. Pull on lever with whole body to lower platen. Repeat as necessary. With luck, some muscles, and a couple of printer's devils (helpers) to keep the clean things clean and the inky parts inked, you could print fifteen or twenty pages per hour!

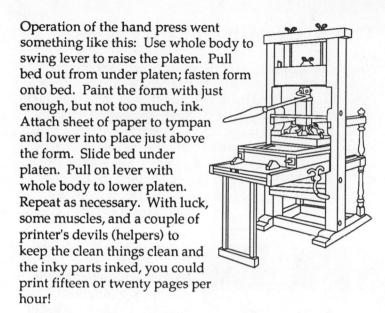

Figure 1.4. Guttenberg-style hand presses such as this one were used for large and small printing jobs for several hundred years.

Printing took Europe by storm. From about 1450 to 1470 there were fourteen European cities with printing presses. By 1480 there were a hundred. At the turn of the century there were nearly three hundred cities with active print shops. Moveable type was here to stay.

Another important printer, whose influence is still with us, also got his start in the late 15th century. Teobaldo Mannucci, a.k.a. Aldus Manütius, founded his Aldine Press in Venice in 1494. As his printer's mark or logo he used the dolphin and anchor, symbols of the popular motto "make haste slowly." Aldus invited prominent scholars (including Erasmus) and technicians to live and work with him. Francesco Griffo, an independent punch cutter, produced the first Italic type while working with Aldus. (In the twentieth century Aldus' name and likeness have been adopted by the software company producing one of the earliest desktop publishing programs – PageMaker.)

The Sixteenth Century

This period saw the rise of the great woodblock printmakers. Now that the problem of moveable type was out of the way, artisans concentrated on developing the woodcut to its highest level. This is the period of Dürer, Rembrandt, Holbein, Titian, Rubens, and many others. Although recognized as artists, many of these, such as Dürer, were also intimately involved in the development of printing, especially in the creation of letterforms or alphabets. Among the famous names in type design which come down to us today are

Fig. 1.5 An early wood block print showing a kite flyer.

Giovanbattista Palatino and Claude Garamond. These, among others, helped take type away from the chancery script style of lettering which attempted to duplicate handwriting, and into the use of the Roman or upright characters which most of us associate with printed text.

The Seventeenth Century

This century brings us a number of famous events and techniques in the history of printing. In the first quarter of the century, two of the most often printed books in the history of the English language made their first appearance: the First Folio of Shakespeare's plays, and the King James Version of the Bible. The King James Bible appeared in 1611, after seven years were spent by forty-seven translators to make the transition to English. A third major literary event was the publication in Madrid (in 1605) of *El Ingenioso Hildago Don Quixote de la Mancha*, by Miguel de Cervantes.

The seventeenth century also saw raised woodblock printing being replaced by relief-cut intaglio printing. Rather than using ink on the surface of raised lines, intaglio prints have

Fig. 1.6 A pleasant day for sailing. This intaglio print is from the late 19th century.

the design cut into the plate and the lines filled with ink. Among the intaglio methods are engraving, aquatint, and mezzotint. These techniques were most often performed on copper plates. Intaglio presses for printing illustrations used a pair of rollers to squeeze the copper plate and paper together and force the paper into the inked hollows. Before or after the illustrations were printed, the text portions of a page were printed using a Gutenberg platen press.

A major landmark in the history of printing was the production of the first newspaper by Johan Carolus of Strasbourg in 1609. The name of his newspaper was *Avis Relation oder Zeitung*.

With the rapid dissemination of information came censorship – governments not always (or even usually) wanting everyone to know what was going on where and how. Government agents closed down, often forcefully, those presses that did not print acceptable or approved news. The first American published newspaper, *Publick Occurrences Both Forreign and Domestick* , was published in September of 1690 in Boston by printer Benjamin Harris. Four days later, the colonial governor and the colony council declared that the newspaper had been published without authority and the paper died after its first issue.

The earliest North American printer was Stephen Day. In 1638, he set up his press in Cambridge, Massachusetts Colony. He and the Reverend Jesse Glover had intended to set up a partnership, but Glover died at sea during the trip to the colony. Day published the *Oath of A Free Man* in 1639 and the *Bay Psalm Book* in 1640. The press was purchased in 1649 by Samuel Green, and was operated until nearly the turn of the century. Green and Marmaduke Johnson printed the first Indian Bible in 1663, as translated by John Eliot.

The Eighteenth Century

This century saw the development of many typefaces which are still used by contemporary typesetters and designers. William Caslon, who started as a gun engraver, turned his hand to creating fonts in 1720. He produced not only the face now named after him, but also faces in Arabic, Hebrew, and Coptic, for The Society for Promoting Christian Knowledge.

John Baskerville started as a writing teacher, then turned to making lacquerware. In 1750 he became interested in printing and aspects of typography, and established a type foundry, printshop, and paper mill. Baskerville's uncomplicated Roman font still bears his name.

On the technical side, the seventeenth century saw the invention of of the French Point and Didot systems of measuring type size (see Chapter 3: Typography for more details), and the first all-iron press. Up to this time, type designers had been calling their type sizes by all sorts of names, and the new systems gave a more common system of measure. For over three hundred years the press had remained essentially the same as that made for Gutenberg by Konrad Saspoch–a mixture of metal plates, wood frame, and wooden screw. In 1799, Charles, Earl of Stanhope, designed the first all-metal press for use at the Boydell and Nicol Shakespeare Printing Office in London.

The Nineteenth Century

By the nineteenth century, it was time for some more technical revolutions. The cost of copper for copperplate intaglio illustrations was out of sight. A playwright-turned-publisher named Senefelder began experimenting with stone as an engraving medium. At first he tried acid etching of the stone to raise or lower the portions to be printed. Then he discovered that he didn't need to have the picture either raised or lowered! Lithography (stone drawing) uses a

greasy crayon or pencil to create the picture on a smooth
stone surface. A greasy picture surrounded by damp stone
attracts and holds special greasy inks that the stone won't accept. If you pass paper over the stone in a scraping and
pressing motion, the image transfers to the paper.

The invention of the typewriter helped
writers as well as typesetters. The mechanically struck letters made composing much
faster and cleaner, as well as much easier
for typesetters to read.

The first powered press was invented in
Germany by Fredrich Koenig, who named it
the Suhler press after the town where he was
living. It featured a flat bed holding the form
and a rotating traversing cylinder to provide pressure. A single cylinder press could produce 800 sheets per
hour and an improved version, 1100 sheets per hour. It was
this improved version, first used by the London Times in
1814, that marked the beginning of modern printing.

*Fig. 1.7 An early manual,
upright typewriter.*

The next major step to speed things up was the Fourdrinier
Paper Making Machine. This device made it possible to
make continuous rolls of paper rather than individual
sheets.

By mid-century, presses were developed that used curved
plates to hold the type. In 1865 William Bullock demonstrat-
ed the first rotary press connected to a continuous roll of
paper. Ten years later, J. Eickhoff built a four-cylinder rotary press that would print both sides of continuous roll feed
paper at the same time.

Two major printing developments took place in the last
quarter of the century. Both were machines which cast and
set type in a single operation, rather than first casting the
type and then laboriously setting the letters in properly or-
dered lines.

In 1886, Otto Merganthaler invented the Linotype machine,
which cast a line of type as a single slug. It operated as a

*Fig. 1.8 A 19th century
cylinder presspress.*

large type mold which held all of the matrices for an entire line of type. The Monotype machine, invented in 1893 by Tolbert Lanston, cast the letters individually but then mechanically assembled them into lines of type. The Linotype machine made possible cheap first proofs (called galley proofs), but the Monotype machine made it easier to make corrections to the proof.

The Linotype machine requires only a single operator, who types the words on a keyboard. The machine then assembles the matrices for those letters, justifies the line by adding appropriate spaces, casts the line of type, and racks it on the form with other lines of type. Once composed, the form is then taken to the press.

A Monotype machine has two components and requires two operators. The keyboard unit creates a punched tape that indicates the order and spacing of the letters. The tape is then

Fig. 1.9 A Linotype machine.

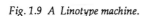

fed into the caster unit. The tape controls the selection of the matrices and the casting of each individual letter. Letters are automatically assembled, in order, on a stick, until the line is complete. Individual lines are then assembled on the form, locked down, and taken to the press.

The last great printing invention of the 19th century was photoengraving. Photoengraving is a sort of extension of the lithography and copperplate processes. Here, a photograph is made of the original artwork, and the negative is used to make an acid-resistant positive on a metal (zinc or copper) plate. The plate is then acid-etched to produce a metal negative. The metal negative is clamped into a press and inked for printing.

The inventions and advancements of the first five hundred years of moveable type printing were fantastic indeed. But the developments of the twentieth century, and especially the period from 1970 to the present, have had an arguably greater impact on millions of everyday people.

Fig. 1.10 A 19th century newspaper pressroom.

The Twentieth Century

Freedom of the press belongs to those who own one.
- *A. J. Liebling*

Liebling is right. Only those who actually own a press truly have the freedom to use that press in any way they choose. In all other situations, the use of the press is dictated not only by those who own them, but such considerations as economics (Will the subject and its presentation sell enough copies to make it worth printing?) and ethics or morals (Do we want our company associated with this stuff?).

As printing moves toward the twenty-first century, the advent of the computer and desktop publishing is allowing more and more people to have personal access to the equivalent of a printing press. In bygone days, it was relatively easy to tell some of the more undesirable publications simply by the nature of their printing methods. Conventional press companies wouldn't touch certain subjects or certain treatments (hate literature, pornography, some religion-related subjects), so such writings were usually self-published via spirit duplicator or photocopied typewritten text. Today, with a microcomputer and some simple software, anyone can produce a high-quality product, regardless of the appropriateness, or tastefulness, of the text. That same hardware and software make you a "vanity press," which means you can charge others to publish books after they have been turned down by conventional publishers.

The premier figure in twentieth century printing is Frederic W. Goudy. He designed and cut well over a hundred typefaces, including Pabst Old Style Roman and Italic (for the Pabst Brewery), Kennerley Old Style, and the Goudy family–Antique, Old Style, and Modern. He wrote two books on the subject: *The Alphabet*, and *Elements of Lettering*.

In the pre-war years, pantographic engraving machines began to take the place of the hand cutting of punches to produce type. Producing type from a pantographic engraving instead of a hand-cut and stamped matrix drastically reduced the labor and cost of having a new typeface created.

In 1904 the first offset press for planographic printing on paper was invented. Copperplate, intaglio, and lithography are planographic printing methods; the image is neither raised nor relief, but on the same plane as the base. The offset principle had previously only been used for printing from stone onto tin. The press that Ira Rubel of New York introduced was made possible by the development of curved metal plates which held the image to be printed. The plates wrapped on a cylinder which ran against, and printed on, a second rubber-covered cylinder. The impression transferred from the metal plate to the rubber cylinder, then from the rubber cylinder the impression was made on paper. The process was called "offset" because the image was offset onto the intermediary rubber cylinder before being printed on paper. Today, offset printing is still the most common method of printing small to medium projects. For projects requiring under 500 copies, photocopying generally is cheaper; but when more than 500 copies are needed, offset printing is increasingly more cost effective and produces a much higher quality product.

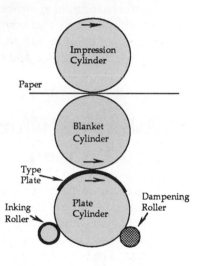

Fig. 1.11 How an offset press works. The type to be printed is etched on a curved metal plate attached to the plate cylinder. The dampening roller moistens the background, but not the type. The inking roller transfers special ink to the dry letters not the damp background. As the plate cylinder turns, the image is transferred to the blanket cylinder, which in turn prints the text on the paper held against the impression cylinder.

Planographic printing more or less eliminated the need for type composition to go through the typecasting stage. Instead, images of letters could be drawn and then photographed. The tiny photos of the letters could then be photographically enlarged or reduced to produce the desired sizes of type. The photographic letters could then be assembled and printed on a planographic plate and transferred from there to paper. The first "photocomposing" machine, which electro-opto-mechanically handled the details of letter choice, size, and boldness at the press of a key, was built in England in the early 1920s.

Except for increases in speed and quality, and an emphasis on multiple-color printing, printing technology mostly stood still from the advent of photocomposing to the advent of computers in the late 1960s. With computers to do most of the drudgery of making typographic and typesetting decisions for composition, today's designers are, relatively speaking, much freer to experiment with different typographic effects. Because the computer allows us to make drastic changes in a number of elements including type style and size, leading, and kerning in less than the blink of an eye, experimenting to find just the right layout and design is much easier, simpler, and considerably less costly.

A Short History of Computers and Printing

One of the earliest "computers" was a mechanical calculator designed and built by Blaise Pascal in 1643. It was a collection of gears, chains, and dials that could add and subtract as the user entered numbers by turning dials to the appropriate digits. The twentieth century computer language Pascal was named after this mathematical genius.

The next major mechanical computer was the Analytical Engine designed by another mathematical genius, Charles Babbage. It was to use punched cards containing coded instructions and data, similar to those used to control mechanical weaving instructions on the Jaquard loom. The problem was that the rest of the technology of the early 1800s wasn't capable of building the precision tools to build the precision parts required for appropriate mathematical accuracy. The device was designed, but not built, during Babbage's lifetime. Babbage's friend, Lady Ada Augusta Lovelace, daughter of Lord Byron, helped in the design of the Analytical Engine. Today, she is considered the first computer programmer, and the computer language Ada was named in honor of her.

We'll now jump a hundred years or so, to the middle of World War II, when the International Business Machine Company got interested in electrical/electronic computers as a way to handle the vast amounts of calculations inherent in technology – computing ballistics, navigation, financial, and other data. In 1944, the Automatic Sequence Controlled Calculator, known as the Mark I, was created. It was over fifty feet long and eight feet high, and it contained over 800,000 parts (including 500 miles of wire). It could add two 23 digit numbers in a third of a second, multiply them in 3 seconds, and calculate a logarithm to twenty decimal place accuracy in a minute and a half! By 1951, the IBM Model 701 scientific computer was 25 times faster than the Mark I.

Fig. 1.12 An early mainframe computer.

Another famous early computer was Eniac, developed by the Eckert and Maunchly (later Univac, later still Unisys) Computer Company, completed in 1946. It weighed 30 tons, occupied 1500 square feet of floor space, and contained over 18,000 vacuum tubes, half a million soldered joints, and used 150 kilowatts of electricity to run. Its calculation capabilities and speeds were better than those of the IBM Mark I, multiplying 500 pairs of ten digit numbers per second. The age of the megacomputer had arrived.

In 1947 the transistor was developed by William Shockley, J. Bardeen, and H. Brattain at Bell Laboratories in Palo Alto, California, for which they would share a 1956 Nobel Prize. This miniscule bit of ceramic and wire replaced the bulky and temperamental vacuum tube, and allowed the development of the second stage of computers – the minicomputers. Rather than occupying an entire room, the main part of a "mini" computer was only the size of a couple of large desks or filing cabinets.

Michael Broussard, Ken Russo

Fig. 1.13 Transistors come in a variety of sizes, all of them smaller than the vacuum tubes which they replaced.

The first commercial transistorized mainframe was the Sperry Univac Model 1050, familiarly called the Solid State. It was first made available to the public in September of 1963. Compared to the hulking giant vacuum tube computers it certainly was smaller, taking up only part of the space of an Eniac-sized machine. Also, it had a monitor screen and keyboard, instead of being controlled by punch card the way computers had been controlled since the days of Ada Lovelace and Charles Babbage. It was a truly "interactive" computer, not just a collection of boxes to which one fed stacks of cards and from which one received a printout.

The first minicomputer was the PDP-1, manufactured in 1961 by Digital Equipment Company (DEC). It only took up the space of three refrigerators. The retail price for this marvel was a mere $120,000 dollars.

These early computers had very little software. If a user wanted to calculate an equation, sort information, or any of the other now-standard computer functions, he would have to use either the machine language or another computer language to create the program to do the job. As time went on, more and more of these programs were written and made available to the computer community. Soon, companies were being formed just to create and market computer software.

The next major invention in the computer world was the integrated circuit (IC), an idea first presented by J.W.A. Dummer, a British radar expert, in 1952.

An IC is a tiny network (circuit) of transistors and other components miniaturized and compressed into "chips" – plastic-covered squares with thin metal connectors on the bottom. Robert Noyce, then working for Fairchild and later co-founder of Intel Corp., and Jack Kilby of Texas Instruments, both filed patents on the integrated circuit in 1959. By 1961

Noyce's Intel Corp. was marketing them. The IC allowed another order of magnitude of reduction in the size of computers, and ushered in the age of the microcomputer – a computer small enough to fit on top of a desk with space left over.

Ten years later, Intel Corp. engineers developed a special kind of IC chip which they called a **microprocessor**. Microprocessors are extremely intricate, microscopic complexes of circuits duplicating all of the detail usually found in the central processing unit of an entire computer. Now the entire computing part of a computer could fit in a square inch or so. Powerful pocket calculators, computers with the power and capabilities of a mainframe reduced to the size of a briefcase, and other uses for the microprocessor exploded on the scene almost overnight.

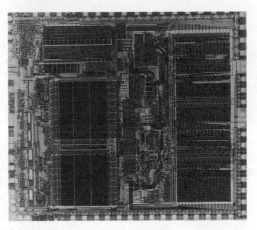

Fig. 1.14 The invention of integrated circuits and microprocessors caused the next reduction in the size of computers, from desk sized to desk-top sized machines.

In 1968, the last Linotype hot-metal typesetting machine was made. The first generation phototypsetters, essentially Linotype-style machines using photographic matrices, had driven the hot metal machines out, and the second generation, electromechanical phototypsetters, took over. For the next ten years, these machines would reign supreme in typsetting. They used mechanical methods to move the photographic impressions of type for spacing as lines and pages were composed. The entire page was then photographed as a unit.

The year 1978 marks a milestone for the introduction, by Linotype, of the first digital (computerized) phototypsetting machines. Several other companies also introduced electronic page composition at the same time, including Intertype, Hell (a European company marketed in the U.S. by RCA), and AlphaNumerics. Time/Life Corporation was one of the first publishing companies to use the new technology. With

Michael Broussard, Ken Russo

electronic composition, they could lay out and compose their various publications at the central offices in New York, and then electronically transmit the magazines to several distributed sites for local printing and distribution around the country. By 1986 there were no new electromechanical phototypesetters being manufactured; everything had gone electronic. In 1989, the last Fleet Street (British) newspaper "went electronic."

Fig. 1.15 Computerized typsetting machinery.

Although other attempts had been made to make simple, low-cost computers available to almost everyone, one of the most interesting, and important to desktop publishing, computer companies is Apple Computers, Inc. of Cupertino, Calif. Steve Wozniak and Steve Jobs literally built the Apple I computer circuit board in Steve Jobs' parents' garage. The Apple I was Woz's contribution to a group called the Homebrew Computer Club, a group of hardware and software hackers who met to trade equipment and expertise in making and using computers. Convinced by their friends, they went public on April Fool's Day 1976 in that garage. At first Apple sold just the Apple I circuit board – no keyboard, monitor, or other parts. Then they started designing the Apple II, a complete and ready-to-use computer, which went on sale in June of 1977.

In 1981, Apple finally got some serious competition when IBM announced its first Personal Computer. By June of 1983 Apple had sold over one million Apple II computers. In January 1984, during the Superbowl, Apple announced the Apple Macintosh, "The Computer for the Rest of Us." The world of computers hasn't been the same since.

What makes the Mac different is its operating system. Other computer operating systems are text oriented; the Mac is graphically oriented. Rather than presenting textual lists of files, programs, etc., the Mac uses icons, or pictures. Because of the graphic nature of the operating system, it is much easier to create and manipulate graphics electronically than on comparable non-graphic system computers. The marriage of text and graphics gives a WYSIWYG (What You See Is What You Get) look at things as they are created, rather than the earlier notion of word processing on personal computers, where things did not print out the way they appeared on screen. The capabilities of the Mac made electronic page layout on small computers a real possibility.

Fig. 1.16 *The Apple Macintosh computer has a built-in graphic operating system that offers the WISYWIG (What You See Is What You Get) creation of text and graphics which is so important for desktop publishing.*

In February of 1984, Paul Brainerd founded the Aldus Corporation, named after Aldus Manutius, the 17th century printer/type designer, and by July of '85 its program PageMaker was being shipped to the public. It was Brainerd who coined the term **desktop publishing** to distinguish what Aldus was doing from the earlier page composition programs on dedicated computers.

Following closely on the heels of PageMaker was a program called MacPublisher, by Boston Software. Another early contender was ReadySetGo! then owned by Manhattan Graphics Co. Interleaf, Inc. announced a publishing program for Sun workstation computers in the same month as Apple announced the Macintosh. Soon, they too would produce versions of their product for the Mac and other computers.

In 1985 John Warnock of Adobe Systems, Inc. introduced the page description language PostScript. Combined with Canon's laser printing engine, the two produced Apple Computer's "smart" high-quality laser printer, the Apple LaserWriter. Printing at 300 dots per inch instead of the 72 dpi resolution common for dot matrix printers gave the power of near-typset quality output created with the ease of use of the Macintosh.

PostScript has become a widely used page description language. If the computer, desktop publishing program, and printer all understand Postscript, then the resolution (printing quality) of the output is limited only by the resolution of the printer, whether that printer is an 18 pin dot matrix

PAST

printer, daisy-wheel printer, or Linotronic 300 typesetting machine that prints at 2450 dots per inch.

Soon desktop publishing spread to other computers. By January 1987 Aldus was marketing an IBM PC and compatible version of PageMaker. Another popular and useful PC desktop publishing program is Ventura Publisher by Ventura Software, Inc., a subsidiary of Xerox Corporation. As with the Macintosh, numerous desktop publishing programs were created or translated for use with PCs. Once the dust settled, the top contenders were PageMaker PC and Ventura Publisher.

There are desktop publishing programs for almost every imaginable computer type, but the main thing that seems to hold back the popularity of desktop publishing on non-Macintosh computers is the lack of ease of use and lack of a graphical operating system. By the time a PC user has added all the extra hardware and software components to a PC to make it do desktop publishing and graphics like a Macintosh, what the user has is a slower, more cumbersome, more expensive imitation of a Mac. The introduction of the OS/2 operating system by IBM should alleviate many of the hassles of desktop publishing on PCs with its built-in graphics capabilities.

In the same year that desktop publishing began spreading to non-Macintosh computers, Boston Software shut its doors, unable to keep up with the competition, and a new contender arrived.

The original version of ReadySetGo! was very limited, almost crippled in some senses. In 1986/87 Esselte LetraSet Corporation, longtime makers of printing accessories such as rub-on display type and color gels, and owners of International Typeface Corporation (ITC), decided to get into the desktop publishing and associated computer graphics business. At first they tried to revitalize the MacPublisher program from Boston Software, but the job of rewriting the code to make it more useful proved too time consuming to meet corporate deadlines. Instead, they purchased the rights to ReadySetGo! Version 3.0 to market under their own label.

Also in 1987, a third contender arose. In the amazingly short time of ten months, a handful of programmers at Quark, Inc. in Denver, Colorado, turned out their entry into the desktop publishing market – Xpress. Having the advantage of watching what features, capabilities, and methods the other companies had used, Quark was able to quickly produce a product that strongly competes with the others.

The newest Macintosh desktop publishing program (as of this writing in 1989) is called Springboard Publisher, by Springboard Software, Inc. of Minneapolis, Minnesota. It has added graphics creation features that none of the other programs address.

Each revision of the desktop publishing programs (roughly every six to nine months) sees new and more impressive features and capabilities being added. What will the future bring? Only time will tell.

Review Questions

1. Who is Frederick W. Goudy?
2. What is planographic printing?
3. Why is a free press so important?
4. Who was Blaise Pascal, and what did he invent?
5. Describe the process of papermaking.
6. Describe the process of hand cutting and casting type.
7. Who was the first North American printer?
8. When were some of the most often-printed books first typeset? Name two of them.
9. Who were Caslon and Baskerville?
10. Who invented the transistor? Why was this invention so important?
11. When was the first all-metal hand press made?
12. What is a Linotype machine? Who invented it?
13. When was the last hot-metal Linotype machine made?
14. When did computerized typesetting first begin?
15. Who are Steve Jobs and Steve Wozniak, and what contribution did they make to computing?
16. Who coined the term "desktop publishing"?
17. Which company created the first desktop publishing program?
18. What is PostScript and why is it important to desktop publishing?
19. Name two desktop publishing programs for the Macintosh and two for the PC.
20. What is offset printing?

Exercises

1. Compose a 1000 word essay or article on some topic that appeals to you. Type it, using a word processing program, and save the file. This essay will be used in conjunction with other exercises in chapters to follow.

2. Print the story you created as an Exercise 1 on a variety of computer printers and examine the differences in resolution.

3. Take the best resolution print from Exercise 2 and, if possible, have it both photocopied and offset printed. Which printing technique is better?

4. Make an electronic copy of the story/article you created in Exercise 1. Using your wordprocessor, format the text into a 3" wide column. Print the text in this format. Using scissors and rubber cement, paste up the text onto 8.5" x 11" pages arranged horizontally, with .5" margins all around and equal spaces between the columns:

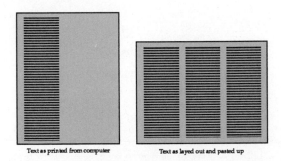

Text as printed from computer   Text as layed out and pasted up

Keep track of the time involved in each step (formatting, printing, layout (drawing the margins and columns on the pages), and pasteup. In later exercises you will see how much more efficient desktop publishing is.

Chapter 2: Text, The Backbone of Publishing

"But above all astonishing inventions, what loftiness of mind was that of the man who conceived of finding a way to communicate his most recondite thoughts to whatever other person, though separated from him by the longest intervals of space and time! To speak with those as yet unborn, or to be born perhaps a thousand or even ten thousand years hence! And with what ease! All through various groupings of twenty simple letters on paper!"

-- Galileo Galilei

Galileo's thoughts ring as true today as they did 400 years ago, and as they will ring true four hundred or ten thousand years from now, despite changes in alphabets and languages. The written word is perhaps man's most significant invention. The ability to remember yesterday and pass these thoughts on verbally is one of the things that separates us from other high-order animals such as chimpanzees and gorillas.

But spoken thoughts are only as good or accurate as the memory of the person hearing those words. Yes, members of pre-literate societies developed remarkable memories for incredibly complex material, but this material was still subject to "data errors" as we would say today. The advent of the written word gave man a quantum leap forward sociologically and technologically. Detailed information could now be recorded, checked for errors, and then reproduced exactly, time and again. The upheaval in European society cause by Gutenberg's development of printing with movable type was phenomenal.

As writers, editors, layout artists, and journalists, we must never forget that the written–not videotaped, audiotaped, spoken– word is our most important tool. This chapter will explore the effective use of the printed word and the many forms it can take.

We will structure →

Typography

Typography *n.* **1.** the art, craft, or process of composing type and printing from type. **2.** the planning, selection, and setting of type for a printed work.

The first definition refers to the artistic creation of the designs of the letters and symbols of an alphabet. Although there isn't space in a book such as this to go into great detail on creating letters, there are several terms which are important for anyone dealing with type–electronic or physical–to know.

TYPE comes from the Greek τψποσ meaning "letter form." From the beginning, the original meaning was the collection of carved or cast alphabet letters and symbols used with a printing press. In computer terms these letters and symbols (as well as spaces and "hidden" marks such as paragraph markers) are usually called characters.

A particular design of an alphabet is called a TYPEFACE. The distinctions among typefaces can be extremely subtle, or as obvious as a Godzilla in a garage. Each typeface is given a name, often that of the designer (Bodoni, Goudy, ITC), the place where the designer lived (London, New York, Helvetica), or some other characteristic (Avant Garde, Helvetica Narrow). There are over five thousand more or less standard typefaces available for composition purposes. In spite of this variety, it is comforting to know that even the typographic experts select only a dozen or less typefaces to compose anything from a four-word sign to a six-hundred-page technical manual! Typefaces that come with most desktop publishing programs or personal computers will be at least adequate for most typographical projects you will need to do. Other typefaces can be purchased and added to your repertoire as needed.

Fig. 2.1 *Some common typefaces.*

Palatino 14 – When in the course of human events...

Helvetica 14 – When in the course of human events...

New Century Schoolbook 14 – When in the course of human events...

Times 14 – When in the course of human events...

Which typeface(s) you use for your documents depend on the feeling you are trying to impart. Are you trying to appear conservative? Hi-tech modern? Traditional? Cute? Avant garde? Do you want to influence readers consciously with blatant typography that helps scream the message like a tabloid newsrag, or influence them unconsciously, below the threshhold of ordinary perception, as does much advertising copy? The typeface you choose can help you express any range of feelings. The feelings you portray with typography will in turn influence the reader in a (hopefully) similar way.

Fig. 2.2 How the typeface can affect the feel of a document. Bookman gives the text a poised, balanced feel, while Old German adds a sense of mystery to the words. Avant Garde lends an extremely clean, modern feeling.

Bookman

We the People of the United States, in order to form a more perfect Union...

Old German

𝕎𝔢 𝔱𝔥𝔢 𝔓𝔢𝔬𝔭𝔩𝔢 of the United States, in order to form a more perfect Union...

Avant Garde

We the People of the United States, in order to form a more perfect Union...

Although we as writers and publishers may not realize it, our cultural heritage and background can influence our choice of type. As one of America's more famous recent designers says:

> "It is easier for Europeans to use Helvetica. It's very difficult for Americans. We can appeal to big corporate executives with Helvetica and to stockholders who read annual reports, but for the great masses of Americans we cannot do that. There are over two hundred typefaces in the world for the masses, and then there is Helvetica. Helvetica is for designers, design students, design instructors, and a few intellectuals and clients, and for the population of Switzerland.
> – Herb Lubalin

TYPESTYLE refers to the seventeenth century division of typefaces into five basic "families" or general appearances: Roman, Italic, Script, Gothic, and Greek.

Roman typefaces are characterized by an upright look. Palatino, which this text uses, is a Roman typeface.

Italic typefaces are Roman typefaces slanted more or less to the right. They are used to emphasize foreign words, quotes, and other special expressions in a normally Roman typeface paragraph.

𝕲𝖔𝖙𝖍𝖎𝖈 𝖙𝖞𝖕𝖊𝖋𝖆𝖈𝖊𝖘 𝖍𝖆𝖛𝖊 𝖆 𝖇𝖆𝖗𝖔𝖖𝖚𝖊, 𝖆𝖓𝖙𝖎𝖖𝖚𝖊 𝖋𝖊𝖊𝖑 𝖙𝖍𝖆𝖙 𝖒𝖆𝖓𝖞 𝖕𝖊𝖔𝖕𝖑𝖊 𝖙𝖍𝖎𝖓𝖐 𝖔𝖋 𝖆𝖘 𝖖𝖚𝖆𝖎𝖓𝖙. 𝕴𝖒𝖆𝖌𝖎𝖓𝖊 𝖙𝖍𝖎𝖘 𝖙𝖞𝖕𝖊𝖋𝖆𝖈𝖊 𝖇𝖊𝖎𝖓𝖌 𝖚𝖘𝖊𝖉 𝖎𝖓 𝖆 𝖘𝖎𝖌𝖓: 𝖄𝖊 𝕺𝖑𝖉𝖊 𝕻𝖗𝖎𝖓𝖙𝖊 𝕾𝖍𝖔𝖕𝖕𝖊.

Script typefaces, such as the Zapf Chancery used for this paragraph, are so called because the letters flow together in imitation of handwritten lettering.

Γρεεκ (Greek) typefaces are those using letters from the Greek alphabet, such as the Symbol font used here to create the word "Greek".

A sixth "family" are those more modern typefaces called Ornamental or Novelty faces. Some try to imitate other things, by having the characters drawn with strokes resembling icicles, dripping blood, or lightning bolts; others evoke a mood by using strokes resembling Oriental brushstrokes, rococco gilt work, stencilled letters, and other embellishments. Some have no alphabet or number characters. Instead, each character is represented by a picture; sort of a modern equivalent of Egyptian hieroglyphics!

Q   W   E   R   T   Y

Another typographic meaning for typestyle is that referring to the differing weights or darkness levels of the lines which make up the letters. These weights are: extralight, light, normal, semibold, bold, and extrabold. Not all typefaces are available in all of these variations.

This is normal.
This is bold.
This is light.

Most desktop publishing software and hardware does not recognize the majority of the "stroke weight" styles; normal and bold are the most common. Some typefaces however, such as Courier and Zapf Chancery on the Macintosh, have a "normal" definition which is actually, typographically speaking, "light."

In word processing and desktop publishing there is a related but additional meaning to TYPESTYLE. That is, the style which one can apply to a given typeface, such as plain, **bold**, *italic*, <u>underline</u>, outline, shadow, ~~strikethru~~, or a *<u>combination</u>* of these styles, which can vary from program to program. In typesetting terms, the computer normal style is the same as Roman typestyle, and italic is truly the Italic typestyle, but the other styles are actually separate faces derived from the original face.

In typographical terms, these separate faces comprise a type FAMILY – a group of all the related styles and sizes derived from a master typeface. Some of the derivations, such as ~~strikethru~~ and <u>underline</u>, add elements (in this case, lines) to the original typeface. Other derivatives (outline, shadow) are created by changing the width or other characteristic of the letter strokes. Additional members of a family can be created by broadening or "extending" the characters' widths to make fatter characters, or by slimming (condensing) character widths to make a narrower font.

Fig. 2.3 The Times 12 point family on the Macintosh.

Plain (Roman)
abcdefghijklmnopqrstuvwxyz 1234567890
abcdefghijklmnopqrstuvwxyz 1234567890

Bold
abcdefghijklmnopqrstuvwxyz 1234567890
abcdefghijklmnopqrstuvwxyz 1234567890

Italic
abcdefghijklmnopqrstuvwxyz 1234567890
abcdefghijklmnopqrstuvwxyz 1234567890

Underlined
<u>abcdefghijklmnopqrstuvwxyz 1234567890</u>
<u>abcdefghijklmnopqrstuvwxyz 1234567890</u>

Outlined
abcdefghijklmnopqrstuvwxyz 1234567890
abcdefghijklmnopqrstuvwxyz 1234567890

Shadowed
abcdefghijklmnopqrstuvwxyz 1234567890
abcdefghijklmnopqrstuvwxyz 1234567890

Combination
<u>*abcdefghijklmnopqrstuvwxyz*</u>
<u>*1234567890*</u>
<u>*abcdefghijklmnopqrstuvwxyz*</u>
<u>*1234567890*</u>

FONT is a widely misused term. A **font** is a complete alphabet, including punctuation and other symbols, of *one size* of *one typeface*. Thus, by technical definition, Times 12 point is one font, while Times 14 point is another and Times 12 point Bold is a third. In the world of desktop publishing, the term *font* is often misused. Many computer people speak of a font when what they really mean is typeface. It is all too common to hear an exchange such as:

"What fonts are you using?"
"Avant Garde for the headlines, and Palatino for the body copy."

The correct question and answer should be:

"What typefaces are you using?"
"Avant Garde for the headlines, and Palatino for the body copy."

or

"What fonts are you using?"
"Avant Garde 36 point bold for the headlines, and Palatino 10 point Plain for the body copy."

Using these typographic terms correctly may not seem important now, but out in "the real world," using them incorrectly can mean costly (in time, effort, and material) misunderstandings if you say one thing and the agency or service you are dealing with hears another.

Desktop Publishing Typeface Distinctions

Proportional vs. Non-Proportional Typefaces

A major difference between typewriting text and typesetting text is that, on a typewriter, all of the characters were created on slugs (metal pads) of the same width, whereas typeset characters are set on slugs that vary with the width of the character. Thus, with a typewriter, every character occupies the same amount of space on a line. Some characters have more white space around them than others – a capital "M" occupies the entire width of the slug, while a lower case "l" has a lot of white space. The common width slug was selected for mechanical reason – to allow rapid typing without jamming things up too badly where the characters met the platen. This style of type became known as "non-proportional," as the slug does not vary in width with the character. Typeset-style typefaces are called "proportional," meaning that the size of the slug is proportional to the width of the character. Early computers used typewriter style characters, because it made them easier for non-typographer computer people to design.

Fig. 2.4 Proportional vs. non-proportional typefaces .

Proportional (New Century Schoolbook)
The time has come, the walrus said, to speak of many things...

Non-Proportional (Courier)
```
The time has come, the walrus said, to
speak of many things...
```

Modern computers used for desktop publishing can be loaded with both proportional and non-proportional typefaces. Proportional typefaces give much more of a feeling of "real published writing," where non-proportional typefaces are often dismissed as "imitation typewriter" faces.
Proportional typefaces are generally the faces of choice when desktop publishing, but non-proportional faces are useful for a radically different look which can help make important text stand out. One common use, when writing about computers, is to use a proportional typeface for the major body copy and then use a non-proportional typeface to illustrate phrases which appear on the computer's screen.

Computer programmers often use non-proportional typefaces when composing their code, because many computers perceive a line of text as being composed of fixed width columns which are either empty or filled with a character. In some programming languages, such as FORTRAN, the exact column position for the beginning of certain command phrases is of critical importance.

Fig. 2.5 FORTRAN Program Code using a non-proportional typeface to ensure correct character positioning.

```
C  Program Name -- Averager
      DIMENSION DATA1(5), DATA2(4)
      DATA DATA1/1.0,2.0,3.0,4.0,5.0/
   *     DATA2/2.0,4.0,6.0,8.0/
      CALL MEAN(DATA1, 5, AVE1)
      CALL MEAN(DATA2, 4, AVE2)
      WRITE (*, 100) AVE1, AVE2
  100 FORMAT (1X, 'Average 1=', F6.2, /, 1X,
   *'Average 2=', F6.2)
      STOP
      END
C
      SUBROUTINE MEAN (DATA, N, AVE)
      DIMENSION DATA (N)
      AN = N
      SUM = 0.0
      DO 10 I = 1, N
         SUM = SUM + DATA(I)
   10 CONTINUE
      AVE = SUM/AN
      RETURN
      END
```

Laser vs. Non-Laser Typefaces

Dot matrix printers are often characterized as "dumb" printers. As essentially hi-tech versions of the typewriter, dot-matrix printers have no computer memory or intelligence. Early, simple versions of laser printers were called "smart" printers, because they could distinguish among two or three fonts or type families which could be loaded into them via a tape cartridge, provided the operators remembered to tell the printer what they wanted to use. More expensive laser printers, notably the Apple LaserWriter, are classed as "intelligent" printers, because they contain not just a limited set of fonts or an abbreviated type family, but a computer language for page description such as Adobe Systems'

PostScript. PostScript manages not just fonts but *whole type families*. It contains descriptions of the type family characters which allow creating of various sizes and styles of type "on the fly." The addition of Postscript to a laser printer allowed users to have a poor man's typesetting machine, that, with limited resolution, could do as much or more as typesetting machines costing tens of thousands of dollars more.

When computers are attached to intelligent printers, there are usually two versions of each typeface involved, the screen display or bitmapped version, and the PostScript or downloadable version. The bitmap typeface is stored in the computer's operating system. The PostScript version must also be available to the computer, because it is downloaded (sent) from the computer to the laser printer's memory at the time of printing. Some laser printers, such as the Apple LaserWriter, have a selection of typefaces permanently stored on a ROM (Read Only Memory) chip inside the printer; other laser printers can have hard disks connected, allowing storage of innumerable downloadable fonts.

Some typefaces, however, exist only in bitmap form. These typefaces will not print correctly on a laser printer. When a laser printer prints a bitmap-only typeface, the characters come out oversized, poorly spaced, and of poor resolution. This affects such things as line spacing, position of words on a line, and more. In some cases unwanted characters are printed in place of the desired characters, when there is no description of appropriate characters.

Fig. 2.6 Enlarged bitmapped (Geneva) and laser (Palatino) typefaces showing resolution.

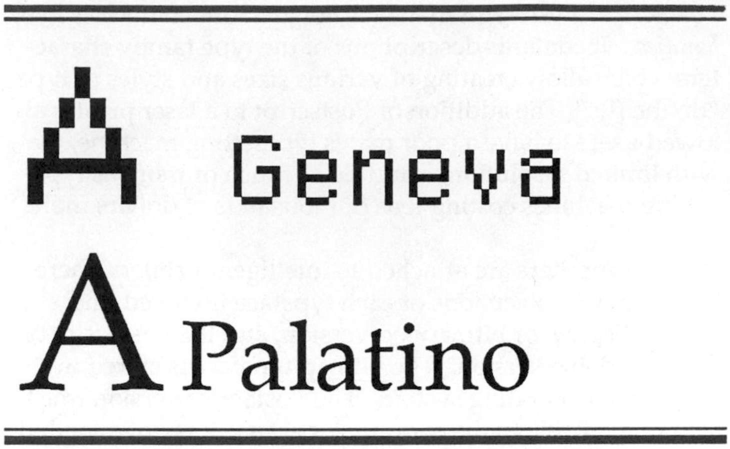

A Geneva

A Palatino

General Rule of Typefaces For Desktop Publishers:
Use only laser fonts when composing a document.

If you need to use non-Postscript fonts in a project, test print them first to see how they look and whether or not they will be usable in the sizes you desire. If, however, a few characters of an ornamental typeface such as Images, Cairo, or London are desired, the printer can be temporarily told to disallow font substitution.   Generally these characters will only print to the quality or resolution that they would on a dot matrix printer –jagged– especially in display sizes.

Character Terminology

In discussing the design of a typeface, or reasons for choosing one typeface over another, there are a few terms which it is important to understand so that everyone speaks the same language.   Figure 3.7 illustrates these terms.

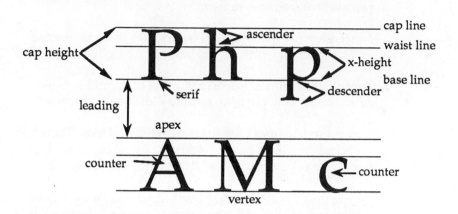

Uppercase letters are so called because hand-set type was arranged so that the compositor could rapidly and accurately select each letter. Two large wooden cases were arranged, one above the other, each divided into as many compartments as the font had characters. In the upper (or least used) case were the larger capital letters, used only for the beginnings of sentences, proper names, and such. Below those, in the lower case (closest to hand) were the smaller letters most commonly used in creating the body of the text. Thus capital letters became known as "uppercase letters" and the smaller ones "lowercase letters."

The **baseline** is the master line used by the typographer when the font was created. The bottom of capitals and the body of lowercase characters rest on the baseline.

X-height was originally exactly that: the height of the lowercase "x" above the baseline. The body of most lowercase characters is designed to be no taller than the x-height. The line used by typographers to define this height when creating a typeface is called the "waist line."

Fig. 2.7 The various parts that make up characters.

41

Cap-height is the distance above the baseline to which uppercase characters are drawn.

Descenders are those parts of letters such as on lowercase *p*s, *q*s, js, and *y*s, which extend below the baseline of the font.

Ascenders are upper extensions, as on *b*s, *t*s, and *f*s, which go above the x-height of an ordinary lowercase character.

Strokes are the lines used to create the characters. There are countless variations on the thickness of strokes. Some typefaces have wide verticals and thin diagonals, others the reverse. In other typefaces one angle of the diagonals will be thicker than the other, or the horizontals will be a different thickness than the verticals. Another series of variations is in the strokes for rounded characters; tapering to various places, or same thickness throughout. Study the design of characters in the fonts shown in this chapter. You may want to try to create a classification system for typefaces based on stroke variations.

Counters are the enclosed or hollow parts of letters such as *o*s, *p*s, *s*s, *c*s.

Serif is a word used to describe light lines or strokes crossing or projecting from the end of a main line or stroke in a letter. From the Dutch word *schreef* via the Latin word *scribere*, meaning *a line*. Typefaces that have no serifs are known as *sans serif*, from a French word meaning *without*.

The serif is perhaps the most readily identifiable characteristic that distinguishes one typeface from another. Serifs are usually found in three basic styles: square, rounded, or triangular. They may extend straight out from the main stroke,

Fig. 2.8 A variety of serifs.

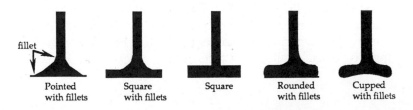

fillet

| Pointed with fillets | Square with fillets | Square | Rounded with fillets | Cupped with fillets |

slope gradually outward with a fillet, or dip inwards towards its center. This is is called a **cupped serif.** **Inscribed serifs** are really a variation on sans serif, except the strokes have a slight flare inwards at the terminals; not all letters in a typeface with incribed serifs will have them.

Although there is no hard evidence to support it, there seems to be a general consensus that serifed typefaces are easier and less fatiguing to read, if the reader is presented with large amounts of small size copy unbroken by illustrations. Indeed, most book-length manuscripts and newspapers are set in serifed type.

With or without serifs, a typeface can have characters that end without serifs. These **terminals** may be horizontal, vertical, or "sheared" (cut off at an angle) inwards or outwards.

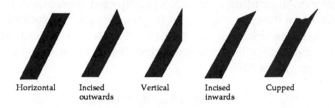

Horizontal   Incised outwards   Vertical   Incised inwards   Cupped

Fig. 2.9 Several kinds of terminals (ends of strokes that are not serifed).

Letters such as "A" and "M" have one or more high points called **apexes**, while letters like "V" and "W" have low points called **vertexes.** These too can take many forms, such as pointed, square, rounded, and serifed.

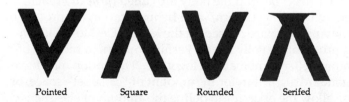

Pointed   Square   Rounded   Serifed

Fig. 2.10 Where two strokes meet, such apices and vertices can also have a number of variations.

Swashes are highly ornamental flourishes on some characters of certain typefaces, which can be used as decorative touches at the beginning or ending of lines of type.

Fig. 2.11 Ornamental flourishes on characters are called swashes.

Ordinary Serif · Calligraphic Swash · Ornate Swash

Ligatures, in metal type, were single characters which contained two or more letters, such as the digraphs fi, fl, ff and æ, which represent single sounds in English. They were common in printing in the 15th to 19th centuries, but the invention of the typewriter with its monospaced characters spelled their doom. In the past twenty years or so, with the advent of computerized typesetting, ligatures seem to be making a comeback.

Ligatures (fi, fl, and æ)

In the final analysis, spaceflight is an æsthetic experience.

Kerning is sometimes confused with ligature. We can observe that certain letter combinations "just don't look right together" because of the spacing between elements of the letters, particularly those with slanted strokes and elements that stick out beyond the body, such as cross bars. The bits which project beyond the body are called *carne* in French, from which we get "kern," and by implication the process of removing the space caused by the kerns. Desktop publishing programs usually have a kerning option, to tuck the offending letter combinations together. The option may have a standard algorithm for the amount of "close set" space, or may allow the operator to define the amount of close set, based (usually) on a spacing algorithm utilizing 18 units of kern space per em of line space. Some programs don't have kerning *per se,* but do allow use of negative numbers (negative spacing) in their letterspacing option, which produces the same effect.

Avenue

Avenue

Fig. 2.12 Unkerned (top) vs. kerned words

Kerning is generally used to improve the overall look of the document; it can however be employed as a copyfitting technique if space is critical.

A **superscript** (sometimes called a "superior") is type that is set a a few points smaller than the normal body copy, and set above (usually about 1/4 of the face size) the baseline of the body, as in the mathematical equation πr^2. Without special adjustment, such text set in mid-paragraph will often adversely affect the line spacing of the paragraph.

Subscripts (or "inferiors") are characters set below the baseline, as in the chemical formula H_2O. Subscripts aren't set quite as far below the baseline as superscripts are above the baseline.

Typographic Units Of Measure

Type is measured by its height; typewriter characters are measured by their "pitch" or the number of characters per inch of line (cpi). This fundamental difference tends to confuse newcomers to computerized word processing and desktop publishing.

Early Systems of Measurement

In the early days of typography, each type designer had his characters cut to whatever heights and widths he felt like; there was no standardization. Instead of referring to typeface sizes in units, they were referred to by names like gem (approximately 4 point), diamond (4.5 point), agate (5.5 point), nonpareil (6 point), minion (7 point), and English (14 point). Some of these names lasted for centuries, and indeed are still in use today. Agate, for example, with its 1/14th inch line height, has come to be the basic unit in advertising copy measure, and especially in classified advertising.

The French System

In continental Europe, the French developed a system of measurement based on the "French inch" (which is just a bit larger than anyone else's.) The minimum unit of measure in the French System is the **didot** (pronounced "dee dough"), named after its inventor François Ambroise Didot. One didot equals 1.07 American System points. The secondary unit of measure is the **cicero**, which is equal to 12 didot.

Didot and ciceros differ just enough from points and picas to prevent mixing up cast type from the two systems.

The American Point System

The American System, derived from the French System, but the American System is based on the "English inch." The basic unit of measurement in the American System is the **point**, abbreviated "pt". One point equals 0.0138 inches, which is close enough to 1/72" that no one quibbles. Thus there are 72 points per inch. Since the point is so small, a more convenient unit evolved, called the **pica**. There are 12 points in one pica, so 1 pica = 1/6". The pica (which is short for "pica Em") was derived from the width of a 12 point typeface's capital "M". M is generally the broadest letter in a typeface.

With typewriters, pitch tells how many letters of a given typewriter face can be set in one inch of line space. "Pica" refers to a size of letter that has 10 characters per inch of line (10-pitch); "Elite" is a 12-pitch letter size, which is roughly equivalent to 10 point type. Electric or electronic typewriters having both pica and elite type available are called "dual pitch" machines.

The point is normally used to measure character height; the pica used to measure line length (especially when doing copyfitting).

The Metric System

Yes, metrics are taking over even the measurement of type with its 300 year old tradition of unique units. However, knowing the resistance of typesetters and typographers to some kinds of change, it will be a while before the majority of type in America is measured metrically. However, several phototypesetting companies and transfer letter makers have "gone metric," and even a few newspapers measure "column centimeters" instead of column inches.

One point equals almost exactly .35 millimeters, so 1mm = 2.85 points, and 72 points (6 picas) is nearly 25.24 mm.

4 Point Type
6 Point Type
8 Point Type
10 Point Type
12 Point Type
14 Point Type
18 Point Type
24 Point Type

36 Point Type

48 Point

72 Point

127

Fig. 2.13 A variety of common body and display type sizes.

Type measurements are not always exact. If you put a "pica pole" or typographer's ruler on various 12 point fonts, for example, you will find that the actual distances from ascender to descender vary radically from font to font. *Chancery 12 pt,* for example is much smaller than Palatino 12 pt. This is because typographers build in a fudge factor so that when type is "set solid" (see below) the descenders of one line of type don't cross the ascenders of the line below. This fudge factor or **shoulder** varies from typeface to typeface and designer to designer; thus the wide variation in the true heights of various fonts of the same nominal point size.

Body type is the range of sizes used to create the main portion of ordinary printed text. Generally, body type is in the 8-12 point size range, but can be smaller (contracts with lots of fine print) or larger (books for the visually impaired). In earlier historical periods, even 4 to 7 point type was considered body type.

Display type is larger than body type, and is used for headlines and advertising copy; generally 14 point and larger type is classed as display type.

Leading (pronounced "ledding") is another use of the point for typographic measurement. Leading is the distance from the baseline of one line of type to the capline of the next line of type below.

Leading is usually expressed as "x points of type on y points of leading," commonly abbreviated to something like 12/15, meaning 12 point type with 3 points of leading between the lines. **Close set type** has the leading equal to the type size – 9/9 for example. **Solid set type** can be used in copyfitting, to keep all of an article in a column, on a single page. The most common leading is to have two points more leading than the size of the typeface – 10/12 or 12/14.

This paragraph is close set or 10/10

Leading is usually expressed as "x points of type on y points of leading," commonly abbreviated to something like 12/15, meaning 12 point type with 3 points of leading between the lines. **Close set type** has the leading equal to the type size – 9/9 for example. **Solid set type** can be used in copyfitting, to keep all of an article in a column, on a single page. The most common leading is to have two points more leading than the size of the typeface – 10/12 or 12/14.

This paragraph is set 10/12

Leading is usually expressed as "x points of type on y points of leading," commonly abbreviated to something like 12/15, meaning 12 point type with 3 points of leading between the lines. **Close set type** has the leading equal to the type size – 9/9 for example. **Solid set type** can be used in copyfitting, to keep all of an article in a column, on a single page. The most common leading is to have two points more leading than the size of the typeface – 10/12 or 12/14.

This paragraph is set 10/14

Leading is usually expressed as "x points of type on y points of leading," commonly abbreviated to something like 12/15, meaning 12 point type with 3 points of leading between the lines. **Close set type** has the leading equal to the type size – 9/9 for example. **Solid set type** can be used in copyfitting, to keep all of an article in a column, on a single page. The most common leading is to have two points more leading than the size of the typeface – 10/12 or 12/14.

Fig. 2.14 Examples of varying leading The amount of leading can influence readability – an important factor in anty desktop publishing project.

Double space type, as on a typewriter or word processor, has one full character height of space between the lines; if you are using 12 pt type, there is one full line of blank space between lines of type.

Desktop publishing software lets you adjust the leading of various portions of text, usually through a "Line Spacing" option. In these programs, leading can usually be expressed in terms of points, inches, centimeters, or percentage of line space.

Creating Text for Desktop Publishing

There are two basic ways to get text into a desktop publishing program so that it can be laid out:

1) create it with a word processing or text editing program on the same or another computer, or

2) type the text directly into the desktop publishing program using its onboard word processor.

There are advantages and disadvantages to both methods. This is neither the time nor the place to learn in detail about word processing or text editing programs, but there are some things you should know about how they work in conjunction with with desktop publishing software. Remember that there are two distinct functions involving words in desktop publishing: **writing**, or composing the words themselves, and **layout**, or arranging the words on the page. Writing may best be done in a word processing program, and layout is best done in a desktop publishing program.

Creating Text in a Separate Word Processing Program

Creating text in a separate word processing program is especially useful when there are several (or several dozen) people who have to write the stories and articles, or check the artwork which you, as the layout artist, will assemble using a desktop publishing program. This way, writers can use their favorite word processor to produce the text as full screen-width copy with minimum fuss and hassle.

There are some problems, however. When text containing elaborate hanging paragraphs, outline structure, or tab-filled tables is imported from a word processor, often the positions of the tabs and other hidden characters used to create these structures do not import exactly, and much labor is necessary to straighten things out so that tables fit the new column width, indents are correct, and so forth. This is even more troublesome when the text was created on word processor on a non-compatible computer (text from an IBM PC word processor or mainframe computer text editor to be used with a desktop publishing program on a Macintosh, for example).

Where text is created on a non-compatible computer and must be "translated" to a form that the desktop publishing computer can understand, the best format to save it in on the originating computer is called "text only" or **ASCII format.** ASCII is an acronym which stands for American Standard Code for Information Interchange. In this form, few hidden formatting characters such as tabs, indents, boldface or underline are recorded, and the translation to the new computer format and importation into desktop publishing will occur with minimal problems. If this is the case, your writers should be told to avoid wasting time formatting tables, and hanging paragraphs, and indicate how they want the results to look by sending you a proof print (made before they save the text in ASCII format) along with the electronic copy of the text.

Once text is translated and imported, there may be strange-looking characters embedded in the text. They must be removed. These characters are the result of hidden formatting characters or unusual symbols that the ASCII format did not understand, and for which it substituted the strange characters that appear. Read the imported text carefully, and use the desktop publishing program's "search and replace" function to remove them. Rather than importing text in ASCII format directly into the desktop publishing program, it is often more useful to open that text with a wordprocessing program (which is compatible with the desktop publishing program) first, and remove odd characters, carriage returns which may be embedded at the end of every line, and so on *before* moving the text to the desktop publishing program.

Rule of Thumb For Creating Text With An Outside Word Processor: Never have more than one article (or other internally consistent text segment) in a given file.

If your writers put three or four short (1-6 paragraph) articles in the same file, you will either have to import the same document three or four times, and each time delete the parts you don't want; or have to create an improbable combination of linked Text Blocks (see below) to get each small article to end up where it is supposed to be in the layout.

Creating Text With the Onboard Text Facility

This method is most useful where you are writer, editor, and layout person all rolled into one. Advantages include not having to rework someone else's well meant but misguided attempts to hang paragraphs, layout tables, not having any translation problems from a non-compatible computer's software, and having fewer problems with after-the-fact copy fitting (you can see how the text is fitting as you create it, and compensate "on the fly"). The text processors in modern desktop publishing programs are generally more sophisticated (but not necessarily easier to compose with, because of the sophistication) than ordinary word processing programs , although some simple desktop publishing projects such as posters or flyers can be accomplished simply by using sophisticated word processing software.

The general technique for creating text with the onboard processor is somewhat different from using an ordinary word processing program. When using a word processor, the program opens to a blank page of a document for which there are default page margins, tab spacings, and perhaps a typeface. There is also a flashing cursor to mark where typing will begin, and in most cases you can start typing immediately.

Layout Masters and Text Blocks

With desktop publishing software, when you first open up the program to begin a new document, you are presented with a *truly* blank page. Generally all you will see are the default margins indicated by a dashed or dotted line. There is usually no flashing cursor, and if you start typing, nothing may happen. This is because the blank page you are seeing is the equivalent of the older mechanical or "blueline" master on which the typeset text would be laid out and pasted up. In most programs, at this point you will have to define the "blueline" or layout by telling the program how many columns you want, how wide and deep they are to be, and how much gutter will be between them. Once the layout has been defined, then you can start to create places to type or put artwork.

Fig. 2.15 Dotted line shows a Text Block placed on a desktop publishing layout.

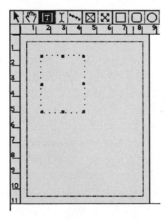

To start typing, you will usually have to create a **Text Block**, a transparent area in which you can position a cursor. This Text Block may be only a few characters wide to hold a headline or title, but is generally used to define the column width and depth. Most programs have a tool that you position at some starting point for the Text Block and then drag until the block is the desired size. The Text Block can then be moved around on the layout with some kind of a pointer tool. The size of the Text Block can also be altered through a "Text Specification" function which allows fine tuning of the position and size of the Text Block, and perhaps other features such as white type, special styles, or runaround capability. See Chapter 4 for other uses of the Text Specification function. Once the Text Block has been created and positioned, you can position the cursor in the block and begin typing.

Actual details of how to create, move, and manipulate a Text Block will vary from program to program and computer to computer. It is up to you to read, understand, and become familiar with the commands, functions, and tools of specific programs you will be using in this course.

Simple Copyfitting

As you type, text can be left in the default typeface until you have filled a block, or you can select and modify finished portions to the desired final typeface as you go, to have a

Fig. 2.16 Copyfitting by reducing column length.

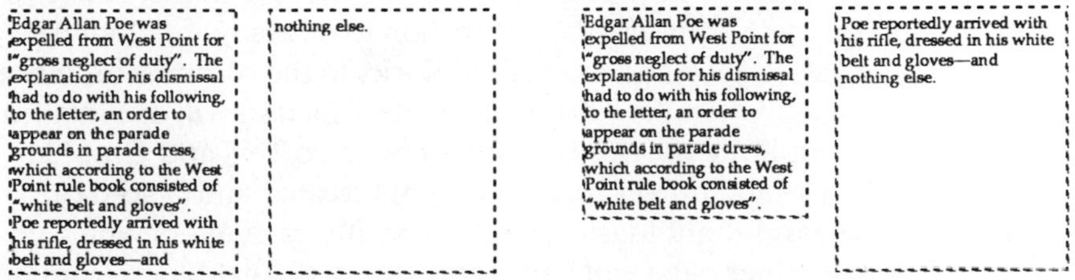

Edgar Allan Poe was expelled from West Point for "gross neglect of duty". The explanation for his dismissal had to do with his following, to the letter, an order to appear on the parade grounds in parade dress, which according to the West Point rule book consisted of "white belt and gloves". Poe reportedly arrived with his rifle, dressed in his white belt and gloves—and

nothing else.

Edgar Allan Poe was expelled from West Point for "gross neglect of duty". The explanation for his dismissal had to do with his following, to the letter, an order to appear on the parade grounds in parade dress, which according to the West Point rule book consisted of "white belt and gloves".

Poe reportedly arrived with his rifle, dressed in his white belt and gloves—and nothing else.

Text As Composed

Text with left column length reduced

better idea of how much of the block is being utilized. If the text being created will be longer than the Text Block in which you are working, you have three options. You could make the Text Block longer or wider, if that doesn't conflict with the layout you have designed. Or you could use combinations of changes to wording, leading, hyphenation, or word spacing to copy fit the text to available space if it will be only a few lines longer than the Text Block. The third option is to create another Text Block and then link the text to create a "carryover" to the additional block.

Widows and Orphans

Widows and **orphans** are the most common copyfitting problem. These are very short lines standing alone at the top (orphan) or bottom (widow) of a page or column, which may consist of a word or two, or even a hyphenated syllable. These may be unavoidable leftovers from the start or finish of a paragraph. Often the simplest way to copyfit a widow or orphan is to lengthen or shorten the widow column so that widow lines carry over to the next colum or the orphan is brought back.

Carryovers

Carryover Text Blocks can be in another column on the same page of the document, or on another page altogether. If the document you are creating is a book, manual, or similar work, this is how pages beyond the first are made. First you use the Additional Pages function to create more blueline masters; then add more Text Blocks to the columns on those pages. Often the Additional Pages function will automatically duplicate not only the layout but also Text and Graphic Blocks and other graphic elements created and placed on Left and Right Master Pages. Usually carryovers which go to another page will have separate small Text Blocks containing the phrases "Continued on page ..." and "Continued

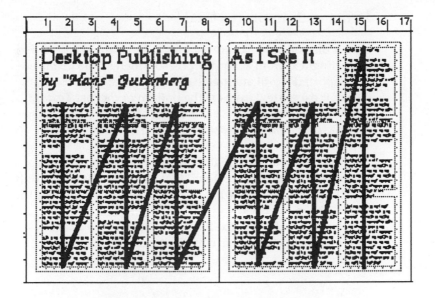

from page..." below and above the respective carryover blocks. Some programs will insert notices automatically or at your command; others require you to create separate Text Blocks containing the "continued" information.

Fig. 2.17 Carryover paths on a facing page layout.

Regardless of whether the carryover is to another column on the same page, or to a completely different page, the next step is to **link** the original Text Block to the Carryover Text Block. In some programs, such as QuarkXpress, links from column to column and page to page are created automatically and must be "uncreated" if carryover is not desired, but in most programs each Text Block stands as a separate entity, and the order in which column links to column and page links to page is under the personal control of the desktop publisher. To create a link, the general principle is to first select the Link Tool, then use that tool to select the Text Block where the text is already in place. Then you select successive Text Blocks on the same or different pages. As additional text is created in a linked Text Block, the excess text "bumped down" will automatically flow to successively linked Text Blocks wherever they may be in the document.

Links with Imported Text

If Text Blocks and links are established in the layout prior to importing text from a word processor, then as the text is being imported it will automatically carry over from block to block. If excess text exists at the bottom of the last Text Block in the linked series, a marker of some sort appears to indicate that more text exists than appears in that block.

Alternatively, you can create a single Text Block and import an entire large piece of text into that block, although the only part that will appear is what fits in the block. Then, once the text has been imported and the importation saved to the document, additional Text Blocks can be created, placed, and linked as necessary to contain the entire text.

Review Questions

1. Define typography.
2. What are the differences among typeface, typestyle, and desktop publishing fonts?
3. List six common typefaces used in desktop publishing.
4. For what are Italic typefaces used?
5. What is a type family?
6. What is the difference between proportional and non-proportional typefaces? When would you use each?
7. How do laser typefaces differ from bitmapped typefaces?
8. Define:

Uppercase	Superscript	Descender
Lowercase	Subscript	Sans-serif
Body type	Kerning	Serif
Display type	Ligature	Counter
x-height	Vertex	Stroke
cap-height	Apex	Ascender

9. List four kinds of serifs.
10. Name three kinds of terminals.
11. What are gem, diamond, and agate?
12. How big is a point? How many points in a pica? In an em?
13. What is the difference between pica and elite type on a typewriter?
14. What is typewriter pitch?
15. What is a didot?
16. What is leading? What is the leading of close set type?
17. If you need to transfer text from one computer to another, what format would you save the file in? Why?
18. What is a Text Block, and how is it used in desktop publishing software?
19. What are widows and orphans?
20. Why would you link two text blocks?
21. What is carryover?
22. When would you use serifed type? Sans-serif type?
23. What is a calligraphic swash?
24. List the advantages and disadvantages of creating text in a separate word processing program versus the on-board text creator in your desktop publishing program?

Exercises

1. Write a basic story on a subject of interest to you, of between 250 and 500 words (1 to 2 pages of 12 point single space type). Use a word processing program, and type the text full width. Make two electronic copies; one in ASCII format, the other in the ordinary word processor format. Save both formats for use in later exercises in this and other chapters in this book.

2. With your desktop publishing program, create a simple layout with two text blocks side by side, with 0.25" between the columns. Import your basic story to the left hand Text Block and then link the left and right blocks together so that the story flows from one to the other. If your story is longer than one page, create a second page with two Text Blocks and link the right column of the first page to the left column of the second.

3. Typeset and print your laid-out story in both a serifed and sans-serifed typeface, each in two different type sizes of body copy. Set the title in a bold display type three times larger than the body type. Copyfit as necessary.

4. Kern one paragraph of your story. Set another paragraph in a non-proportional typeface. Condense the type in a paragraph and expand the type in another. Indent one paragraph on the right, another on the left, and a third on both sides. Print the story again, and observe the results.

5. With your desktop publishing program, create a single large Text Block that covers the entire page. In 12 point type, make a keyboard map of all the possible characters, by typing each key in all its uppercase, lowercase, and optional combinations (A-Z, a-z, 0-9, and symbols). Make a type family (like the Times 12 Point family shown in this chapter) for each of the 12 point typefaces available on your computer.

Chapter 3: Art & The Computer

In this age of computer typesetting and photoprinting, it is easy to forget that just a few years ago books were printed from brass and copper plates. Finely illustrated books, for example, required massive marble plates [for the illustrations] and an acid etching process. The D'Aulaires, a husband-and-wife team who have written and illustrated dozens of children's books, used this process. Hand drawings were laboriously transferred onto the marble slabs, which they could never get themselves to throw out. The plates accumulated in their apartment until the inevitable happened – the floor began to cave in under the weight.

–The Writer's Home Companion

Although today our computer-generated graphics may be weighty in terms of the storage space they take up, it's highly unlikely that even the most fanatic computer artist today will have a problem with the mass of disks that the D'Aulaires had with their marble storage!

In the early days of computers, the 1950s, most people thought of computers as gigantic adding machines capable of nothing more than doing (very) rapid mathematical manipulation. Yet even then, some of the early computer hackers experimented with having the computer screen display crude pictures by writing programs to place letters and other characters at various places on the screen. Over the years, this kind of symbol drawing developed into relatively sophisticated art. Nearly every big mainframe computer site had a number of these drawings which it could print out at the command of the operator. The symbol drawing shown on page 62 was taken from the Sperry Univac 1100/72 mainframe that was, for years, the primary computer for student and faculty use at the University of Utah Computer Center.

A major step forward in computer graphics came when it was realized that the computer screen (or printout paper) could be arbitrarily divided into tiny rectangles (called **pixels** for **pic**ture **el**ements), each of which could be made to print (black) or not (white). Later still, with sophisticated monitors and printers, numerous shades of gray and colors could be assigned to a pixel as well. Each pixel has a unique location on the screen, expressed as an X,Y coordinate, and programmers developed various ways to tell the computer which pixels were black or white (on or off).

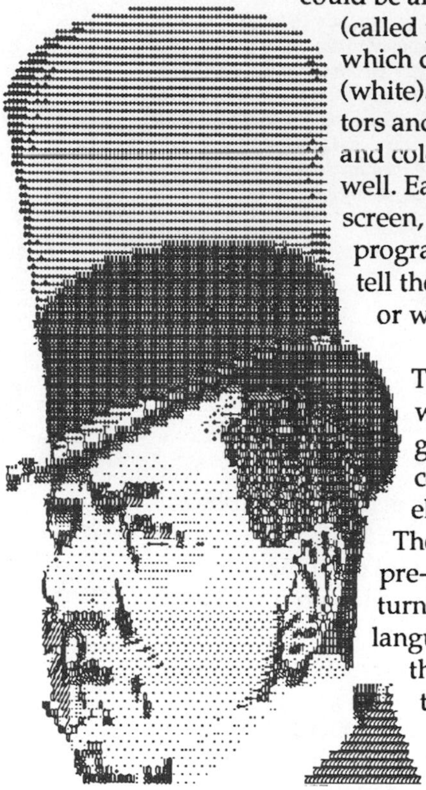

The most difficult method of drawing with the computer is to write a program which does nothing but tell the computer in intricate detail which pixels are to be black and which white. There is no drawing involved, just a pre-plotting of which pixels are to be turned on, and then using a computer language to create a program which tells the computer, "Turn on these locations." The programmer can use graph paper to create the drawing, as if it were an unmarked paint-by-number picture. This method works, and is still in limited use today, but is so complicated that it is outside the realm of this book to attempt to teach it. For more information, visit your campus computer science department.

Fig. 3.1 Vintage comedian W.C. Fields as rendered by a symbol drawing program. This picture was ported from a Univac 1100/72 to the Macintosh. What appear to be dots in this reduced image are actually 6 pt. high non-proportional characters in the full page version.

One of the most important advances in computer art was the development of the **mouse**, by Douglas Englebart of the Stanford Research Institute. The first mouse, constructed of wood, rubber bands, and a switch, simply served as a substitute for the cursor arrow keys, which moved the cursor (or active typing spot) around on the computer screen. Later revisions of the mouse were adapted to locating a particular pixel on the screen. When a push button located on top the mouse was pressed, the pixel directly under the pointer (or cursor) was enabled to change its state from off (white) to on (black) and *vice versa*. With this innovation, computer graphics came of age.

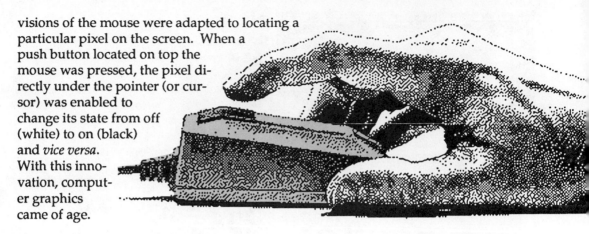

Fig. 3.2 *Invention of the mouse was a major step forward in creating computer graphics quickly and easily.*

Drawing with Microcomputer Graphics Programs

The modern mouse makes computer drawing programs simple and easy to use. No longer does the budding computer artist have to master a computer language to create art. It is simply a matter of adopting previously learned techniques to the tools and effects possible with a particular program.

Now, a "toolbox" presents icons of tools which the artist can use to create the drawing. Common tools include oval/circle and rectangle/square makers, straight line creators, and random polygon tools. There are tools for erasing all or part of a drawing, duplicating parts of the picture, rotating or mirror imaging graphics, modifying line thickness and shade or pattern, and adding shades or patterns to the picture.

To draw something, the user moves the mouse around on the tabletop, which in turn moves a pointer shape on screen. At first this feels cumbersome, like trying to draw with a deck of cards (or a brick) in your hand rather than a pencil,

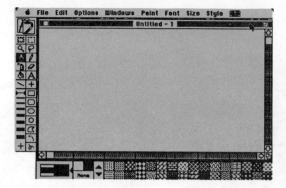

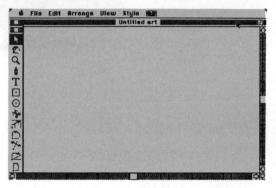

Fig. 3.3 Toolboxes from Super-
Paint, Illustrator, MacPaint, and
MacDraw.

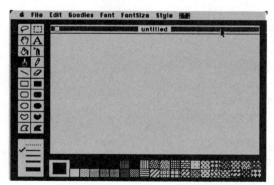

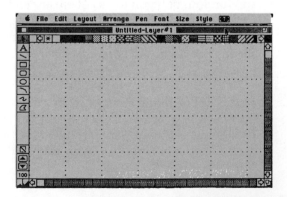

but the movements soon become second nature. Tools are selected by clicking a button located on top of the mouse when the pointer is directly over the desired tool. The pointer usually changes shape to indicate which tool is in current use, and the artist positions it where the desired drawing is to begin. Pressing the mouse button and holding it down activates the portion of the drawing program that darkens pixels wherever the pointer is moved, and a dark line appears on screen.

There are a great many microcomputer graphics programs available for the Macintosh, IBM PC and its compatibles, and advanced workstation micro- and minicomputers. They can be divided into two major classes: bitmap programs and object-oriented programs.

Fig. 3.4 Computer graphic artists at work.

Bitmap Graphics Programs

Bitmap graphics programs use the oldest of all methods of recording the shapes which are drawn – recording the size, black or white status, and X,Y coordinates for each and every pixel in the available drawing area. This approach is simple; yet, because the program records the location and status of every pixel, such drawings tend to take up a lot of storage space. These programs are also relatively slow in their operation. The major problem with such a recording method is that it also records the size of the pixel (generally about 1/50 to 1/70 of an inch square). This, in effect, limits the resolution of the drawing to the size of the pixel, regardless of the resolution of the output device that prints the drawing. A common complaint among early users of MacPaint on the Macintosh was this limited resolution, and the almost woodcut effect it gave to most drawings. However, one program, MacCalligraphy, takes advantage of this effect by creating tools that mimic Japanese *sumi-e* brush painting techniques! IBM PC programs also suffer from the resolution problem if the monitor is not of sufficiently high quality and small pixel size.

Fig. 3.5 A typical bitmap graphic drawn in MacPaint on the Macintosh.

In a bitmap drawing program, straight lines running horizontally, vertically, or at 45° across the drawing will appear as thin, straight lines on the screen or in print. But as the artist tries to create smooth curves, the curved line intercepts not just single pixels, but clusters of them. The result is that curves are actually composed of small straight line segments. The lines tend to appear very jagged ("the jaggies").

It takes a great deal of time and effort to eradicate the "woodcut feel" of graphics of this nature. The artist first has to create the entire drawing as cleanly as possible. The artist then goes to a "magnifying glass" mode, where the drawing is enlarged as much as 800% and only a tiny portion of the drawing can be viewed at one time. In this mode, nearly every pixel has to be examined, and a determination made as to which pixels are really needed to create the curve, shading or other effect, and which can be eliminated. The results can be very good indeed, but may not warrant the amount of time spent to produce them if other alternatives are available.

Commonly Used Bitmap Graphics Programs For Mac & PC

Macintosh	IBM PC and Compatibles
MacPaint	Pixel Paint
Full Paint	PC Paint
HyperCard	PC Paintbrush
SuperPaint	EGA Paint

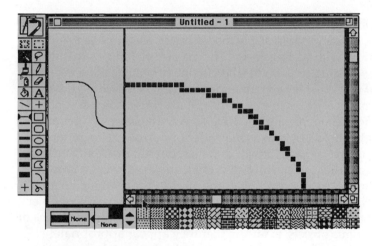

Fig. 3.6 A typical bitmap graphic curve. At the left side of the screen, the curve appears as it will print; on the right, the curve is magnified to show how the "jaggies" approximate the true path of a curved line.

Object-Oriented Graphics Programs

The second type of microcomputer graphics program does not record the location of every pixel. Instead, it essentially records a mathematical description of where the cursor goes. It then displays this description as lines on the screen. This type of computer drawing is much faster, in most cases, than drawing with a bitmap graphics program. The primary advantage of this method, however, is that the resolution of the artwork is limited only by the resolution of the output device, not by the size of the pixel.

For every advantage there is a disadvantage, and the disadvantage of an **object-oriented graphics program** is that the monitor on which the artist views what is being created generally has a very poor resolution (roughly the same as a bitmapped graphics program,1/50 to 1/70 inch square pixels) compared to the output from laser printers or higher resolution printers. This means that what is seen as it is being drawn isn't nearly as good as the quality of the drawing when it comes out of printers such as a laser printer with 300 dot per inch resolution, or a Linotronic Model L300 with 2400 dpi resolution.

Object-oriented programs operate much the same as bitmap graphics programs: the mouse is still used to select and draw with various tools. The major difference is that there is no "magnifier" mode wherein one can manipulate individual pixels. This is because the program is recording the *locations of objects* – lines, circles, or polygons as units – and *not the locations of the pixels* which create the object. Lines and other objects can be made wider or narrower, longer or shorter, as with bitmap graphics, but not manipulated on a magnifier level. How crisp or clean the edges of a line or border are is a function of the output device, remember? Object-oriented graphics programs which have a magnifier mode intend that it be used to better observe the junctions of various objects, to ensure that they appear appropriately aligned when printed even at the highest resolution.

Another advantage of object-oriented programs is that the objects which are drawn– lines and polygons can be re-sized and/or reshaped *as a unit* at any time. With bitmap graphics, once a line or polygon is drawn, it is just a collection of pixels. To reshape or resize, individual pixels must first be erased, and then redrawn. But with object-oriented graphics the object can be selected at any time and then instantly re-sized or reshaped as desired.

Fig. 3.7 Top, an object-oriented graphic show at its on-screen resolution. Bottom, the same graphic shown at its printing resolution.

Commonly Used Object-oriented Programs For Mac & PC

Macintosh   **IBM PC and Compatibles**
MacDraw II   Pixie
SuperPaint   Draw
Drawing Table   Harvard Graphics

PostScript Graphics Programs

Although there are numerous ways in which object-oriented graphics programs can record a drawing, perhaps the most well known (and most efficient) is the **PostScript** page description language invented at Adobe Systems, Inc. When Apple Computers, Inc., adopted PostScript as the language to be used by the graphically oriented Macintosh with its LaserWriter laser printer, a revolution in computer graphics began.

At the time, only some of the very finest output devices for high resolution text were using PostScript as the language to format typesetting output on machines costing tens of thousands of dollars. The then-current laser printers for microcomputers used cassette tapes containing descriptions of a small selection of typefaces. These laser printers were intended as a small-scale, medium-resolution (300 dpi) printers for word processing documents.

The advent of the Apple LaserWriter with PostScript residing in its internal memory sent shock waves through the computer and publishing industry. For less than the cost of a single typesetting machine, practically anyone could own what amounted to a personal electronic publishing company, able to compose text and graphics and print them at medium resolution on a LaserWriter, or with a simple wiring hookup print directly from the Macintosh to the highest resolution typesetting machines. Today, PostScript has become a standard microcomputer page description language not only for graphics, but for text as well, and is the basis for the ease of use and popularity of desktop publishing programs.

There are several graphics programs which record artwork directly in the PostScript language, and some of these allow the user to edit that language to produce even more interesting effects than the basic program allows. Such editing is not simple, because it requires an intimate knowledge of

computer programming. Other graphics programs must un-
dergo a kind of translation from their method of information
storage to the nearest PostScript equivalent. With a Post-
Script-recording graphics program you are assured very
high-quality graphics capabilities to the limit of your printer.

PostScript graphics programs work much the same as other
object-oriented graphics programs, although the tools vary
somewhat. PostScript programs have a wider range of tools
and more possible options. They may be a little more difficult to learn initially, but the results are well worth the effort.

*Fig. 3.8 This PostScript-
generated rose was created in
Adobe Illustrator.*

Why is it no one ever sent me yet
One perfect limousine, do you suppose?
Ah no, it's always just my luck to get
One perfect rose.
  —Dorothy Parker

Commonly Used Postscript
Drawing Programs

Cricket Draw
Illustrator
Freehand

Drawing with Desktop Publishing Program Tools

In addition to using specialized graphics programs to create art, desktop publishing programs normally contain some drawing tools for creating common types of art in the publishing world such as horizontal and vertical rules, boxes and ovals, and patterns for text reversals (see Chapter 4). Object-oriented drawing tools are used to create this art. The tools are used exactly the same way as those in standard graphics programs, except that the drawing is made directly on the desktop publishing layout. Graphic elements of a layout may be added when the initial design is created and before text and pictures are added, or after the fact, to improve the look of the laid-out page.

Graphics Techniques

Some desktop publishing programs, such as Springboard Publisher, contain a relatively complete graphics program as a subset of the main program. In these programs the user activates the graphics mode to create a complete drawing, then electronically moves the finished artwork into the layout.

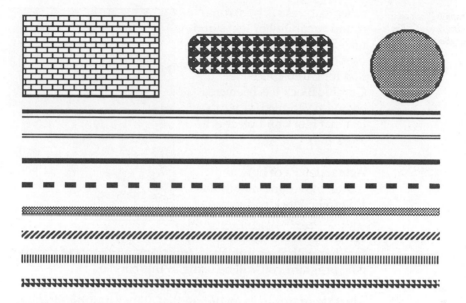

Fig. 3.9 Typical graphics from desktop publishing programs useful for creating rules, boxes, and other page enhancements.

In most cases, however, complicated line art must be created in a specialized graphics program to take advantage of the more sophisticated drawing tools and capabilities. Once created and saved, the drawing can be used in numerous desktop publishing applications, in a variety of different layouts.

To add a graphic created in a specialized drawing program to a desktop publishing layout, the first step is to open the layout and decide where the artwork will go. Then a Graphic Block large enough to contain the picture must be created.

The **Graphic Block** is a special transparent area on the blueline or layout where artwork can be placed. It may be as small as a line or as large as an entire page. Most programs have a Graphics Tool that you position at some starting point for the Graphic Block and then drag until the block is the desired size. The Graphic Block can then be moved around on the layout with some sort of pointer tool. The size of the Graphic Block can also be altered through a Graphic Specification function which allows fine tuning of the position and size of the Graphic Block, and perhaps

73

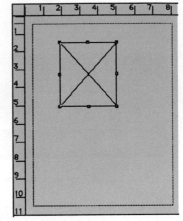

Fig. 3.10 A Graphic Block on a desktop publishing layout. The program is ReadySetGo! on the Macintosh.

other features such as runaround capability or text standoff. See Chapter 4 for other uses of the Graphic Specification function. Once the Graphic Block has been created and positioned, you can select that block and place artwork in it.

Actual details of how to create, move, and manipulate a Graphic Block will vary from program to program and computer to computer. It is up to you to read and become familiar with the commands, functions, and tools of the specific program you will be using in this course.

Most programs have an option that allows graphics to be imported directly to a selected Graphic Block, without having to go through a separate "open the graphics program, copy the picture, close the graphics program, open the desktop publishing program, choose where to paste, then paste" process. Instead, all the user has to do is select the Graphic Block and then choose the Import Graphic option. A list of accessible graphics documents is presented and the user selects the desired document. That picture then automatically appears in the selected Graphic Block.

Scaling and Cropping

Many times it is easier to find or create a picture at one size in a graphics program, but have it appear smaller or larger in the desktop publishing layout. To this end, desktop publishing programs allow the user to **scale** (change the overall size of) and **crop** (choose a particular portion of) a graphic once it has been imported.

Scaling of pictures is most often accomplished through the Specification for the Graphic Block in question. Pictures may be scaled proportionally (both axes reduced or enlarged the same amount) or non-proportionally (axes reduced or enlarged by different amounts) for special effects.

Cropping is handled in one of two ways. There can be a separate tool which, when placed inside the Graphic Block, allows the user to move the picture around within the block. Only the portion within the Graphic Block will then appear when printed. The other method re-forms the Graphic Block over an appropriate portion of the picture.

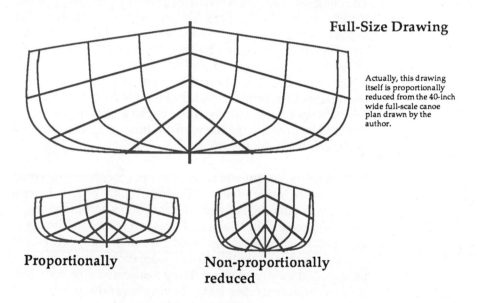

Full-Size Drawing

Actually, this drawing itself is proportionally reduced from the 40-inch wide full-scale canoe plan drawn by the author.

Proportionally

Non-proportionally reduced

Fig. 3.11 An original drawing plus a proportionally reduced and non-proportionally reduced version.

Scanning – Computer Art Without Grief

Scanners or **digitizers** (see also Appendix D) allow the non-artist to create and include computer art in desktop publishing documents. Artwork which has been created in another medium such as pencil, chalk, oil, or photograph can be electronically recorded at various resolutions and stored, displayed, or printed in numerous ways. Software that accompanies the scanner or that can be obtained from other vendors allows the desktop publisher to manipulate the scanned images in various ways.

The simplest scanners work like a printer in reverse, producing bitmap graphics images. The scanner temporarily replaces the printing head, and the software causes the scanner to record pixel-by-pixel, line-by-line, the status of each pixel-sized area on the page. The art to be recorded must be photocopied or otherwise be capable of passing through the platen rollers of the printer. When the art is recorded, the software allows limited editing. Images can also be manipulated by opening the file with a bitmap graphics program and using the program's tools.

High-resolution scanners work like a photocopier in reverse. The artwork is placed on a glass-covered flat bed. When the software is activated, a beam of light passes across the artwork and records it. These scanners can record in bitmap mode, or in a "laser bitmap" mode where the pixels are 1/300 inch square. In this latter mode, the scanned art can be recorded in several ways: **Gray Scale mode** (records the art as a continuous tone image having several hundred graduations from black to white); **Halftone mode** (imitates the mechanical process of screening a continuous tone image, breaking it into various dot patterns for printing); and **Line Art mode** (for black and white art with no middle tones of gray).

Recordings can be saved as bitmap images, object-oriented images, or in a variety of "universal" formats which can allow different kinds of computers to read the image. The most common universal formats are **TIFF (Tag Image File Format)** and **GIF (Graphics Image Format)**. Saving the artwork in TIFF, for example, allows a Macintosh user to create the image using the AppleScan scanner. The user can then electronically transfer the file so that an IBM PC user can incorporate the picture in a document created with Ventura Publisher. TIFF and GIFF are also the formats of choice when recording high-resolution gray-scaled or half-toned art for high-resolution printing. TIFF and GIFF files, because of the level of detail they are recording, may be massive.

The TIFF file for the picture of the woman on page 78 contains 314K bytes. The scanned image was manipulated using the program Digital DarkRoom. The resulting EPS file is 956K bytes. The original picture is a wallet-size color photo.

High-resolution scanner software allows the user to manipulate aspects of the image such as contrast and brightness, and to edit the document to remove unwanted portions. Special software for working with scanned images offers more complete tools, similar to those in graphics programs, which let the user perform sophisticated image modification such as watercolor-like washes, chalk-like blending of patterns and shades, and much more.

When scanned images are imported into desktop publishing programs, they can be scaled and cropped like any other imported graphic.

Some scanners are capable of taking text from typed manuscripts, books, and other materials, digitizing it, and turning it not into graphics, but into text which can be manipulated by word processing programs. These digitizers are called **OCR (optical character recognition)** scanners. This technology can be very useful if you need to use text electronically which was typewritten, but you can't afford the time to retype the text into a word processor.

Some Post-processing Software

Macintosh	**IBM PC and clones**
ImageStudio	Scanning Gallery
	Picture Publisher

Legal Aspects of Scanning

Remember that art, like text, may be protected by copyright and trademark laws. It is illegal to reproduce in any form (including scanning) copyrighted artwork which you have not obtained written permission to reproduce. Violation of

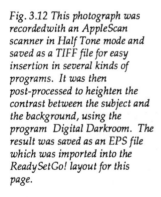

Fig. 3.12 This photograph was recordedwith an AppleScan scanner in Half Tone mode and saved as a TIFF file for easy insertion in several kinds of programs. It was then post-processed to heighten the contrast between the subject and the background, using the program Digital Darkroom. The result was saved as an EPS file which was imported into the ReadySetGo! layout for this page.

copyright or trademark laws can lead to a federal court trial, fines, or even jail. Make sure of your sources, and make sure that you have *written* permission to use any artwork not created by your own art department or an artist working for you on a contractual basis.

Clip Art Collections

Not all of us are artists, especially computer artists, yet as desktop publishers we often need graphics to illustrate the text. If you can't draw what you need, or your artist will take too long to produce a scannable graphic, there is another resort: clip art collections. **Clip art** is art not protected by copyright, and it may be used without obtaining any kind of permission. Originally clip art was published in large format books, and desired graphics were literally clipped from the book and pasted into a layout. Today there are also electronic clip art collections. The advantage of electronic clip art is that you need not destroy the original when you use it; instead you make a copy electronically of the original, and use the duplicate. Two kinds of collections are available: public domain and commercial.

There are numerous "public domain" collections throughout the country, that contain art which is not protected by copyright. Pictures may be electronically copied, modified, and generally used in whatever manner you choose. Such art can vary wildly, from pornographic to saccharin, from crude to exquisite. It's almost always worth your time to hunt through these collections; you never know what gems you might turn up.

Commercial clip art collections are essentially the electronic equivalents of the earlier printed books. You buy from the creator a collection of art documents on disks. Generally each disk has a theme or subject. When you buy the disks you are purchasing a license for the right for your unlimited use of the artwork. This does not mean that you can legally pass the disks around and let others make copies of the disks for their own use.

Electronic clip art, like the programs which are used to create it, can be bitmapped art or object-oriented art such as PostScript-created graphics.

Fig. 3.13 Clip art from the University of Utah Computer Center collection.

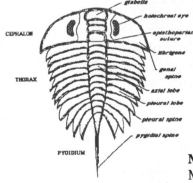

Some Clip Art Collections

Macintosh
MacArt Library Series
Springboard
Works of Art Series

IBM PC and Compatibles
Arts and Letters
MicroGraphics Clip Art

Fig. 3.14 *Commercial clip art.*
Mountain scene and samurai
from the den now e maki
Japanese Clip Art collection;
Magus and Washington
Monument from the
Springboard Works of Art
collection.

Non-Digitized Art in Desktop Publishing

Yes, this can be done; no, it isn't a sin to have occasional pieces of mechanically pasted up artwork!

The technique is to use a Graphic Block to make a space on the page to hold the photo or other art. The original is used to create a halftone or continuous-tone positive which is then pasted into place on the printed master copy. This master copy is throughput from desktop publishing software. For a multitude of copies it can then be taken to a printer. The printer takes the master copy with photo in place, and reproduces that as the published document.

Infographics
Having Your Pie Chart and Eating It Too

Infographics are graphics that present hard technical information, usually statistical in nature – pie charts, bar charts, line charts, or scattergrams. Sometimes the information is presented as stretched or stacked pictures of the topic being discussed, such as coins or bills when talking about budgets, airplanes when discussing passenger miles or crashes per flight hour. A real promoter of this kind of information presentation is the Knight-Ridder Newspaper chain, publishers of *USA Today*.

An advantage of doing infographics electronically is that you don't have to draw all those pies, columns, or bars, or worry about whether the column heights match the numbers or how correctly the pie is divided. The infographics programs do all that for you! All you have to do is type in the correct numbers for comparison, choose the appropriate type of graph to display the information, and make minor cosmetic changes to the fonts.

The earliest infographics were developed as parts of spreadsheet, database, or integrated (spreadsheet and database combined) software. Resolution on screen and with printers, as with ordinary graphics, was the main stumbling block to developing useful software, but all that has changed with the advent of smart laser printers and PostScript compatible software.

Some of the more interesting programs let you create icons or pic-

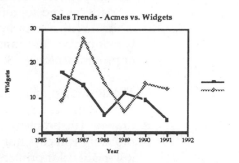

tures that are stacked or stretched by the program to indicate relative values. Other programs let the user make custom versions of another useful infographic – the calendar.

Fig. 3.15 A variety of infographics plots created using CricketGraph on the Macintosh.

Some Infographics Programs

Macintosh	IBM PC and compatibles
Cricket Graph	Pixie
MockChart	Harvard Graphics
PictOgram	

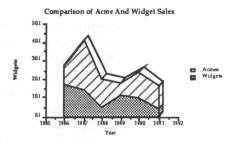

Color and Graphics

Most, if not all, of the graphics programs today allow you to work with color. If you have a black and white monitor, of course, you won't see the colors, but you can specify them for patterns and solid fills as you use them in black and white. With a color monitor, you not only see, but can easily manipulate, the range of colors that the monitor, system, or program allows – 8, 16, 32 , even 256 colors.

The desktop publishing programs will allow you to import, and in some cases manipulate, color graphics after they are drawn. The problem in working with color has been, and probably will continue to be, the dearth of high-quality/ low-price color printers.

If you have access to a high quality color printer, then producing color graphics and color desktop publishing documents is straightforward. Create the graphics in the desired colors, import them to the desktop publishing program, and then integrate them with black or colored text. When you print the document on the color printer, everything comes out as it should.

Color Separations

Without a color printer, the standard method of obtaining color output from black and white is called **four-color process printing**. The four colors are: yellow, cyan (blue-green), magenta (purple-red), and black. Yellow, cyan, and magenta can, in color theory, be combined in various proportions to make any other color in the spectrum, including black. But, since printers inks are in the real world, not in the realm of theory, black is added to the process to help produce the deeper shades of the other colors as well as enrich the three color black.

To create the color picture, four halftone photographs are made, each one recording only the specified color as a pattern of dots. The halftones are then printed sequentially on the same piece of paper, each with its own separate color of ink. The overlap of the four color prints produces the varying shades and solid colors that make up the picture. If the **registration**, or correct relationship among the four prints is not exact, not only will the colors be off, but the final image may be so chaotic as to be almost unrecognizable.

Drawing an illustration to be color-separation printed takes a bit of pre-planning. An object-oriented drawing program that permits the creation of overlay layers is a real bonus. On one layer you can create the complete drawing, and on subsequent layers copy and paste just the red areas, just the blue parts, etc. The program will then let you view, manipulate, and print each layer independently.

Although this textbook is being printed in two colors only, the illustrations on page 86 show the steps and results of creating and printing a four-color separation graphic.

Graphics of all kinds will enhance the look and tone of your desktop publishing efforts. As with everything else, however, a little bit goes a long way. Don't try to incorporate every known kind of electronic and other art into the same document! Pick a style of art reproduction and stay with it, at least within a given project.

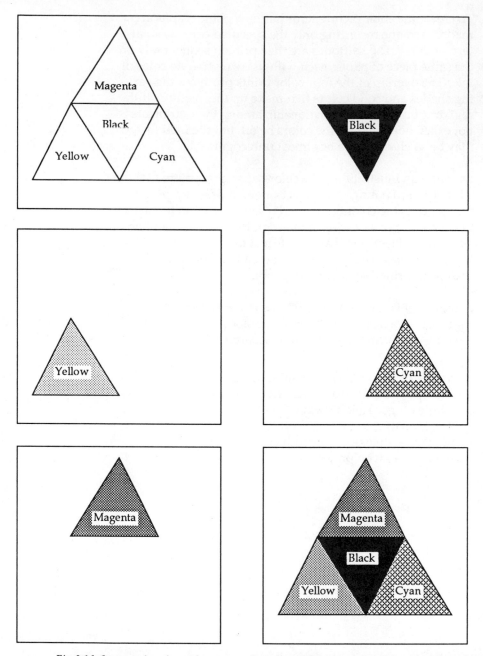

Fig. 3.16 Sequence for a four-color process. Opposite, top left, shows the whole unshaded graphic. Successive illustrations show each area as it is shaded and photographed. The last illustration, above, shows full color graphic as it will be printed when the four separate colors are printed.

Review Questions

1. How were early computer drawings created?
2. What is a pixel?
3. What is a mouse, and how is it used in creating graphics?
4. Name six different tools used in commonly used graphics programs.
5. What other things do graphics toolboxes include besides line and object-making tools?
6. Define bitmap and object-oriented graphics, and give advantages and disadvantages of both types of graphics programs.
7. What is PostScript?
8. How can screen resolution and printed resolution differ, and why?
9. Why is PostScript an efficient way to record a drawing?
10. What kinds of drawing tools do most desktop publishing programs include?
11. What is a Graphic Block?
12. What is the general technique for importing a graphic created in a drawing program into a desktop publishing program?
13. What is the difference between proportional and non-proportional scaling?
14. What good is a scanner?
15. Name four different methods of recording a scanned image.
16. What is gray scale art? Halftone art?
17. Discuss the legal aspects of scanning artwork.
18. What is the difference between public domain and commercial clip art collections?
19. What is the basic technique for including non-electronic art in a desktop published document?
20. Define infographics.
21. List at least three kinds of infographics.

Exercises

1. Create a picture of something interesting to you using a bitmap graphics program. If the software is available, duplicate your drawing using an object-oriented drawing program. Print out your handiwork. Save your drawings electronically for use in other exercises in this chapter and others in this book.

2. Make a copy of both the bitmapped and object-oriented pictures. Using the copies, scale your picture both proportionally and non-proportionally to see how well both kinds of graphics programs allow scaling. Print the results.

3. Using copies of your original drawings, experiment with the effects of different patterns on the look of your drawing. Try signing your name electronically. How close can you get to the look of your ordinary signature? Print your experiments.

4. Save copies of your drawings in forms that are readable by your desktop publishing program. Open the desktop publishing program and create two Graphics Blocks. Import the bitmap version of your picture into one block, and the object-oriented version into the other. Crop the graphics and print out the results. Undo the cropping, and scale the drawings using the publishing program's scaling option. Print copies of your drawings scaled 200%, 150%, 50%, and 25%. Which type of graphics scaled the best?

5. In your favorite graphics program, create a column chart
   infographic the hard way – draw the axes, columns, type
   in the numbers, etc. Record how long it takes you. Print
   your infographic.

6. If the software is available, use an infographics program
   to create a column chart using the same numbers you
   used in #5. How much faster was it to create the infographic this way? Import the infographic into your
   desktop publishing program and crop and scale it. Print
   out both the original and the scaled or cropped versions.

Chapter 4: Special Techniques Combining Text and Graphics

A picture is worth a thousand words.
-- Chinese proverb attributed to Confucius

Confucius was right. A thousand words comes out to a little under 10K of computer storage. So does a modest sort of picture.

-- Ted Nelson in Computer Lib and Dream Machines

This chapter will discuss several interesting and useful (although sometimes complicated) ways to combine both text and graphics on a page layout. These techniques add a great deal of life and interest to documents which, under other circumstances, could be boring blocks of text separated by lonely graphics standing amidst acres of white space. In this chapter you will learn how to meld text and pictures tastefully into an integrated whole that makes a statement – about the overall visual impact of the message as well as your abilities as a designer.

Layout is transparent to most readers, but its effect is very powerful. A good designer can psychologically manipulate the reader with the visual impact of the page well before the first sentence is read. Display type (in a sense a kind of graphic) can scream a headline:

WAR!

Or suppress it;

War in Middle East Reaches New Heights

Express sorrow or joy;

HEINLEIN DEAD
– SciFi Fans Mourn

The Lighter Side

Or otherwise prepare the reader for the content of the story.

The placement and treatment of graphics help set the tone of the story or publication. Geometric placement of pictures within or across columns suggests a solemn, formal approach. Graphics crammed between paragraphs can tell the reader that the pictures were added as an afterthought, or can present an impression of attempting to cram the maximum information in the minimum space. Pictures in a sea of white can indicate an attempt to cover up a lack of body copy, or point up the importance of the image. The space between graphics and text can play up or play down the importance of a graphic.

The size, kind, and number of graphics and how they are integrated into the layout are vitally important in getting subliminal messages across to your reader. Collect examples of what you consider good and poor integration of text and graphics, and then try to analyze why they are good and poor; what you like and don't like about them. A scrapbook of such samples can be an excellent "idea book" when you are trying to find just the right look for a client. Remember, you as the designer are responsible for the psychological tone of the article as expressed in the relationships between the text and graphics on each page of the document. The "right look" can sway the world; the "wrong look" can cost reader understanding, revenue, or your job. In what follows, we will look at some ways to create the "right look."

The Runaround

The **runaround** is not what you get instead of a date on Saturday night. It is a technique for pulling text closely to two or more sides of a graphic, to avoid the look of a picture floating in white between two rigid blocks of text. Runarounds are also valuable space savers. As much as 50% of the length of a document can be reduced by appropriate use of runarounds. Such space savings of course also saves the client additional money – something we all try for as much as possible. In the "old days" cutting body copy around a graphic was time consuming and tedious (and expensive); with desktop publishing, runarounds are a snap.

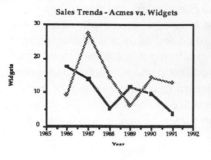

There are two basic ways that text can be run around a graphic. The first is to run the text around some arbitrary **frame**, a non-printing shape within which the picture sits. The frame can be explicit: actual lines forming a rectangular or circular border. Or it may be implicit: the text justified around the rectangular or circular shape without a border. Running around the frame is conventional and dignified, suitable for standard sizes and shapes of photos, charts, diagrams, tables, and many types of line art.

Fig. 4.1 Two kinds of runa-round. Above, text running around the frame that contains the graphics; below, text running around the graphic itself.

The second method is to run the text around the shape of the graphic itself. This technique is more avant-garde or free-flowing. It is best used with unframed art, cutout photos, informal line art, etc. It intimately links the graphic and the text discussing the picture.

Runarounds can of course be placed anywhere on the page, but they have the most impact when the paragraph(s) describing the picture are those which run around it. This is especially true when running text around the shape of the graphic itself.

Always Run Appropriate Text Around a Graphic

We've all seen inappropriate runarounds: the story of the devastating forest fire wrapped around a picture of a boy and his dog romping in a park; the picture of Item A in the middle of the description of Part B. These runarounds are usually caused by different artists laying out text and art, or failure on the part of someone to proof the layout before it is printed. Use common sense. Put the map of the hike location in the middle of the section describing how to get there, not in the dissertation on what clothes to wear for different weather conditions. Triple check to make sure the picture of Fred goes next to his biography, not with Jim's, and that the picture with the chicken cacciatore recipe doesn't look like baked ham.

Runaround Technique

The first step is to find the right graphic and get it into a form which your desktop publishing program can use. If the graphic is a photo to be mechanically pasted, make sure you have the final dimensions handy. Chapter 3 discusses where to obtain free or low-cost computerized art as well as the various forms it can take. There too is a discussion of the various kinds of computer graphics programs that you (or someone with artistic talent, if you don't have it) can use to create your own computer art.

Secondly, the graphic should be stored where you can readily access it (on a hard disk with everything else, or on the storage or program disk along with your document) without having to perform numerous disk swaps or spend time later loading the graphic. With the Macintosh, store often-used graphics such as logos in the Scrapbook so that they are readily available for any program. Similar graphic storage utilities are available for IBM and compatible computers.

If the Text Blocks have been created and the copy is already typed in or imported, the next step is to create the Graphic Block where the picture will be placed.

A few desktop publishing programs still require you to duplicate old fashioned cutting and pasting, by having you cut and reshape Text Blocks electro-manually to fit around a Graphic Block. Most programs, however, let you simply create a Graphic Block and move it on top of one or more Text Blocks. When you do, the underlying text automatically flows away from the Graphic Block. This text flow will take place whether the text was previously entered, is imported from a word processing file, or is typed in after the Text and Graphic Blocks have been arranged.

The best time to create a Graphic Block for runarounds is when you are in the View Full Page mode. That way you have an overall view of the effect of the graphic on the look of the page. Zoom in to the 100% View to make sure that the Graphic Block is near the appropriate paragraph. Use the Graphic Block Specification item to fine-tune the size or position of the block if necessary.

If the graphics are to be the dominant element in the layout, it is often best to place them (or at least Graphic Blocks which will contain them) on the page first. This approach works best for projects such as catalogues or brochures, where a "picture is worth a thousand words" in selling or describing the object, and the text is secondary to the visual impact.

For catalogues and similar projects, the most common format is to have exactly the same layout from page to page, with pictures in the same locations on every page (or mirror image locations). Desktop publishing programs normally have some kind of Master Page layout where you can place items such as page numbers, rules, Graphic or Text Boxes, and other items that occur on every page. The Master Page lets you create a separate Left Master Page and Right Master Page, for alternating the positions of page numbers, headers and footers, and other items. In a catalogue project, use the Left and Right Master Pages to create, apportion, and position recurring Graphic Blocks and Picture Blocks. Whatever is laid out on a Master Page appears in the same location on every page, regardless of whatever else is placed in that location during the regular layout process. Items on a Master Page can sometimes cause confusion if your carefully designed layout is overprinted by items that you placed in the Master Page and forgot.

Stand-off

Stand-off, or the separation between the edges of the runaround text and the graphic, is an important element in
achieving the right look. Too much space, and your picture
floats in white; too little space, and the impact of the graphic
is lost in the body copy. Some programs require that you
hand position the associated Text Blocks to achieve the correct stand-off. Others let you specify the amount of stand-off
in the Graphic Block Specification item. In either case, it is
important to take the time to get the stand-off right.

Generally the right amount of stand-off can be determined
using the 3-to-5 Rule. The top stand-off should be 3 units to
the bottom stand-off's 5 units. What the units are – points,
picas, millimeters, or inches – is irrelevant. The important
factor is that the bottom have more stand-off than the top.
Side stand-off should be the same as, or slightly less than,
the top stand-off.

At this time, only a few desktop publishing programs allow
individual control of top, bottom, left, and right stand-off,
but this feature will become more common as time goes by
and desktop publishers demand more from their software.

Captions With Runarounds

If your graphic needs a caption, the caption should be placed
in its own Text Block and positioned below (or at least near)
the Graphic Block. This way, if changes are necessary, the
caption and graphic don't have to be cut from the desktop
publishing program, placed in the graphic program, modified, and then pasted back into the publishing document.
The caption Text Block can be made a runaround in the Text
Block Specification item of some programs; in others you
will have to position the main text blocks around it as well
as the Graphic Block. To make it distinct, caption text is usually set 2-3 point sizes smaller than the body copy; it can be
in the same font as the body copy or in a different font for
added distinction. With a captioned graphic, the stand-off

between caption text and body copy should follow the 3-to-5 Rule. Set the stand-off between the graphic and caption to one unit distance.

Placing The Graphic

Now that you have taken up the right amount of page space for the graphic, electronically paste it in place and scale it to fit the Graphic Block. Decide whether you want to run the text around the frame or the graphic itself, and make that setting for the Graphic Block. Once the text is running around the graphic, you may find it necessary to adjust the position of the graphic on the page, so that it stays in or with the appropriate paragraph(s). The result should look something like Figure 4.2.

Fig. 4.2 Text flowing around a graphic in a desktop publishing layout. These kinds of techniques are very easy to do in desktop publishing; very difficult in conventional typesetting publishing.

Spillover

When you put Graphic Blocks on top of Text Blocks and tell the program you want to do a runaround, the text is displaced to other locations in the body copy column(s) and some of the text may disappear at the bottom of the last affected Text Block. This is especially critical where Text Blocks linked from page to page may cause text to flow onto other pages, disrupting other layouts. Make sure you don't lose any of your copy or affect other pages with widows or orphans. If you know you are going to run a particular graphic with a story, it is often better to create the Graphic Block before placing the text, so that the space for the graphic is already allocated in the columns on the page. Then as you enter the text, either manually or by calling it in from another file, the text will automatically flow around the Graphic Block and the chance of dropping a word or line of text is minimized.

Running Around Photos

If you need to have text running around non-digitized photos (because of limitations in quality or the effect of the digitization on the artwork), the technique is to create Graphic Blocks and size them to fit the photos, as described above. The block can be framed with integral drawing tools or unframed as desired. When printed, the unfilled Graphic Block leaves a blank space on the page. Once the document is printed, the photo, positive print, or screen is mechanically pasted in the appropriate blank.

Running electronic text around a cut out photo (around the "graphic" as opposed to around the "frame") can be an interesting option. Cut the picture out of its background, then photocopy the silhouette. Digitize the photocopy of the silhouette and electronically paste that into the Graphic Block. Proportionally scale the silhouette graphic 1-2% smaller than the desired finished size and set the Specification so that the text will flow around the graphic. The text conforms to the shape of the silhouette and the silhouette will be just small enough to hide behind the photo which will be mechanically pasted onto the printed master.

The Large Initial Capital Letter

When books were hand written, a large initial capital letter (often illuminated with detailed pictures entwined about it) was often inscribed on the first page of a chapter or as the first letter of the first word of the opening paragraph. This letter served several purposes. It gave the calligrapher a break from the tedium of copying the miniscule text; it served as a convenient way to indicate chapter breaks in manuscripts that usually didn't even have paragraph breaks (to save space on costly vellum). The illumination served to liven up the content for the reader, by its colors and figures. It also accomplished the additional task of celebrating the glory of God, an important factor for the early churchmen-scribes.

With desktop publishing, the **large initial capital** can still serve as a break for the publisher. It can also serve to help indicate chapter or section headings along with chapter titles labelled Chapter Three: The Dawn of Civilization. If you can find or create them, illuminated capitals, because of their "picture letters," can also be used in some publishing projects such as achievement scrolls or certificates, fancy public notices, flyers, and brochures.

Two kinds of large capitals can be created with desktop publishing programs; the raised large capital, and the embedded large capital.

T his paragraph begins with a raised large capital set in

the same font as the body copy. The raised large capital is created by specifying a font size two or three times larger than the body copy. This paragraph's large capital is three times as large as the body copy.

T his paragraph begins with a raised large capital set in a

different font from the body copy. The raised large capital is created by specifying a complimentary font and a size two or three times larger than the body copy. This paragraph's large capital is also three times the size of the body copy.

O ften the large initial capital is additionally empha-

sized by adding Bold, Italic, or other features to its style, as in this paragraph's shadowed capital O. These features are added with the font processing characteristics of the programs. They will vary depending on which desktop publishing program is used with which printer.

N otice how the size and style of the initial capital have affected the line spacing between the first line and subsequent lines of the paragraphs above. The solution is to change the line spacing of the entire paragraph, and then use the default line spacing for the rest of the article. This paragraph has had its line spacing set to 12 points of line spacing. The "auto" setting was changed to the normal spacing for the font size, forcing the lines to close up. Subsequent paragraphs return to the "auto" line spacing.

T he second type of large initial capital is the **embedded initial capital** as seen in this paragraph. This type of initial capital is created by using a separate, runaround Text Block for the capital. The capital Text Block specifications are set so that it is just large enough to contain the letter in the size required, and has minimal or no stand-off. If the desktop publishing program does not allow Text Blocks to be specified as runarounds, you have to create the runaround effect by putting the large capital in a Text Block and then cutting and shaping portions of the body copy Text Block to fit around the Text Block containing the capital, just as you would with a runaround.

I lluminated capitals, such as the French Manuscript style "I" beginning this paragraph, can be created using clip art and fonts together in a graphics program, and then importing the combined graphic into the desktop publishing program. The resulting graphic is then placed in a runaround Graphic Block, and the body copy flows around it. Some illuminated alphabets are available as pure graphics, and need only to be cut and pasted into place and specified as runarounds. Using these techniques, you can custom design illuminated letters for specific purposes such as sports events posters, art and theatre programs, business flyers, or club event notices.

To create illuminated letters, the best type of graphics program to use is one that lets you create and save images directly in the PostScript printer language. With this kind of graphic, the resolution is limited only by the resolution of the printer – from dot matrix through PostScript-compatible typesetting machines. However, many graphics programs are not PostScript compatible, and you will have to settle for the best resolution you can get. See Chapter 3 for more detail on the various kinds of graphics and graphics programs.

Illuminated capitals can be ultramodern, conservative, or traditional, to suit the feeling of the document in which you use them. Just make sure to match the style of art in the

illumination to the feel of the document. The French
Manuscript "I" on page 102, wouldn't work very well in The
American Chemical Society Newsletter – it's too flowery; but
letters illuminated with Ehrlenmeyer flasks, a titration appa-
ratus, or made into large versions of the symbols for the elements might be just the right touch to take the stodginess
out of the copy. "Creative but not cute" is the effect you
should strive for in this as well as other uses of graphics and
text in your various desktop publishing projects.

The Sidebar

Sidebars are those bits of information, found in boxes ac-
companying magazine articles, that contain explanatory or
expository text relevant to the subject at hand. The sidebar
is a form of footnote. If the same article were to appear in a
scholarly journal or book, most of the sidebar information
would be condensed into footnotes or chapter notes.

Sidebars may be written by the author of the main article, by
another author contracted to produce just the sidebar, or by
the staff of the publication, to fill in details that the main article author missed or ignored but which the editor feels are
important to the story.

Don't use sidebars for trivial information; keep them in your
bag of layout tricks for emphasizing important data. Sidebars can fill out poorly written or incomplete articles with information which
may possibly be
written in a radi-
cally different
style. Repeated-
ly using any
technique causes
the reader to
begin ignoring it
and its impact.

A Sidebar About Sidebars

What makes a good sidebar? If the author ram-
bles about anecdotes or data that are interesting
but not immediately relevent to the discussion,
those paragraphs can make a good sidebar. Other
possibilities occur when an author goes into excessive detail or jargon when you requested a simple,
straightforward article written in plain English.
Pull quotes, a single phrase or sentence set in
larger type than the body, are a kind of sidebar

Variety is important, but too much variety can be distracting.

Sidebars may be set in the same typeface and size as the main article, in the same face 1-2 points smaller than the body copy, or in a different face and size entirely. They can be set in plain black type against the paper color, screened against a gray or complimentary-colored background, or **reversed out** with white lettering against a black or colored background. In addition to or in lieu of screen techniques to set it apart from the main article, the sidebar may also be boxed by graphic lines of various kinds and sizes.

A sidebar may be the same width as a normal column or smaller than column width. Or it may extend across several columns. Regardless of its placement, a sidebar rarely takes up as much as half a page. Of course, there are always exceptions to the rule, as in the sidebar shown below. The magazine editor set the sidebar in normal body size, added a photograph, byline, and judicious white space, and used it to fill a page for which an advertising deal fell through at the last minute.

Fig. 4.3 This is an example of a sidebar which grew large enough to occupy an entire page. All it took was a photo and a little creative layout on the part of the editor.

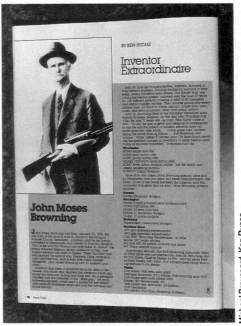

Sidebar Technique

The basic technique for creating a sidebar is to place it in its own Text Block. You could just type the sidebar text in the main body and then change its font and size, but you are limited to in that the sidebar can be no wider than the existing column. "Hanging" the sidebar will create a clumsy amount of white space. Creating a separate Text Block for the sidebar lets you shape the sidebar to column width or less or across two or more columns at any time; and then make it a runaround, or not, depending on circumstances. If you create the sidebar in the body copy Text Block, and then later decide you want the sidebar to carry across columns, you've created lots of extra work for yourself. By putting the sidebar copy in its own Text Block to start with, you leave yourself many more options.

Regardless of the width of the sidebar, its Specification item should be set for runaround if the desktop publishing program allows. This way, the position of the sidebar on the page can be modified instantly without having to manually readjust the main body copy. It is done automatically as the runaround sidebar is moved.

Reversals

If you really want textual information to stand out, the most dramatic technique to use is to reverse it. Where the eye is accustomed to seeing black letters on the white page, the sudden occurrence of white letters against a black background is almost guaranteed to cause the reader to pause and read the new message. **Reversal** can be applied with equal dexterity to body copy or a sidebar; in either case, the effect is striking.

The abilities of the desktop publishing program you are using will depend on how you go about creating a reversal. On one hand, a program such as Pagemaker will let you make all of the text in a given Text Block white lettering by choosing that option in the Text Block Specification item. The black background is created using the Pagemaker drawing tools to make a rectangle or oval and to fill it with black. This black shape must then be positioned behind the text. In some programs this can be very disconcerting because you can't see the results immediately. With the lettering set to white, the Text Block seems empty until it is placed on the black Graphic Block, and can be hard to locate if you are working with a Block only a single line deep. If the black shape is left on top of the white lettering, lettering will not appear when the page is printed.

If you really want textual information to stand out, the most dramatic technique is the black and white or color reversal. Where the eye is accustomed to seeing black letters on the white page, the sudden occurrence of white letters against a black background is almost guaranteed to cause the reader to pause and read the new message. Reversal techniques can be applied equally to body copy or a sidebar; in either case, the effect is striking.

Fig. 4.4 Two varieties of reversal. White on black in body copy, and below, black copy on 30% gray as a sidebar.

With the program ReadySetGo!, reversals are much easier to create, and the results are more WYSIWYG. In this program you create a Text Block, type the text, choose White Type from the Specification menu, and then choose a pattern or shade of gray from the Fill menu. The text block itself is filled with the shade. There is no need to create or manipulate both a Text and a Graphic Block.

If you really want textual information to stand out, the most dramatic technique is the black and white or color reversal. Where the eye is accustomed to seeing black letters on the white page, the sudden occurrence of white letters against a black or shaded background is almost guaranteed to cause the reader to pause and read the new message.

Still other desktop publishing programs, notably those for IBM PC and compatible computers, allow neither of the above capabilities, and require you to create both the black background and white text in a graphic or other program and then import the result as a graphic, which cannot be edited as normal text.

Color Reversals or Separations

Text reversals need not be just black and white or shades of gray. You can also have white lettering against a colored background, colored lettering against a white or black background, or colored lettering against a complementary colored background. Which combination you should choose is determined by the project design and budget. Adding a single color to a nominally black and white project can quadruple the project cost.

Color reversals – and the choice of colors themselves – help to maintain a consistant look. Combining red and black on one page and blue and white on another, for example, can create truly ugly, unreadable documents. Experiment with color reversals to see how they will affect the document well before going to final press. Know what your final product will look like. Don't be surprised when the proofs come back!

The technique for producing color text reversals is similar to that discussed in Chapter 3 for creating color separations for graphics. In this case, the Blocks are created as described above, and given a specified percentage of intensity and color, such as 20% blue for the background and white for the text. A separate print is made of the laid out page for each color used, plus black. These prints show only those items on the page to be printed in each specified color. This is most often done with a printing option called something like Print Color Separations.

The printer then makes a negative for each color used in the layout, overlaps them in the darkroom, and makes an color **interneg** or **multicolor print** which is used to produce the multicolor printed page. **Registration marks** (tiny marks on the edges of each color separation which do not show up on the final print) allow the printer to align the different negatives of the page precisely. If the registration marks are not aligned accurately, the resulting multicolored final page appears double or triple printed and blurred – a distracting and costly error. To avoid this problem, copy the page electronically several times and then delete all but one color from each copy.

Rotated and Contoured Text

Special effects with text and graphics can certainly be attention grabbers if they are done tastefully. Such is the case with **rotated text**. In some instances, text set at a shallow angle or at right angles to the body is just the ticket to grab the reader. Edge-keyed reference materials, long complicated headlines running the length of the page, and SALE! proclaimed diagonally across the top of a flyer are good examples of rotated text used effectively.

Fig. 4.5 Text contoured in the shape of a mountain by raising characters to varying heights above the baseline. Only the "C" in Collect and final "h" in High are on the baseline.

The mirror image text in Lewis Carrolls' poem Jabberwocky, from *Through the Looking Glass, and What Alice Found There* is a classic example of a creative use of rotated text. Alice finds the poem and discovers that it can be read only if she holds it up to a mirror.

Other special text effects can be obtained by "contouring" the text – placing words at varying levels to create a picture, such as the mountain shown here.

Jabberwocky

'Twas brillig, and slithy toves
did gyre and gimble in the wabe.
All mimsy were the borogoves,
and mome raths outgrabe.

Beware the Jabberwock my sone,
with jaws that bite, and claws that catch
Beware the the jubjube bird
and shun the frumious bandersnatch.

He took his vorpal sword in hand,
long time the manxome foe he sought.
So rested he by a tumtum tree
and stood awhile in thought.

And while in uffish thought he stood,
a Jabberwock, with eyes aflame
came whiffling through the tulgey wood
and burbled as it came.

One, Two, through and through
his vorpal blade went snickersnack.
He left it dead, and with its head,
he went galumphing back.

Oh hast thou slain the Jabberwock,
Come to my arms my beamish boy!
Caloo, callay,
he chortled in his joy.

'Twas brillig, and slithy toves
did gyre and gimble in the wabe.
All mimsy were the borogoves,
and mome raths outgrabe.

Fig. 4.6 The poem Jabberwocky *as printed in various editions of* Through the Looking Glass, and What Alice Found There. *Read the text while looking in a mirror to see the image correctly. The effect was created by typing the text in MacDraw and using the horizontal flip function to make it a mirror image.*

Lewis Carroll's other classic use of effect is the mouse's tail
tale from *Alice's Adventures Underground*. Dodson created
this wordplay as a visual play on "tale" and "tail":

Fig. 4.7 "The Mouse's Tale"
from the facsimile edition of
Alice's Adventures
Underground.

Creating these effects on a traditional typesetting machine, or by hand pasteup is a laborious and time-consuming process. A simple project such as the impression of the mountain shown above can take twenty minutes if done by traditional cut and paste techniques. Doing them with desktop publishing and computer graphics programs, however, is relatively easy and fast; the "electronic" mountain was done in less than five minutes.

Fig. 4.8 Rotated text can be used effectively in a variety of situations. Here, the normal 18 pt. section heading has been rotated 45° to the left.

Rotated Text Some desktop publishing programs allow you to type text in a Text Block, and then select and rotate the entire Block to a specified degree. Other programs make no provision for these effects, and you will have to create the rotated text in a graphics program and then import it as a graphic. If the rotated text is imported as a graphic, the body copy should be specified to runaround the graphic rather than the frame. In this way the body copy adjusts to fit the angular shape. Running around the graphic will cause excessive white space above and below the angled text.

In either case, the degree of rotation is important to the reader's grasp of the content. As a general rule, it is best to stick to standard angles of rotation – 15°, 30°, 45°, 60°, 90°. These are the angles at which most readers are used to seeing things tilted. Non-standard angles like 36° or 69° tend to decrease readability as the reader's eye takes longer to decipher the wording at the unusual angle.

If, on the other hand, the entire layout is slanted to accomodate a design, then it is best to rotate everything to the same angle. In such cases, text set to a "standard" angle will clash with, and disrupt the feel of, the overall design, and readability will be decreased.

Fig. 4.9 Above, three uses of rotated text as a graphic element to emphasize a point.

Contoured Text

Placing text in some overall shape is a much more limited special effect than rotated text. Most often the effect is more cute than creative. However, in some situations, the impact of **contoured text** can be very dramatic.

Fig. 4.10 PostScript is used to program text to fit within the outline of a star.

Some desktop publishing programs have provisions for creating contour effects semi-automatically. In others you will have to tab and space the words manually into the contoured shape, using graphics or other programs and importing the result as a graphic. To be able to create contoured text most easily, both the desktop publishing program and the printer need to use PostScript, a computer language which contains numerous special effects for text, including contouring to predefined shapes. Learning to manipulate PostScript commands, however, is not particularly easy. For most purposes, using the techniques below will create adequate contour text.

Creative Word and Line Placement

Most desktop publishing programs allow you to specify the placement of a selected letter or word above or below the baseline of the text. Sometimes these functions have built-in settings for the superscripts and subscripts used in science and mathematics:

$$\pi r^2 \qquad H_2O$$

If the program allows arbitrary setting of the upper and lower location of words and/or letters, you can easily create effects such as:

$$H^{i^{g^h}} \qquad \text{and} \qquad L_{o_w}$$

by manipulating the position of the letters within the line. In these examples, the first letter of each word was left on the baseline, and succeeding letters raised 2, 4, or 6 points above the previous line.

Another effect is the ability to adjust the spacing between letters of a word, such as:

BRAKE and S l i d e

orbetweenwords,asinthisparagraph,wherethespacesbe- tween the words in the first line are compressed 90% and the words in the second line are expanded to 225% of normal, while the remainder has normal word spacing.

Combining these effects with the ability to change the point size of the lettering, gives you a wealth of possibilities for creating contoured text. See if you can duplicate the example below using your desktop publishing program.

The bu^{m}py road c^{u}r$_v$e^d as it

went o^{ver} ^{hi}l$_l$ and d$_{own}$ dal^e.

Graphics Fonts
and Custom Logo Fonts

A **dingbat** is one of a number of special graphics or symbols used by typographers. The most commonly available dingbat font for desktop publishing is the ITC Dingbat family:

Fig. 4.11 ITC Dingbats is a very useful typeface for desktop publishing purposes. The figures are useful for books, reports, brochures, forms, etc.

These graphics find frequent but restrained use in creating brochures, forms, flyers, and similar projects. Overuse of dingbats becomes cute.

Other graphics fonts replace ordinary letters and numbers with fanciful **pictograms** – sort of modern-day hieroglyphics, which can be used in a variety of ways as well. One common use is to replace an ordinary font character in an embedded or raised capital. Another is to choose a pictogram which replaces the first letter of the first word and has something to do with the paragraph or chapter in question – a locomotive in an article about trains, for example. Here again, the tone or feel of the document is important. Graphics fonts generally have no place in formal documents, but look their best in *avant garde* publications, club newsletters, and similar projects.

The Images bitmap font is a good example of a pictogram typeface:

Fig. 4.12 Pictogram typefaces, like dingbats, can be used in many desktop publishing projects. This is the Images font for the Macintosh.

Another kind of graphic font is one that you create with a graphics program and use as standalone artwork. In this case, the letter itself is either created from strokes that are graphics, or overlaid with art (as opposed to being surrounded by art as illuminated letters are).

The "net U" was created for a University of Utah Men's Basketball Team program. Originally, a conventional artist was commissioned to create the "U," but that person worked for 2 hours and completed less than one fourth of the letter. The client approached a typesetter to see if the emblem could be created quicker but with equivalent sharpness and precision. The typesetter could not create the logo letter to the standards of the project manager, and a last attempt was made by the author, creating the "U" using a Macintosh and MacDraw II. The "U" as shown was completed in less than one half hour.

Fig. 4.13 Typography as a graphic. In this case, the "U" from "Utah" is made to look like a basketball net. Using MacDraw II, the author created the shape of the letter, filled it with black, and then created a single white line. The line was then duplicated at regular intervals and the set of lines grouped together. The grouped lines were also duplicated, and the duplicate flipped and overlaid on the original lines to produce the diamond effect.

Custom Logo Fonts

Using special computer programs, it is possible to design your own font, or create a version of a standard font where one or more characters display and print a graphic instead of a letter.

On the Macintosh there are two programs that allow you to make your own fonts – Fontastic and Fontographer. Fontastic allows users to generate bitmap fonts for use with dot matrix printers, while Fontographer allows making of fonts whose definitions are recorded in PostScript for use by laser printers and other devices which use PostScript. Using these programs you can create your own fanciful or elegant styles of lettering, or recreate historical alphabets.

You can also use an existing font and modify a little-used character such as "~" into your personal or corporate logo. The font behaves as always, except that whenever you want the log there is no need to cut and paste from a graphics program to a word processor or access a large TIFF file of the scanned logo from a desktop publishing application. Just tap the appropriate key and the logo appears. Like other characters the logo can be enlarged or reduced by choosing a different font size to suit the particular application. Choose 96 point or 127 point to type the logo in a letterhead, or choose 6 point or 8 point to add the logo as a flourish to your signature block.

Creating your own specialty or logo font can be time-consuming and tedious, and such an effort should be undertaken only if the alternatives are either totally unsuitable or outrageously expensive. Of course, if you've nothing else to do for a couple of days, and just happen to have a font-making program, such projects do help while away the time, and they can be very useful. Below is the first alphabet created by the author using Fontographer. This is supposedly the alphabet used by the Anglo Saxon people prior to the Norman Conquest. Even with the ability to copy, paste, and shrink capitals to their lowercase form, the project took some 12 hours to complete. Creating an entire alphabet is much more complex than the "U" shown above.

ΛBⅭDЄFGHIⱩL∞NOPRSⱵUⱷXYZ
abcdeᵽꝫhiklmnopꝓꝛꞇuꝗxyzꝺþꝹÞ™ꝑ
Ðe᾿ qꞇc Noꝛman ᵽox ꝫumpeꝺ opeᵽ þe᾿ lazy Saxon ꝺoꝫ

Custom designing fonts and logo fonts can be very useful to an advertising agency or publishing house which could use the creation repeatedly. However for "small publishers," such effects can be overly time consuming for a one-time use.

PostScript Wizardry

PostScript is a graphic computer language used by many laser printers and other output devices to present extremely crisp text. The language stores absolute descriptions of characters, so the quality of output is limited only by the resolution of the output device. PostScript text on a Macintosh LaserWriter prints at 300 dpi, while the same file printed through a Linotronic L300 printer can be printed at up to 2450 dpi.

Many people don't realize that PostScript has a great many standard text manipulation routines that, given a program which lets you access them, can be used to create interesting and unusual effects. Among the PostScript effects are drop shadows, special shading effects, binding of text to follow outlines of standard and generated shapes, and much more. Working with PostScript is not easy, but the results can be dramatic.

The program codes for many standard effects such as these are readily available and can be modified without a great deal of trouble. The program code to produce the falling word effect shown on page 120 is given on Page 121. The word which falls appears in the fourth line in parentheses, the shades of gray used are established in line 12, and the font is set in line 14.

Fig. 4.14 *Three examples of PostScript-generated special text effects. Although not easy to create, the effects certainly are striking. Top, the Falling Word; Center, Spiral Text; Bottom, Radial Text.*

Postscript Code To Create the Falling Word Effect

```
% Modified from Adobe Systems Incorporated code by
Kenneth S. Hulme
gsave
0 -200 translate
/firstname (Typography) def
/lastname (Systems) def
/inch {72 mul} def
/fallover
{gsave 90 rotate
.9 -.2 .3 {setgray 0 0 moveto firstname show -22.2
rotate} for
grestore
0 0 moveto
.1 setgray firstname show
} def
/Palatino-BoldItalic findfont 72 scalefont setfont
/leftmargin 8.5 inch firstname stringwidth exch sub add 2
div def
gsave
leftmargin 5 inch translate
fallover
grestore
grestore

showpage
```

PostScript effects can be very dramatic, but are you willing to take the days or weeks necessary to learn how to program in PostScript? Maybe. But don't pick up a PostScript manual today, and promise a given effect by tomorrow!

Review Questions

1. What is the first thing readers will notice when they look at a page?
2. Give three examples of ways that the designer can influence the reader.
3. Why is it usually advisable to do runarounds?
4. Name the two kinds of runarounds.
5. What is the 3-to-5 rule for standoff?
6. What purpose does a Master Page serve in a layout?
7. How can you avoid spillover?
8. List three purposes for a large initial capital.
9. What are the two kinds of large initial capital?
10. When do you put copy in a sidebar?
11. What are three sources of sidebar material?
12. Why reverse text?
13. What is the basic purpose of any text or graphic special effect?
14. List three things that rotated or angled text can accomplish in a design.
15. Why would you want to take the time and effort to create a logo font?
16. How is contoured text created?
17. When would you create a graphic font or alphabet?
18. Define PostScript.
19. Does PostScript work with text or graphics?
20. When would you use PostScript to create an effect?

Exercises

1. Import the graphics you created in Chapter 4 into your desktop publishing program. Place them in Graphics Blocks. Import the story you wrote for Chapter 3 and lay it out in two Text Blocks 3.5 inch wide and 10 inch deep with a .25 inch gutter. Drag one of the Graphic Blocks across the gutter and make the text of both columns run around the graphic. Scale the other Graphic Block so that the art is narrower than the column width; lay this graphic flush with the left side of the right hand column. Add a runaround caption to one of the graphics.

2. Type the entire opening paragraph of the Preamble to the Constitution. Duplicate the text so that you have three copies. Replace the ordinary "W" of "We" with 1) a raised large capital; 2) an embedded large capital; and 3) an illuminated capital from a clip art collection or one of your own creation.

3. Lay out the basic story that you wrote for Chapter 2 in two columns, with a .25 inch gutter. Now write a sidebar of at least 150 words which expands, explains, or adds to the initial story. Create a sidebar that crosses the gutter, and make it a 50% gray reversal.

4. Contour the following: Jack and Jill went up a hill to fetch a pail of water. Jack fell down and broke his crown, and Jill came tumbling after.

5. With a graphics program, create a graphic or illuminated capital letter at least 2" x 3". Import it into your desktop publishing program, and lay out your basic story around this letter.

6. If the software is available, experiment with producing various effects using PostScript. Many word processing and desktop publishing programs (such as Microsoft Word and ReadySetGo!) have ways of specifying pieces of text as PostScript code which will be printed as PostScript effects rather than ordinary text.

Chapter 5: Basic Design and Small Publications

Space is the most flexible of all the raw materials we use in making printed pieces. Using it intelligently can make a good piece more vivid, more sparkly, more original—more interesting to look at. Using it insensitively can make a good piece mediocre and easy to disregard.

— *Jan V. White*, The Grid Book

The common denominator of all publications is layout. Thus the importance of learning the basics of layout and design. Once that is out of the way, we'll go on to see how to apply those principles to the tremendous variety of publications collectively known as miscellaneous or "small" publications. Book, magazine, and newsletter layout and design are covered in separate chapters later in this book.

One of the more famous creators of miscellaneous publications got into a lot of legal trouble over his works. The pamphlet *The Case of the Offices of Excise,* based on personal experience, got the author fired from that office, whereupon he emigrated to the not-yet-United States. In January, 1776 he published another pamphlet that caused revolutionary uproar around the world – *Common Sense.* The author, of course, was Thomas Paine.

Elements of a Layout

Layouts have a number of common elements. As in typography, learning the correct terminology for these elements is important for understanding among those who will be involved in a project. The following elements can be found in many layouts, but any given layout won't necessarily use all of the elements.

Heading – The line of type, usually heavier and larger than the body copy, which sits above the main body of material. Also known as a **Head** or **Headline**. Headings may be in the same typeface as the body, or in a typeface chosen for its contrast, applicability to the body copy (ornamental faces for example), and so forth.

Subhead – Secondary material set smaller than the heading but larger than the body, which usually appears between the head and the body.

Illustration – Also called **art** or **artwork**. Any kind of illustrative material. Illustrations can be humorous, decorative, explanatory, and in any medium – electronic art, photograph, pencil, chalk, or oil. *The* illustration is the major piece of artwork in a design.

Secondary Illustration – Smaller, supplementary artwork. Art used to help the balance of a design or to create a common feel from page to page of a design. Often called a **graphic element**.

Caption – Text which explains an illustration, usually set in smaller type than the body, and placed under, over, or alongside an illustration separate from the body.

Body – Also called **text**. The typed material which contains the main message of the page.

Logo – A design or symbol representative of a company or organization. Also known as a **trademark**.

Signature – The name of a company or organization. Usually set in type that is distinctive to the organization or its logo. Also called a **logotype**.

Just arranging these elements on a page isn't enough. Even though the resultant design may be pleasing to you, remember that the goal of a designer is to integrate these elements with the typography, the message that the client wants to get across, and make this page stand out against the wealth of other pages that the reader will encounter.

Hard and fast rules for design are difficult to define, because a design is a complex composite of the designer's talent, knowledge, and experience, combined with the content of the page and the editorial directive. The following Design Rules of Thumb are not intended to be inviolable laws of design, but things that every designer should consider at the start of each new project.

Design Rules of Thumb

The design must reflect the aim of the publication.

An informal design works with a chatty publication but not with serious subjects. If the target audience is professional, design a professional-looking publication; conversely, design less formally if the audience is less formal. If the aim of the publication is to show off exciting or dramatic artwork, keep large areas of text to a minimum. Technical subjects generally require less artwork.

Establish ground rules with the production team.

To avoid conflicts during the production process, it is best to assemble all the writers, editors, designers, artists, and others that will be involved with the project, and define exactly each person's responsibilities, deadlines, etc. Periodic group meetings before and during production will help alleviate conflicts, answer questions, and give the production team a sense of unity that will be reflected in the design and contents of the publication.

Design in miniature first.

Designing miniatures or "thumbnails" of the major pages helps the designer and others see what the publication will look like. Designs can be discussed, altered, re-altered, and finally approved in miniature before time or money is spent in actual layout.

Consider how columns define the design.

Newspapers tend to use four or five columns, magazines two or three columns, books one or two columns. The number of columns you choose for a publication subliminally gives the reader a message as to the kind of information that can be expected.

It is generally best to use standard column sizes, as defined by desktop publishing programs, because it is all too easy to decide on an oddball size, create a few pages with that size, then forget and lay out others in a standard size. The resulting mishmash, if not detected until the publication goes to press, results in a poor visual impression.

Avoid narrow justified columns, because they are hard to read and contain too much hyphenation. A minimum of thirty characters per line should be maintained for readability. Likewise, avoid overly broad columns, regardless of justification. If lines are too long, the reader gets lost because the eye has trouble tracking back to the left for subsequent lines. The size of type and line length must be coordinated for optimum reading.

Use graphics to help communicate key concepts

If you are creating a "coffee table book," then art for art's sake is the whole purpose of the publication. Otherwise, the overuse of art or inappropriate artwork can confuse the reader. Use only as much artwork as is necessary to help communicate concepts. In some cases, "a picture is worth a thousand words" is certainly true, and an illustration obviously uses less space. A table or chart graphic is better than a prose description; and a line art sketch can clarify prose at a glance. If so, use the art. But if you have 15 pictures and only three are useful, don't include all 15 just because they're there!

Contrasting elements help visual appeal and reading ease.

The use of larger, bolder elements viewed against smaller, lighter elements creates visual interest. The most common technique is the **pull out** also called a **call out** or **pull quote**. These are important, interesting, or provocative phrases taken from the body copy, enlarged, and set off from the body and headlines by boxing, white space, rules, etc. They help draw the reader into the body of the piece.

Break up long "gray" passages.

The pull outs, mentioned above, are one way to break up **gray pages**, those pages that are all body copy type and visually uninteresting. Subheads are also very useful for helping to organize, summarize, and draw the reader's attention to specific points. In headlines and subheads, avoid using all capital letteres and capitalizing the first letter of every word.

Use white space effectively.

White space will draw the reader to whatever element is within or below it. It also helps organize elements by setting them off from others. Too little white space yields a gray page that is visually uninteresting, and conveys a sense of massive amounts of dry, boring reading. Whether the text is boring or not, good use of white space makes it more appealing to the reader.

Minimize the number of typefaces.

This is a problem especially found among beginning designers and desktop publishers. Just because you have 15 or 50 typefaces available doesn't mean you have to use them all! A maximum of two or three typefaces per publication is best: headline, body, byline or caption are all the distinctions most designs need. Choose typefaces that reflect the nature of the publication and audience (see Chapter 2 for more detail on typography).

Be consistent in placing and spacing.

Avoid widows and orphans. If some new sections start on new pages, all of them should. Be consistent in the amount of spacing between the end of one paragraph or section and the start of the next paragraph or section, the space between a head or subhead and the copy for instance. Not having consistent spacing is the sign of someone who didn't design carefully or proof the publication before it went to press. Also, the reader picks up cues from spacing and placing of elements, and varying them causes confusion, "Wait a second!" the reader puzzles, "Is this section part of the bit above, or does it go with the rest below?"

Record design specs for posterity.

If you record the design specifications, six months or a year from now, when you need to design a similar publication, you will have handy the specifications that were approved before. Modifying an existing specification is easier than re-designing the wheel with every new project. Most of the desktop publishing programs today include templates or pre-designed standard formats that can be used as masters for your publications. Modifications to a template's design specifications should be saved in the template (rather than the publication created with the template) for future use.

Basic Design Structures

In spite of a lack of hard and fast rules for page design, there are a few basic arrangements of the essentially rectangular space of a traditional printed page. Page design is, at its simplest, an exercise in space management. There are four basic structures, or ways in which page space can be managed.

- Symmetrical
- Asymmetrical
- Bordered
- Grid

Fig. 5.1 Symmetrical design normally centers on one axis, as shown in this poster.

Symmetrical Structure

The **symmetrical structure** implies stability, sincerity, trustworthiness; all those great qualities that corporations and institutions such as schools and colleges like to tout to their public. Consequently, this style of layout is often found in corporate publications and similar documents where the reader will not be challenged, but presented with the facts.

The name says it all: a symmetrical layout balances. Equal areas left and right, and top and bottom.

The poster in Figure 5.1 contains five basic layout elements:

Heading: Collect a Rocky Mountain High
Subheading: at ABS '91
Illustration: The tree
Body: "Featuring... " and "Collect..."
Signature: "The Bonsai Club of Utah...

All of the elements are aligned on a single vertical axis through the center of the page.

Asymmetrical Structure

Asymmetrical page design is much more subtle than symmetrical design. It presents an image of informality, freedom, balanced constraint. To handle asymmetrical layout well requires skill, and a sense of balance, proportion, and weight, that usually comes with experience. But since experience is the Great Teacher, don't avoid this design structure; rather, practice until you get it perfect!

Fig. 5.2 This classically designed bonsai illustrates the Japanese mastery of asymmetrical symmetry. The tree is displayed in the Fall without its leaves to accentuate the beauty of the fruit and the design of the trunk and branches.

The Japanese are masters of asymmetrical balance. Bonsai, the miniature trees of Japan, illustrate their mastery of the concept. Branches are never opposite each other, the tree is never centered in the pot, and yet the whole composition has a "rightness" about it that derives from the asymmetrical balance. (The concept of asymmetrical balance pervades the entire culture.) To understand asymmetry, study Japanese art.

The basic technique for designing an asymmetrical page is to pick a corner of the page and

Fig. 5.3 Aymmetrical design using the same poster design elements as in Fig. 6.2, with the addition of a logo.

weight the elements toward that corner. Done correctly, the most important element of the design will be at the heart, or focus, of the other elements. Asymmetrical pages are thought to have a very modern look, but as we have seen, the concept is thousands of years old. By combining elements correctly, a designer can deliver a sense of balance and proportion.

In addition to the five elements used for the symmetrically designed page above, the asymmetrical design in Figure 5.3 includes a logo created from a Japanese ideogram. The flow of the design is sinuous, beginning at the upper left corner and twining down the page.

Border Structure

This class of design uses the perimeter of the page, or border, to focus the reader's attention on the elements contained within it. Like asymmetrical design, the border is neither old fashioned nor ultra-modern. It can convey either feeling, or both, depending on the choices of border art and style, typography and content. **Border structure** designs are often used for title or introductory pages. They give the designer almost unlimited opportunities for decorative design. Borders need not be "four square." They can also appear just on

Fig. 5.4 Two bordered designs utilizing the same elements as in the previous examples. Left, the elements are arranged symmetrically within the border; right an asymmetrical bordered design.

diagonally opposite corners, tops and bottoms, or opposite sides of a page. Repeating the design motif of a title page as secondary illustrations or graphic elements on interior pages can be an excellent way to tie the feeling of an entire publication together. Elements within a border are generally symmetrical, but asymmetry can also be used to great effect.

Grid Structure

The previous design structures use an intuitive sense of design to provide balance with a minimum of restrictive organization. The grid, however, is the epitome of rigidity. The advantage of this structure is that it does impose discipline

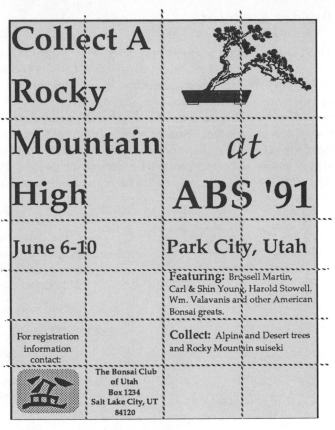

Fig. 5.5 Grid designed version of our convention poster. Here, the elements must be fit within whole blocks of space. They can fill the block, as the first part of the headline ("Collect...") does; or, they can occupy only a portion of the block like the 0 in the date.

Collect A Rocky Mountain High

at

ABS '91

June 6-10

Park City, Utah

Featuring: Brussell Martin, Carl & Shin Young, Harold Stowell. Wm. Valavanis and other American Bonsai greats.

For registration information contact:

Collect: Alpine and Desert trees and Rocky Mountain suiseki

The Bonsai Club of Utah Box 1234 Salt Lake City, UT 84120

on novice designers, but there must still be some skill. Once you learn how things *should* go together, however, it is easier to see which rules can be broken to create truly artistic layout designs. Using a **grid structure** gives a design a sense of continuity and conformity, and lends a sense of unity to multipage documents.

With a grid design, the page (or two-page spread) is broken into columns and rows. Each resulting rectangle is a grid block. Any element which appears in the design *must* be fit to an entire grid block or multiple of whole adjacent blocks. Some desktop publishing programs offer an adjustable background grid display as an option to aid the designer.

On the opposite page, the elements of our poster design are laid out according to a grid. Each element *must* be contained wholly within a major or minor grid block or combination of blocks. In this case the subhead was broken down into secondary subheads consisting of the date and place, and each of those arranged as separate elements.

Pages

Up to this point, we have been unconcerned with how many pages must be designed for a project. A single-page project will utilize just one of the layout structures. Multipage documents can repeat, mirror, alternate, or otherwise mix layout structures. It is important to know, in advance, how many pages a project will utilize and how you will need to organize those pages.

In desktop publishing there are several kinds of pages. First, there is the **page size** that you tell the program you want to use, such as letter (8.5" x 11"), legal (8.5" x 14") or tabloid (11" x 17"). The page-size setting function creates a "virtual page" of those dimensions, which appears on your computer screen. A **virtual page** is the unit that will be printed when you tell the computer to print one page.

Second, there is the **actual page**, which is the size of the page of the printed document. An actual page can be made up of one or more virtual pages, or less than one virtual page, depending on how the Text and Graphics Blocks are laid out.

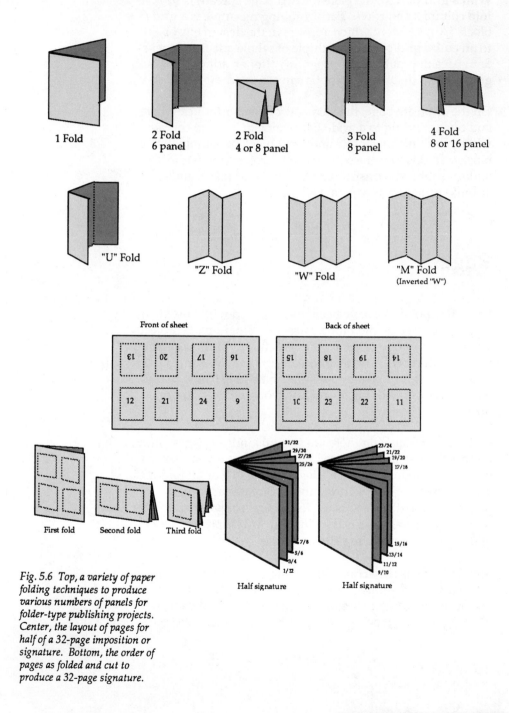

Fig. 5.6 Top, a variety of paper folding techniques to produce various numbers of panels for folder-type publishing projects. Center, the layout of pages for half of a 32-page imposition or signature. Bottom, the order of pages as folded and cut to produce a 32-page signature.

138

Actual pages can be as tiny as a fraction of an inch, or as large as a tabloid newspaper page (although that is a practical upper limit). Think of a page as a unit to hold one complete layout structure with all the necessary elements. That page can, of course, be part of a much larger piece of paper; this can be a limiting factor in the design of the overall project.

Most common computer printers work only with letter- or legal-sized paper, so, to print a tabloid page, a process called **tiling** is used. The computer breaks up the virtual tabloid page into letter-paper-sized pieces and prints as much of the virtual tabloid page as it can on one piece of letter paper (with appropriate overlap to avoid missing anything). These printed pages must then be mechanically pasted up to form a camera master page for the printer.

Pages are often referred to as **sides** because each piece of paper, of course, has two sides, each of which can be a page or more. If there is more than one **page** to a **side**, then the pages are usually called **panels** and the side is called a **signature** or **imposition**. Confusing, isn't it? The illustrations on the opposite page should help.

Small Publications

There really isn't any better single term than "small" to cover the wide variety of publications projects that don't fall under book, magazine, or newsletter and newspaper labels. On the other hand, even though the name isn't that impressive, the subject matter is probably the most fun for designers. Most of these publications are **one shots**; that is, you'll seldom do the same thing twice in a row, and that's what keeps designers on their toes (artistically speaking). One day you'll design a two-fold brochure for a conference, the next a booklet on stocks and bonds, and the day after you'll work on flyers for three separate club meetings. Working in this aspect of design and layout is a real challenge!

There are several categories into which small publications fall, depending on their size:

- Leaflet or Card
- Folder
- Broadside
- Booklet or Brochure

A major criterion of all of these publication types is that they should be single-function publications. Don't try to combine more than one purpose in a single publication. If the message is to inform, sell, influence, or educate, let a given publication do only one of those things; otherwise, the designer gets frustrated trying to cram too much into too little space, and the reader gets confused as to what message really is being given. In general, the functions of a publication can be classed as:

- Image Building or Prestige
- News
- Advertising
- Proselytizing

In any case, the designer must know, or help the client define, the target audience. What kinds of jobs do they have? What are the beliefs about religion, politics, philosophy? In what age group is the audience? Education? Without information such as this the designer of any publication is just shooting in the dark. With this information, the designer can create a publication that will appeal to precisely the audience that the client is trying to reach.

Leaflet and Card

Leaflets are also called **flyers** or **posters**. They usaully occupy one page – one side of one sheet of paper (usually letter or legal sized). A card is something that occupies less than a standard printed page, such as an advertisement. Regardless of the type of project, the challenge of designing these projects is to see how much of the critical information you can fit into the restricted space, and still make the design eyecatching and get the message across. A major consideration in projects like these is keeping the balance among white space, copy, and graphics. Too much white space means the message is lost; too much text forces it down to a size so small as to be unreadable; too large a graphic and you won't have room for the necessary words.

Leaflets

With larger-size projects such as flyers, posters, and leaflets, you can more or less let your design imagination go, as long as you get the message across. Everywhere you look there are hundreds and thousands of flyers or posters announcing lost dogs, sub-atomic physics colloquia, rock concerts, or the opening of a new deli.

The basic design criteria can be summarized by the old military acronym K.I.S.S. (Keep It Simple, Stupid!). The most readable, simplest, most understood message is the one that will get across to the audience. More complex messages need a different kind of publication such as a folder or booklet.

There are three kinds of leaflets:

- Come To The Meeting
- Educational
- Get On The Bandwagon

Come To The Meeting leaflets are simple announcements of date, time, place, and subject, and are usually one-shots. **Educational leaflets** are intended to teach, and may or may not be part of a series. **Get On The Bandwagon leaflets** are intended to sway opinion, rally readers around a cause, etc. They are usually part of a series: political campaigns often use Bandwagon leaflets to sway readers to their cause for instance.

With leaflet-sized projects, the distribution method to be used should affect the design. If the leaflet is to be mailed in an envelope, it needs no special care in design, but if it will be a self-mailer, there must be adequate space designed in for the mailing information block (usually 3" x 5"). If the leaflet is to be posted, the design should be big and bold, to catch the attention of passersby among the myriad of other items of the bulletin board, phone pole, or whatever. If the leaflet will be placed on literature shelves in libraries, bookstores, or similar areas, the design should feature a short keyword title in the top third of the page and heavy paper stock so that if the storage place is vertical the leaflet won't flop over and obscure the message.

Cards

A great many of these projects are ads for newspapers and magazines. There are also interesting projects like the 1" x 1.5", six-page signature, miniature recipe book which comes attached to bottles of oriental cooking sauces from Lee Kum Kee Co., or the ads and coupons on the back of cash register tapes. Phone book ads and direct mail coupons (the ones that get hung on your doorknob once a week) are other interesting small projects.

Fig. 5.7 The variety of leaflets and cards is truly astounding. These examples were collected in a matter of minutes near a campus bookstore.

Incidentally, designing phone book ads is a great way to get design experience. Every population center that produces a phone book has one or more agencies that do the contract ad design for the Yellow Pages. Many of these agencies are now using desktop publishing and graphics programs to generate their ads, and they are more than willing to hire part-time designers. The pay may not be great, but the design experience can hardly be beat! Check it out; from what you'll learn in this book, you may be able to work your way through the rest of your schooling *and* end up with a couple of years of experience.

The primary consideration in ad-type projects is the orientation of the design – vertical or horizontal. Everything else proceeds from there. This dimension may be defined for you by the client or target publication or left entirely to your discretion. If you are given a choice, study the master publication and the area in which your project will appear. Remember, your goal with this kind of design is to make the reader pay heed to your client's information rather than that of a hundred other plumbers, astrologers, or desktop publishing companies on the same page or in the same publication. If the majority of similar ads are vertical, designing a horizontal layout for your client will certainly make the ads stand out of the crowd. If most ads are bordered, try unbordered; if they use bold blocky typefaces, try a thinner look.

The smaller the project, the more critical readability becomes. Use fewer words in larger type. Subtleties of the typeface may be lost, but stroke weight becomes important. Ads are a good place to practice the Grid style of layout. Each element of the ad: name, message, address/phone, and graphic can be placed in a separate grid, and the grids manipulated to find the most pleasing design that optimizes the effect that the client wants.

Folders

Folders are perhaps the second most popular small publication; they are found in almost every area of business, industry and eduction. A folder is a publication printed on both sides of single sheet of paper, that has two or more panels (four times as many panels as the number of folds). Each panel can be considered a page when it comes to design, and adjacent panels or panels at each level of fold can be designed as spreads.

Fig. 5.8 Folders are a very useful and popular way to present a lot of informaiton in a small area. They can vary in physical size as well as the number of folds, to produce a variety of effects.

Where leaflet projects run to 36 pt. or larger display type, folders often use 7-9 pt. body copy, 12-14 pt. heads, and a 24 pt. title. Folders allow much more space to get complex messages across, because the type is generally much smaller. Generally, each panel of a folder should be a single column of text, although two or even three columns can be utilized to present bulleted or enumerated lists of things in reduced size type. As with leaflets, the distribution method affects design, with an "outside" panel being designed as the mailer, the title in the upper third of the front panel, etc.

Carefully design the placement of information in the folder, relative to the sequence of unfolding or opening. Get the important points visible first, then the secondary points as the folder is opened again.

Broadsides

A **broadside** can be thought of as a giant folder. It is generally printed on both sides of tabloid or larger stock. The design criteria are the same as for folders.

The scope of a broadside is much larger. With the right organization, an enormous amount of information can be presented in a very readable manner. A major design flaw is to have text that continues onto a panel not in the next logical sequence of opening. It is perfectly all right to require the reader to open a broadside all the way to get the complete message. It is not right that the reader should have to open a broadside all the way to follow a single item.
An interesting design possibility is to use one side of a broadside to present a verbal message and the reverse to present a high-quality photo or graphic, suitable for hanging on a wall as a poster. If the poster side contains a minimum of text identifying the organization which sent it; the message on the other side will stay in the viewer's consciousness as long as the poster remains hanging.

Booklets and Brochures

Booklets and **brochures** give excellent scope for getting very complex messages across to an audience. They are multi-page publications with almost the capability of a book or magazine, but with a single subject.

The most common sizes for these projects are half page from standard letter or legal paper (each piece of paper is folded in half to produce four sides 8.5" x 5.5" or 8.5" x 7"). Each piece of paper then becomes a signature, and the signatures are stacked for binding. Up to 12 signatures (48 pages of 1-3 columns each) can be stacked and **saddle stitched** (stapled at the fold) to a Bristol board or other heavy stock cover without the necessity of trimming page edges due to thickness. Larger booklets or brochures require cutting the signatures in half at the fold and side stitching. **Side stitched** booklets require more design consideration, because the booklet will not open flat, and thus a wider page margin is necessary to avoid losing text in the binding.

Standard magazine and book design techniques are applicable to booklets and brochures. For more information see Chapters 6 and 7.

Fig. 5.9 Brochures and booklets are excellent projects for desktop publishing. They can be created easily by folding standard letter and legal-sized paper in half and printing on the resulting four-page signature. Two signatures can be just slipped together; with more signatures, they should be stapled or otherwise bound.

Review Questions

1. List the eight basic elements of any layout.
2. Why will a designer work with thumbnails?
3. How do the number and size of columns affect the design?
4. Define pull quote.
5. Explain two ways to break up gray pages.
6. Why does a designer limit the number of typefaces to only two or three?
7. What are the four basic structures of page design?
8. Compare and contrast symmetrical and asymmetrical design structures.
9. Define at least two kinds of pages used in desktop publishing.
10. A publication should only fit only one of four publication classes; what are they?
11. List four kinds of small publications.
12. What are the three kinds of leaflets?
13. What are the advantages of a folder over a leaflet?
14. What are the disadvantages of a broadside?
15. What is a half-letter booklet?
16. Sketch four different paper folding techniques.
17. What is a signature?
18. What is the difference between a virtual and a real page?
19. List four rules of thumb for design.
20. What are the advantages and disadvantages of designing by the grid?

Exercises

1. From the following information and no more than two graphics of your choice, design a leaflet a) symmetrically, b) asymmetrically, c) bordered, and d) by the grid.

   There will be a meeting of the Inner City Garden Club on March 13 at 7 P.M. at the Main Branch of the City Library. The feature speaker is Ralph Busch, and his subject is "Beautifying Our Slums: window box gardens for tenament dwellers." Ralph is a nationally recognized expert on the subject and has even addressed the American Governor's Conference on this important subject.

2. Design three versions of an advertisement. Pick an ad from your local Yellow Pages, and re-design it in three different ways. Turn in a photocopy of the original ad with the assignment.

3. Design a two- or three-fold folder on some subject of interest to you. Create new copy or use previously saved text as greek text (space filling text) for the body.

4. Design a tabloid-sized broadside on some subject of interest to you. Use previously saved electronic text as greek text for the body, if necessary. Design the broadside so that only one side is text. Sketch or electronically draw a poster to be used on the reverse of the broadside.

Chapter 6: Designing Magazines

The only way to describe the magazine business is to say that it is ingenuity-intensive.

-- W.H. Paul, Vice President of the Magazine Publishers Association

Magazines, even more so than newspapers, are the reading material of the masses. Newspapers are for keeping track of rapidly breaking news and other stories of human interest. Books are for contemplative education and specialized research. Magazines give the reader more depth, more specialization than a newspaper, more timeliness and less depth than a book.

The *Writers Market Annual* guide to publications lists over four thousand magazines on topics ranging from Alternative Lifestyles to Veterinary Medicine, and everything in between. Writing for speciality magazines, such as hobby publications, is an excellent way to break into professional writing; most of these publications are hungry for manuscripts from people who not only know the hobby intimately, but who can also string together words in a way to make their knowledge interesting to others.

To begin the study of magazine design, the best place to look is at some of the wide variety on the newsstands. It will be helpful to have a few samples around while reading this chapter, so that you can see real-world examples for the principles and techniques which will be discussed.

The Basics

A magazine must be logically arranged, clearly organized, legible, neat, and above all, it must have content. A magazine with the greatest page and spread designs in the world, the most impressive photos and graphics, is doomed if the contents – the words and what they say – do not meet the readers' expectations. "A picture is worth a thousand words" is true only if the pictures are an organizing element of the story, which derive *from* the story, and are not just added later to make it pretty or fill up space. Pictures, graphic elements, and text are the three major elements of a magazine which must be integrated, or the publication may not succeed.

After studying a few magazines you will begin to notice that, for the most part, regardless of subject matter, nearly all magazines have several types of functional page layouts in common:

- Cover
- Contents Page
- Departments
- Feature Openers
- Editorials
- New Products
- Late-Breaking News

Of course, not every magazine necessarily has all of these page types: *Bazaar* magazine, for example, has no editorial page, while *People Weekly* has no new products reviews, and the *Journal of Lightwave Technology* has no departments.

The overall look and feel of a magazine is the sum of the design of the various parts. So although we will study the design of the parts separately, keep in mind that if and when you get the opportunity to design a new magazine, every one of the various page types must have a sense of continuity.

The Cover

The logical place to begin learning about magazine design is from the outside in. If the design of the cover does not reach out, grab the browser, and demand READ ME! BUY ME!, then the magazine may fail. Remember, there are several thousand other magazines out there competing for your potential purchasers' dollars. Until a magazine has developed tremendous reader recognition and a reputation for having the best contents, it competes with similar publications (from the buyer's viewpoint) strictly on the appeal of its cover design. Thus, when starting a new magazine, you must spend more time and effort to get just the right look for the cover than for other pages. From the cover design will come elements which will affect all of the other pages in the overall design.

There are four elements in any cover:

- The basic format
- The illustration
- The logotype, graphic logo and auxiliary information (date and volume)
- Cover lines

Format

The format must be standardized for reader recognition and familiarity from issue to issue. If issues appear too radically different, your potential buyers will have a lot of trouble recognizing your magazine among the hundreds on a newsstand and may buy something else if they can't spot your title immediately!

Standardization of the format also simplifies the production process. Design it once; then for each issue all you have to do is vary the the contents of the other elements to create a new but recognizably similar look. Of course, too much standardization can be stifling. Don't be so rigid that if something world-shaking comes along you can't break the mold and take on a form appropriate to whatever happens. A major announcement, death of a well-known figure, etc., should be in a somewhat different format so that it truly stands out.

Fig. 6.1 Six variations on the placement of the elements of a magazine cover.

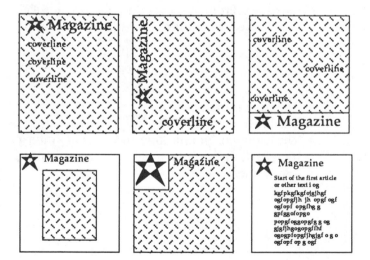

If the subject isn't illustratable or there are few good illustrations available, then the format must be built around something else, and the picture will either be small or absent. A large logo or logotype could be the focus, as could a color block which can vary from issue to issue. Something large must be the focus of the format so that variety is possible while still retaining visibility and reader recognition quality. Most of the magazines published by the Institute of Electrical and Electronics Engineers, Inc., are totally text, or complicated mathematical equations (not the best of illustrations). To have something big to focus on, they have chosen to put the table of contents in a box in lieu of a cover illustration! All the other elements of the cover are there as well, but each issue features the contents as the major element of the cover design.

Illustration

The size of the cover illustration depends on whether or not the subject matter lends itself well to illustration, and the long-term availability of good "cover quality" art (photos, line art, paintings, etc.). A magazine devoted to theoretical chemistry would probably have an illustration worthy of a cover only occasionally, while *International Bonsai* could come up with thousands of suitable cover photos and line art.

One advantage of specially created cover artwork over stock or freelance photos is that the art can be created from the beginning with the predesigned cover format in mind. Artwork, as opposed to photography, is easier to work with in this respect.

Regardless of size or type, cover illustrations must attract interest. If they aren't attractive, get rid of them and redesign around some other element. Look at popular magazines for ideas.

Logo, Logotype, and Other Information

The logo and logotype are the trademarks of a publication. A logo is generally more graphic in nature, like a monogram; while the logotype is the name of the magazine, usually in something more than plain old type. The logo/logotype are used not only on the cover, but on stationery, promotional materials, etc. Although the typeface may be out of the ordinary, it should have a family relationship with the typefaces used inside for titles, headings, and so on. This continuity of visual character is a major link in tying the magazine and its contents into a cohesive whole.

Often the logotype will be condensed or kerned in unusual ways, outlined, shadowed, or otherwise distinct but similar to internal type. Distinctive lettering styles, regardless of readability, can add to reader recognition. It is very important that the reader recognize the logo and logotype. With good design choices, the logo and logotype can stand a variety of treatments, such as varying intensity of shadows, changing color of fills and borders, etc., to add issue-to-issue variation while maintaining the same basic appearance.

Where do the logo and logotype belong in the format? If the magazine is sold strictly on the newsstands, the method of display demands that these elements be placed at the top; preferably the top left corner, because newsstands display publications overlapping. Otherwise, there will be no recognition of the publication. If the publication is primarily distributed by mail, however, then placement is much freer. In this case, many magazines opt for a lower-third or left edge logo with text running bottom-to-top. If the illustrations are not strong and the format depends on the logo, then the logo or logotype should be the first element seen, regardless of placement.

Cover Lines

Cover lines are teasers to draw the reader inside to read particular features. There should be more than one cover line only if there is more than one major story inside. If there is only one cover line, the cover illustration should relate to the cover line, and the cover line should act as the caption to the illustration. If there is more than one cover line, the illustration can relate to any of the cover lines, but the one it relates to should be distinguished in some way (color, size, etc.).

The emphasis that publications put on cover lines varies from not using them, to subdued placement at the head or foot, to gaudy displays splashed all over the illustration. Some publications vary their use of cover lines from issue to issue, depending on the contents. The purpose of cover lines is always to encourage the reader to open the magazine. If they don't do that, eliminate them from the format.

Should the cover format incorporate a frame? Generally no, if the intent is to frame with a thin or hairline border. The problem is that when the magazine is trimmed, more often than not it is not trimmed square, and thin frames appear crooked. The result is a shoddy appearance. If you must frame, make the frame broad enough and dense enough to stand on its own no matter what happens to the edge of the cover. A **full bleed** of color (color all the way to the edge of the page) is better than any kind of frame. With a bleed, poor trimming has no visual effect on its relationship to the edge of the page.

Many magazines, with saddle stitched (stapled) bindings, cannot use the spine as a format element. If a magazine has a spine, it should become an important part of the format. The spine is what you will see when magazines are stacked in piles or on shelves, and here is the perfect opportunity to help your reader. Not only should the logotype, date, and volume be on the spine, but condensed cover lines make an excellent quick reference. *National Geographic* is an outstanding example of good use of the spine.

Fig. 6.2 These magazine covers show some of the many design possibilities. Many magazines today are turning to desktop publishing as a means of reducing their cost of operation.

The Contents Page

Once the cover has done its work and convinced someone to pick up the magazine and open it, the reader will do one of three things: go directly to the cover story or a cover line story; skim the issue, stopping when something attracts attention; check the contents page to see what else besides the cover or cover line story is worth spending his time and money on.

A contents page must present its information in a format that makes it easy to find things. It must stand out, to show importance of the material inside. The exact location is not as crucial as its appearance on the same page in every issue. One of the easiest ways to irritate the constant reader or sub-scriber is to change the contents page location from issue to issue.

There are generally four different kinds of readers who use the contents page: those who know what they're looking for and use the contents as a quick index; those who need to be sold on the contents; those who want capsule summaries of the articles without the bother of wading through pages of text; and info-searchers who are thumbing through stacks of magazines trying to find a particular remembered article or piece of information.

For the first user the information must be well organized, with titles and associated page numbers easy to spot. The second kind of user wants the headlines to jump out, with perhaps a secondary line of text explaining what use the sub-ject of each article will be. The third kind of user wants more detailed explanations of the contents of each article such as abstracts or capsule summaries, but with the boldness and focus of headlines desired by the second type of user.

It is difficult if not impossible to create a contents page that will be all things to all readers. As designers, we can but try to present the editorial decision as to which group of users the contents page should cater. The major problem arises from the sheer amount of information often found on the contents page other than just the titles and locations of articles. Below is a list of information that can appear on a contents page.

- Page label – "Contents" or equivalent
- Table of Contents showing departments, headline, secondary line, byline, photo credits, page number, etc.
- Logo
- Miniature of the cover with caption and credits
- A paragraph describing "coming attractions"
- Small pictures to illustrate articles
- Magazine slogan
- Historical reference to magazine's longevity or purpose
- Date of publication, volume and issue numbers
- Promotion of a special article by enlarging type, boxing, or other special treatment
- List of editorial staff, including name and function
- List of business staff, including name and function
- Lists of advisors, committee members, board of directors, etc.
- Affiliations such as AP, UPI, scientific and technical
- Masthead: parent company and officers, address, frequency of publications, office addresses, manuscript policies and address for submissions, subscription information, change of address information

Much of the information above is required by law to be somewhere in the magazine (to get special mailing privileges). It makes sense to lump it together as much as possible, even if fitting it on one page means some things are set in very small type. If there is too much information for a single page, the most common solution is to move the masthead information elsewhere.

Some magazines try to design their contents pages to appeal to as many of the user types as possible. Their solution is to have two pages of contents, with a more or less standard table of contents on the left and abstracts of the feature articles on the right. This format also gives increased room for fitting the many other elements.

Fig. 6.3 A selection of contents pages showing some of the
variety possible in placement and organization of information.

If types of information aren't adequately grouped – set off from other groups by space, boxing, or other techniques, it becomes very difficult to distinguish where one set of information ends and another begins. Staff names and titles are important to the staff, but not overly so to the readers. Other contents page design problems to watch out for are insufficient grouping, staff names and titles too large compared to other information, and the possible clash between the tabular format of the table of contents and the paragraph format of the coming attractions and cover information.

The major solution to most content page design difficulties is to establish a hierarchy of type sizes. Then assign a level of importance to every group of information and set it in the appropriate size. U.S. Postal Service regulations may *require* that some things be on that page, but the readers will *demand* that the actual table of contents be readable or else they will go elsewhere. The basic ploy with a contents page is to be as simple and logical in your organization of information as possible.

The actual organization of the contents page will vary with the editorial goals for that page (which kind(s) of users you will cater to), kind of publication, number of pages available for listing contents, number and type of pictures available for accenting article titles, readership, and more.

Departments

Technically, magazine departments are all those pages which are not occupied by feature articles, the cover, or advertising. Most of what we are talking about here, however, are those (rarely more than a single page) columns written by magazine staffers, which appear in every issue, and which discuss some specific aspect of the magazine's subject matter. For many readers, the departments of a publication are as important if not more important than the feature stories. Features are sometimes thought to be full of fluff and hype journalism, where departments are nitty gritty writing. Readers expect straight talk from department columnists, and usually get it.

Usually the departmental pages contain many ads. Departments must be distinctive, yet part of the overall image of the magazine. The reader must be able to recognize these scattered pages as part of the editorial content of the magazine and not lose them among the ads. Therefore most departments must have a consistant format, which is *never* changed, and that will give them a family resemblance to the other parts of the magazine and allow them to be spotted as such even at the most casual glance.

One way distinguish departments is to create a format that is big and bold, offering lots of contrast between wide rules, hairline rules, light and bold type, and white space that still follows the same basic typographic style as the rest of the magazine. Bold black and white contrasts will definitely stand out against brightly colored ads.

You can also underplay the presentation: make it as plain and bland in its textual presentation as possible. If the ads have a garish, chaotic quality, the quiet serenity of a department will provide good contrast.

An alternative format will make departments recognizable as well. Use a different number of columns or column measure, or rules or boxes when things aren't normally ruled or boxed. This way departments will not only differ distinctly not only from from the ads, but also from features and other parts, so much so that they will be recognizable as separate entities. To tie them into the magazine as a whole, relate them to the cover, features, etc., with similar typography, use of the logo, similar white space arrangements, and so on.

Whatever format you develop, the elements must be repeated precisely from department to department, issue to issue. Department formats generally contain a department label, rules, a photo or sketch of the columnist, the author's byline, and a headline. They may also have a signature block or a **30 bug** a small dingbat that signifies the end of the column. All of the items contained in the department format must appear in exactly the same relationship in every department and every issue. Alter the department format and you may lose readers.

Fig. 6.4 Departments must be distinct from the ads that surround them. The illustration shows several ways this can be accomplished.

Feature Openers

Openers are the first right hand page or first spread of feature articles. Every feature has an opener, but a **First Opener** is the opener of the initial article in the feature section and is usually given a bigger, bolder play to signal to the reader, "Here's the meat of the issue." A First Opener is especially useful in magazines that produce theme issues, where all features in an issue are on a given topic. The First Opener sets the tone and style for subsequent openers. There really should be at least twelve pages of feature articles to make the time and effort of creating a First Opener worthwhile .

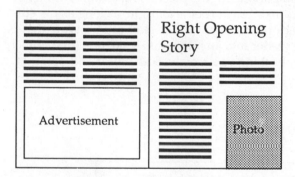

Right Openers

A **First Right Opener** is a small single page. The page opposite is usually sold to advertisers as a "preferred position" (for more money). It contains large ads. To separate the First Right Opener adequately from the ads, more gutter is needed as a white wall, which cuts down on useable space.

Every opener must be visually exciting to draw the reader into the story. Simplicity is the key. Is there a good illustration? If so, a large illustration, headline, and a few paragraphs of body are all that are needed. The best illustration for a First Opener may be a reproduction of the cover (provided the First Opener feature is the cover story as well). The cover already has recognition value to the reader. The space available on a First Right Opener can use a less than 50% reduction of the cover. No good illustration? Try lots of white and an enlarged headline to make a visual impact. Famous author? Enlarge the byline to show the magazine has enough pull to get such a big name.

A miniature of the magazine logo, when incorporated into openers, can be used as a tie-in element to signal the reader, "All these are part of the whole." The typography should be consistent throughout, just more flamboyant (different width, more leading, initial cap on the first paragraph).

The basic technique for finding out what to use for visual impact in the opener is to analyze the feature story and define the order of importance of the pieces: illustrations, author photo, byline, text. Any order is all right, as long as the editor defines the order so that the designer can translate that order for the reader into an integrated sequence. Remember, in desktop publishing you may be both editor and designer.

Spread Openers

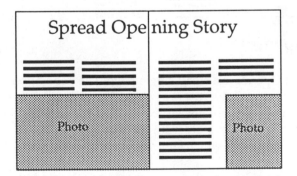

If the magazine uses a **Spread Opener** as the First Opener, it loses the additional income from the preferred position advertising opposite but gains the ability to have a much greater visual and editorial impact. The impact of a two-page spread is considerably greater than twice that of a single page. A good spread for a Right First Opener combines text and illustration so the left-hand page of the spread is a full page, full-bleed illustration, and the right-hand page contains the headline, byline, and copy. The illustration must be of superb quality, however, to stand full-page treatment.

A spread is much more effective than a Single First Opener, provided the magazine has an adequate supply or source of good-quality illustrations.

Left Openers

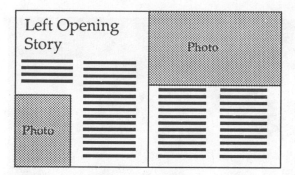

When articles open on the left-hand page, you have two choices, depending on the nature of the issue. If all the features in the issue are related to a topic, *every* Left Opener, more so than other openers, needs to make the interrelationship between all of the features obvious. Left Openers are more difficult for readers to see, because even though we read from left to right, most people, when flipping through a magazine, tend to scan the right pages first.

The **First Left Opener** sets the pattern, and all subsequent openers must follow it as much as possible within the constraints of title length, illustration availability, etc. A common element such as a logo, color box, or bold rule is very useful for tying all left-opening features together.

The second (and more common) situation occurs when the features of an issue are not related, except by the general subject of the magazine title. Here, the First Opener, whether Left, Right, or Spread, is not a pattern setter. The openers from feature to feature should vary as much as possible to avoid a mechanical look. In this case, each feature is a First Opener, and each opener should make the story beginning clearly distinguishable from anything else in the magazine. In an unrelated feature section, a common concession to the First Opener idea of establishing the start of the section is to full-page bleed the first feature opener with a distinct color.

Whichever style of First Opener is chosen, that style must be carried over from issue to issue, so that the reader will always be able to realize the importance of the material.

Fig. 6.5 Feature Openers are signposts to the reader. They identify the beginning of a story and excite the reader's interest.

Michael Broussard, Ken Russo

Editorials

Editorials are often classed with departments, but they really serve a different function. Departments and features tend toward factual journalistic reporting. Editorials, on the other hand, are think pieces which may pontificate, make guesses and pronouncements, present opinions, and generally show a more judgemental slant. Editorials are the author speaking directly to you, not dryly presenting facts.

Because of their nature, editorials must look different from, yet similar to, the rest of the magazine. Their nature can be either very serious and weighty, calling for large type, a bold headline and extra white space; or informal and chatty, where large type is still useful and a headline can be dropped in favor of a "Dear Reader:" start.

The elements of an editorial include:

- The text itself
- A headline
- The editorial label ("EDITORIAL" or some equivalent)
- The signature block of the author
- The editor's picture (optional)
- A cartoon tied to the topic, or a separate editorial cartoon with its own byline for the artist

As with many other parts of the magazine, the placement of the editorial cannot vary from issue to issue. Exactly where the editorial is isn't as important as the fact that it's always in the same place. It's placement is not nearly as important as what goes opposite or on the same page. These are also preferred positions for ads; but an advertisement for a Smith & Wesson revolver opposite an editorial promoting gun control clashes to say the least!

Desirable characteristics in an editorial format are simplicity of design (don't clutter important matters) and a larger-than-normal scale (to point up the importance of the contents). There are several techniques which are useful for achieving these characteristics:

- Employ a wide moat of white (or something else) to act as a barrier between the editorial and adjacent advertisements.
- Set in type of the same family as the rest of the magazine, but larger and with more leading for additional readability (12/16 instead of normal 9/11 body copy, for example).
- Avoid overcrowding the elements.
- Utilize different justification as an added difference.
- Place in a standard location from issue to issue, for recognition. But don't be so rigid that the format can't be opened out to a spread if a more lengthy coverage of a subject is occasionally wanted.
- Design with the same graphic elements as a regular department, if desired, but set off with a different number of columns.

Fig. 6.6 The designers of these magazines have chosen distinctive ways to set off their editorials.

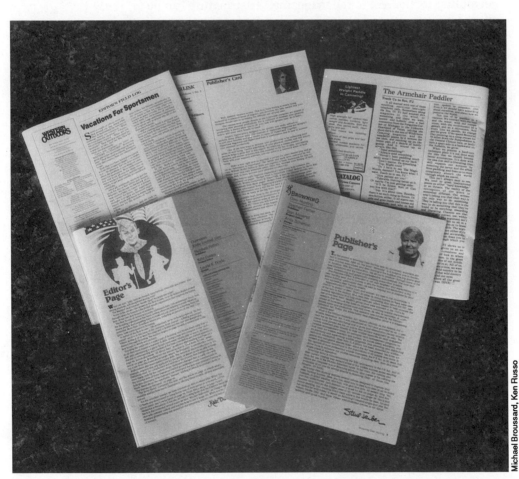

Michael Broussard, Ken Russo

Products

Most specialty publications find that new products pages
are near the top in reader interest. However, often the New
Products Editor position is shuffled off onto the newest em-
ployee because the more or less standard "New Products
Department" format with a label and two or three product
releases per page is boring. Despite the boring nature of
new product information for editors, the readers really crave
such information, and it is up to the designer to find better,
more interesting ways to present the news.

Here's a couple of other ideas to try.

- **Product as a Story.** Here a single new product is
  written about in depth, tested or used, if possible and
  the results presented in the same format as a feature,
  complete with opener.

- **Product as News.** In this instance, a new product is
  written about in news style: Dateline Washington,
  sources close to the developer. Straight reporting
  rather than PR hype or feature style.

- **Product Service Article.** This is a variation on the
  Product as a Story, but the emphasis is not on a single
  new product. Several similar products (old or new)
  are compared and contrasted.

- **Product Catalogue.** This can be either a special section in each issue, or a separate annual/semi-annual
  supplementary issue. Use of a different texture and
  color of paper will make a recurring section stand out
  more. The emphasis is on catalogue-style presentation of the products.

Michael Broussard, Ken Russo

Fig. 6.7 If you become a New Products Editor, try breaking the monotony by designing an entirely different look for your section.

Late-Breaking News Pages
(Flash Forms)

Flash forms are a relatively recent innovation in magazine design, intended to give the magazine an up-to-the-minute feel. Of course, no magazine can be as timely as a newspaper, but the intent is good. Including late-breaking news has been found to be a very positive attribute of specialized (more technical) magazines. Because of the positive effect, some publications use a **pseudo-flash form** as a way of separating news from features, editorials, or departments.

A pseudo-flash form looks like an ordinary flash form, but doesn't carry truly late-breaking news. Other national publications such as *Outdoor Life* use a pseudo-flash form look as an insert to make regionally-relevant versions of their magazines. There may be six or eight flash forms, each with separate contents, detailing news in each of the regions that the magazine considers important.

A true flash form is a two-, four-, or eight-page insert that goes to press at the last minute and is bound into the publication as the last step in the production process. The elements that make up a flash form format are given below.

- **Stock.** Flash forms use a different color and texture of paper to make them stand out from the rest of the publication. Preferred colors are yellow and buff, but any pale color can be used so that the type stands out well. The texture of a flash form can be more glossy than the standard stock, but the usual method is to use a much rougher stock.

- **Logo and Label.** The magazine logo ties the flash form to the rest of the magazine, while the label lets the reader know just what this special section is.

- **Date.** Not just the month, but Month, Day, Year. This gives the flash form more of a sense of immediacy.

- **Writer's Byline and Picture.** Included if the flash form is indeed written by one person.

- **Decorative Elements.** Rules, borders, and other effects are used to distinguish the flash form from other sections.

- **Typography.** There are three basic approaches to the typographical look of a flash form.

  a) Use large type, a wide measure, bold lead-ins rather than headlines.
  b) Use normal type and measure with headlines.
  c) Use a typewriter (non-proportional) typeface to reinforce the "late-breaking news" or "newsletter within a magazine" look.

The typographic approach chosen gives the greatest impact on the look of the flash form. Style (a) uses boldfaced lead-ins stacked left or run-in with the body. Style (b) uses ordinary stacked headlines which can be hung or span the columns. Style (c) can use typeset headlines but it destroys the "so fast we couldn't wait for typesetting" look of the rest of the form; a large typewriter font can be used with some success.

With style (c), never use typesetting conventions such as boldface to emphasize something. Use typewriter tricks such as underline or enclosing words in asterisks (*very*), to maintain the illusion of a typewriter. Another useful ploy when using Style (c) is to frame the text and design a look of a "page within a page" giving the illusion of a photo of the typewriter page reduced and printed on the magazine page.

Whichever style or format is used, flash form stories must be written briefly and concisely. An ideal length for a single flash form page is 3-5 measure (column width) lines per story. Certainly, flash form stories should never exceed one-third of the page in depth.

Review Questions

1. What are the three major elements of a magazine that must be integrated for a magazine to succeed?
2. List the basic page layouts of a magazine.
3. What are the four elements of the magazine cover?
4. List at least ten elements which can appear on a Table of Contents page.
5. Define the four different kinds of Table of Contents users and what they want to see.
6. How can you make Departments pages stand out from the rest of the magazine?
7. Define First Opener, Right Opener, and Spread Opener.
8. How do Editorials differ from Departments?
9. How can you make an editorial simple in design and larger than life?
10. What are preferred position advertisements?
11. Discuss four ways to present new products in a magazine.
12. What elements go into making up flash forms?
13. Why should many magazine elements occur in the same place issue after issue?
14. What purpose does the article opener serve?
15. When would you use a Left Opener?
16. What elements go into an editorial page?
17. Discuss the contents of a flash form.
18. What are the three basic approaches to flash form typography?
19. What is the basic purpose of publishing a magazine?
20. Why is it so important for a magazine to have unity of design in all its elements?

Exercise

Design a magazine on some subject of interest to you. Use greek text or previously saved electronic text to fill in body copy, but create titles, headlines, captions, bylines, etc. Leave appropriate space for illustrations (or include electronic art if it is available). Create a cover, a contents page (single or spread), a department page, a feature opener, an editorial page, and either a new product or flash form.

Chapter 7: Designing Books

For books are not absolutely dead things, but do contain a potency of life in them to be active as that soul whose progeny they are; nay, they do preserve as in a vial the purest efficacy and extraction of that living intellect that bred them.

-- John Milton, in a 1643 address to Parliament on the dangers of censorship.

In the early days of publishing, the book publisher, printer, bookseller, and often the author were all one and the same person. Books were lovingly designed both typographically and artistically to appeal to the reader. Today, desktop publishing allows a return to that kind of operation.

By the eighteenth century, the advent of mechanical printing processes and the myriad of (sometimes ghastly) typefaces had led to very poor designs of books. The author wrote his work and sold the manuscript to a publisher for a fixed sum. The publisher (sometimes doubling as the printer) then shipped the manuscript off to a printer, who was usually given free rein to typeset the book as he saw fit. The resulting hodgepodge of typefaces was then bound and sold in turn to the bookseller, who handled distribution to readers.

By the beginning of the twentieth century, the process of book publishing had changed again, to what we recognize today. The author writes the manuscript, and the publisher acts as a sort of middle man to handle the details of printing, binding, and distribution. The author gets a 10-20% royalty (10-20% of the retail price of the book) as long as the publisher keeps the book in print. The remaining 80-90% of the retail price goes to the publisher to pay for editing, design, production, promotion, distribution, and of course a margin of profit for the publisher for all his work.

Up until World War I, however, the changes in the book production process were not reflected in changes in book design. Most books were still pretty ugly.

After the first World War, a movement towards better book design began in England and the United States. Alfred A. Knopf became the premier publisher in terms of design, and his company still produces some of the best designed books in America. The Knopf formula was to use classic Roman typefaces with decorative borders appropriate to the subject at hand.

About the same time, in Germany, there arose an artistic colony called The Bauhaus. In this German version of Greenwich Village, there arose the concept of book design: "Form follows function." If the function happened to be the rather stark, highly organized education of children, the resulting books were also severe. Rigidly geometric, the books designed in The Bauhaus school were still well conceived and executed, beautiful in the starkness of their presentations, and a cut above most of the other books of the time.

It wasn't until the early 1950s in America that book design really changed radically. The reason was that publishers began seeing their sales drop off in favor of that newfangled contraption – television. Television and other media competition (a wealth of magazines also appeared about this time) caused book publishers to take a second look at what attracted readers. The result is the "modern" design concept of visual appeal – utilizing more and better art and artistry. Good design may not push sales of a book, but bad design can definitely hurt sales.

Today, the advent of desktop publishing is allowing an efficient, relatively inexpensive, yet high-quality way to return to the early notion of the author, publisher, proofreader, spelling checker, editor, and other functions all being wrapped in one person – in the modern case, that person with the help of a trusty computer and laser printer.

Design Styles

There are two modern approaches to book design, the invisible design and the mood design.

An invisible design is so subtle that it doesn't intrude on contents of the book or the reader's consciousness. It simply is. Reading such a book is effortless. From the designer's standpoint, such designs are the safest to create, but not necessarily particularly challenging.

The mood design, on the other hand, is definitely a challenge. And fun. But much harder to do. Without being outrageous, the design must set the stage for the reader, so that through typography and choice of illustration styles, the reader is "set up" as to what to expect from the contents of the book.

For example, a friend of the author's was given the task of writing and helping to design a college textbook on the computer language Pascal for a company making its maiden imprint of a computer science textbook. Now, there are dozens of Pascal textbooks on the market, but the proposal that sold the company on this writer was his idea that the previous textbooks were all stodgy and old fashioned in their presentation of the subject, and that he could turn out a very modern text that would snag a significant portion of the sales of textbooks in that subject. The author/designer spent weeks and months delving into book design and typography, looking for just the right layout, and an equivalent amount of time poring through type catalogues searching for just the right combinations of typefaces that would say to the reader subliminally, "Here's all this wonderful information; yes, it's a subject that's been done to death, but look how interestingly we've put this together so that you can understand it." For a textbook, it fairly shouts at the reader "Here I am, see how neat this is!"

Besides contemporary textbooks, some of the best book designs being done are in the field of children's literature. Here, as in textbooks, the designers have to work harder to try to design on two levels – for the buyers or choosers (professors, textbook committees, parents) and for the readers (children and students).

Book Design Considerations

Unity is very important to book design. There must be a uniformity of elements from opening page to closing page.

When a designers takes on a book project, they don't literally design every page, but like a magazine designer, work out the appearance of the major page types that will appear in the finished product. Where a magazine designer turns over mundane tasks like copyfitting, dummy pasteup, etc., to the production editor, the book designer is more subservient to the production editor. In book publishing, the production editor usually hires the (often freelance) book designer, who works under supervision. The book designer is given a budget and editorial limits by the production editor which must be followed.

In magazine design, the various page types can be designed simply from knowing the general "feel" or subject matter of the publication, without ever seeing the text that will go into the columns, tables of contents, and editorials as discussed in Chapter 6. Book design usually evolves after a significant portion (usually all) of the book is written. The contract that the author signs specifies a "proposed book size" in number of pages. But until book designers see how verbose or terse the authors actually are, they can only do a preliminary design, not carry the project through to completion.

Other things a book designer has to consider are the use that the book will be put to. If it is to be a mail order book (a Book Club edition), thinner interior and cover stocks need to be used to keep postage down. Coffee Table books need to be large format and expensive looking (even if they aren't). Tradebooks need special attention to jacket and cover designs so that they have good marketability. Books intended for sales to libraries need extra tough bindings and covers to stand up to heavy use. Textbooks need lots of color to keep the attention of elementary and high school students. All of these items affect the cost of the book, and must be juggled to fit within the budget.

Paper

A major budgetary item of concern to the designer is the **stock**, or paper that will be used for the interior pages of the book. From 2% to 5% of the retail price of a book goes to cover the cost of the paper on which it is printed. There are a number of different kinds of book paper, applicable to many situations.

Antique book paper is heavy, tough, absorbent stock. It is available in a number of textures and weights. The advantage of Antique stock is that its surface is non-glare and therefore easy on the reader's eyes and excellent for books without illustrations.

Plate stock, also called **English Finish stock** is a smooth out version of Antique stock. It has a much harder finish and is generally a good paper to use with ordinary illustrations because of the way it takes the ink.

Coated stock is even smoother than Plate stock. It has been treated to produce a semi-gloss to glossy finish that is very rich looking and excellent for high-quality photographic and illustration reproduction (colors and shades seem richer, and edges much more crisp on such paper). The major drawback is that is expensive.

Offset stock is a special paper used in offset printing. Because the printing process involves liquids other than ink, the paper has been specially treated to be moisture resistant. It is a smooth textured paper that has a harsh white color, and it is often utilized in magazines.

Bible stock is that ultra thin but opaque paper originally used only for producing Bibles, but now used wherever a massive volume is produced and weight of the finished book is a consideration.

Elements of a Book

Here, in order of appearance, are the parts of a nonfiction book that the designer is concerned with. Not every book will have all of these parts, of course. The elements, up to the first page of Chapter 1, are called the **Frontmatter**, or **Preliminaries**. The illustrations show some of the variations possible with each element.

• **Half Title Page.** In the old days, books were often sold without covers, and the Half Title page protected the much prettier Title Page. Normally the Half Title page contains only the title of the book.

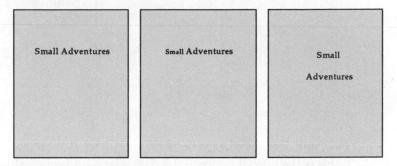

• **Advertisement Page.** A list of the author's other books by this publisher, etc. Sometimes the Advertisement page is combined with the Copyright page (see below).

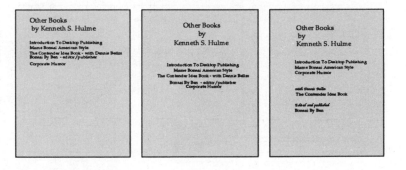

• **The Title Page.** The trend today is for a spread title page rather than just the right hand page. Spread openers, as with magazines, are much more impressive. The Title page may also contain the name of the publisher and the copyright date.

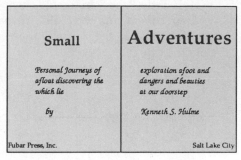

Right Title Page   Spread Title Page

- **The Copyright Notice and Catalogue Number Page.** This is the official notice of the date, place, and ownership of the copyright on the book. Found here too is the ISBN number and the Library of Congress card catalogue listing (see page 183).

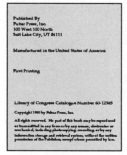

- **Dedication Page.** "To everyone who suffered with/ helped me…" The author gets a chance to dedicate the book to someone.

• **The Table of Contents.** Lists the name and locations (in terms of page numbers) of the chapters, appendices, glossary, bibliography, etc. Like magazine tables of contents, the book T.O.C. may also be illustrated with "teaser" pictures to entice the reader. The Table of Contents can start on either a **recto** (right-facing) or **verso** (left-facing) page.

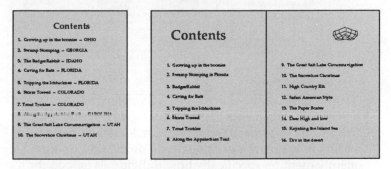

Single Page and Spread Styles of Contents Pages

• **List of Illustrations.** This list usually contains not only the names and locations of illustrations, but often contains the credits for those who created the illustrations (see page 186). The list of illustrations should be be first recto page after the Table of Contents.

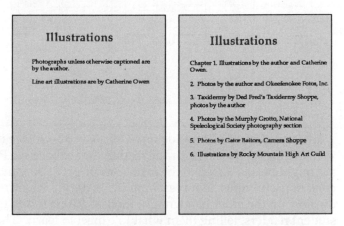

• **Preface or Foreword.** A Preface is written by the author; a Foreword is written by someone else. Either gives some detail about how the book came into being, how the author intends the reader to use the book, or other "stage setting" information.

Preface	Foreword
	by
	Neil L. Smyth, Famous Outdoorsman
You don't have to be Odysseus or Sir Edmund Hillary or Thor Heyerdahl to have adventures. Likewise, you don't necessarily have to travel to Amazon jungle, Darkest Africa or the vast wastelands of the Gobi desert to put your life at risk (if that sort of thing appeals to you.	You don't have to be Odysseus or Sir Edmund Hillary or Thor Heyerdahl to have adventures. Likewise, you don't necessarily have to travel to Amazon jungle, Darkest Africa or the vast wastelands of the Gobi desert to put your life at risk (if that sort of thing appeals to you.
There is plenty of adventure, both high and low, dangerous and idyllic, right in (relatively speaking) your own back yard. As you will see, I've managed to find a surefit of outdoor adventures within the confines of major American cities, or within an hour or three drive thereof.	Ken Hulme, the author of the book you are about to read, has found plenty of adventure, both high and low, dangerous and idyllic, right in (relatively speaking) his own back

- **Acknowledgements Page.** "Without whom this book could never have been written...". Acknowledgements are usually much more extensive than a dedication, and frequently mention specifically how individuals helped the author – research help, illustrations, moral support, typing or computer work, etc. The Acknowledgements can also appear as part of the Preface.

- **Introduction.** An Introduction is similar to a Preface in that it helps set the stage for the reader. In textbooks, a Preface might be addressed to the instructor or professor, and contain useful hints about teaching the material; the Introduction, on the other hand, might then be addressed to the student readers, telling them what to expect to learn. The Introduction should be the first recto page after the Acknowledgements.

Three sample layouts with "Introduction" headings.

• **A Second Half Title Page.** Should be identical to the first. The second Half Title page is optional, but if used, the next page should be the first page of Chapter 1.

Three sample layouts showing "Small Adventures".

• **Chapter 1.** Chapters have Left, Right, or Spread Openers, just as magazine articles do.

Three sample layouts: "Growing up in the boonies" and spread pages.

• **Subsequent Chapters.** In some books, chapters may be grouped into sections which will then have their own Section Openers. Below are some examples of imbedded graphics and quotes which also must be designed for the book.

• **Appendices.** An Appendix will contain information that is useful to the reader, but not necessarily part of the direct line of discussion of the book. This book, for example, primarily discusses desktop publishing from an non-denominational standpoint, i.e., not program or machine specific. The appendices contain specific information about various desktop publishing programs, computers, printers, and other devices.

• **End Notes.** These are necessary only if notational materials aren't included in the text as footnotes or as chapter end notes. This type of notation is going out of style, as readers demand more rapid access to notes. Holding one finger at the back of a thick book to mark the beginning of the End Notes can be literally painful!

• **Bibliography.** This is a list of every book the author even thought about reading to prepare for writing this book. Sometimes the bibliography is dispersed, with additional reading matter relevent to each chapter located at the chapter's end.

• **Glossary.** A listing of what all those big words the author used really mean. Glossaries are most often found in technically oriented books where a great deal of new jargon is presented to the reader.

• **Index.** A comprehensive listing of topics and individuals mentioned in context. A good index includes all references to a subject, with distinguishing characteristics denoting major discussions. Many of the index-generating functions of word processors will create listings of every occurence of a particular word, but that may not be helpful to someone looking for a particular answer. These functions can be used to create the initial listing, which is then cross-checked for simple one-word references versus in-depth discussions of the subject.

• **Colophon.** A colophon allows the designer to tell readers who care about such things some information about the typography used in creating the book. One of the more interesting (and lengthy) colophons is found in the small book *Observations on the Mystery of Print and the work of Johann Gutenberg* by Hendrik Willem van Loon. This book was created as a souvenir for visitors of the 1937 Book Manufacturers' Institute, Inc. Book Fair. It reads as follows:

AN APPRECIATION
These "Observations" of the work of Johann Gutenberg, written by Hendrik Willem van Loon, are printed and published for the New York Times Second National Book Fair at the Book Manufacturing Exhibit of the Book Manufacturers' Institute, held at Rockefeller Center, New York City, November 5 to 21, 1937. The typography has been suggested by Frederick W. Goudy, set at the Lanston Monotype Machine Co., Philadelphia, in Italian Old Style type designed by Mr. Goudy; plates made by The Haddon Craftsmen, Inc.; Camden, N.J. The illustrations were drawn by the author of the book, who also designed the jacket. Illustration plates are by the Chromatic Photo Engraving Co., New York; dies for the cover design by Truart Reproduction Co., New York; advance copies printed by American Book Bindery-Stratford Press, New York and bound by J.F. Tapley Co. and J.C. Valentine Co., New York. Binders' Board was furnished by Binders' Board Manufacturers' Association. The cloth is Aero Natural Finish furnished by Holliston Mills, New York; Roll Leaf supplied by Griffin, Campbell, Hayes, Walsh, Inc., New York. The paper is Ruskin Egg-Shell Text, manufactured by D.M. Bare Co., Roaring Spring, Pa. and distributed by Whitaker Paper Co., New York; ink by John P. Carlson, Inc., New York; glue and paste by Manhattan Paste and Glue Co. of New York. Books printed on Miller Two-Color Automatic Press, courtesy Isaac Goldmann Company, New York and Miller Printing Machinery Company, Pittsburgh, Pa.

This is an extreme example, chosen because the author liked it. Most colophons are simple five or six line celebrations of the printing process which give the typeface and one or two other details. The colophon can also appear on the copyright page.

The Appendices, End Notes, Bibliography, Glossary, Index, and Colophon make up what is called the **Backmatter** or **Endmatter** of the book.

Usually the designer will spend the most time creating just the strategic pages such as the Title, Table of Contents, a Chapter opener, and a facing page set of a chapter to show how running headers and footers, page numbers, and sub-heads will be handled. The designer then provides a **Specification Sheet** that lists such details as:

- **Trim size of the pages.** Hardback books are usually 5.375 x 8.0, 5.5 x 8.25, or 6.125 x 9.25 while paperbacks are either 4.125 x 6.375 or 4.125 x 7.0. Current trends are towards the squarer formats, especially among books with large numbers of graphics. The book's size is chosen for the "least waste" cutting from the width of paper stock that the printer has available.

- **Margins.** White space is 50-75 percent of the total space in a book. Keep the white on the outside edges. The narrowest margin is at the gutter, but the combined gutters on facing pages is larger than any other single gutter. The widest margin goes at the bottom, outside margins are narrower than the bottom, but wider than top margins.

- **Size of copy area.** This may or may not be the same as the trim size of the page minus the margins. Some books use a reduced copy area to fill out the thickness of a book when the text isn't very long.

- **Typestyles, sizes, and leading.** These are specified for running headers and footers, chapter titles, subheads, captions, embedded quotations, etc. Generally only two or three typefaces are selected.

- **Paragraph indent style and amount of indent.** Generally first paragraphs of chapters aren't indented, whereas the rest are; sometimes first paragraphs below subheads also are not indented.

- **Long quote style.** Quotes can be indented in from one or both margins. They can also be set in larger or smaller type, or in a different typeface than the body.

- **Footnote style, if applicable.**

- **Page number typesize, style, and placement.**

- **Typography of titles, subheads, initial capitals.**

- **The "drop" white space. Drop** is the distance from the Chapter title to the first line of body copy on chapter openers.

- **Styles for frontmatter.** Details for the Half and Title pages, Table of Contents, and Preface.

- **Styles for backmatter.** Specifications for the Glossary, Bibliography, and Index.

Design Stages

The designer takes a copy of the manuscript, and after a thorough reading, comes up with a design for the strategic pages, then a printer typesets the sample pages for editorial approval.

The next step is called **casting off**–counting the number of words or characters in the entire manuscript. Then the designer must **copyfit** the manuscript to see how many book pages it will produce relative to the contractual book length. Long manuscripts may require smaller typefaces and tight leading, short manuscripts may need larger faces and broader leading to fit within the "designed length" as established in the author's contract. If possible, the designer tries to make all of this come out as some even multiple of 32 – there being 32 pages in the normal book signature.

After the copyfitting and editorial approval of the basic design, the manuscript is **typeset**. A copy of the typeset pages is used by the designer to paste up a **dummy** of the book mechanically to check the copyfit calculations. A layout artist makes a **camera-ready pasteup**, using the dummy as a guide. Finally, the book is sent out for printing and binding.

Desktop publishing is changing some of the steps in the book design and production process so that, according to Alexander Burke, President of McGraw-Hill Book Company, "…ideally there should be no separation of author, illustrator, and designer … Communication through word, picture, and design is, or should be, a simultaneous act of creation."

With word processors, authors can give the designer exact word or character counts. From a couple of word processed sample chapters, the designer can create the strategic page designs and then have the author dump the text into a desktop publishing program to lay out the book according to the Specification Sheet. The dummy is a laser print of the layout produced in minutes instead of days. Corrections are made directly to the layout, and the camera-ready pasteup is printed out on a high-quality printer in a matter of hours. The cost savings in man hours of typesetting and layout can be significant.

Review Questions

1. Compare and contrast modern book publishing with its pre-twentieth century predecessors.
2. Compare and contrast invisible design and mood design of books.
3. What are some elementary book design considerations?
4. List five kinds of book stock and what they are used for.
5. List and define at least ten elements of a book design.
6. What is a colophon?
7. List the common sizes for hardback and paperback books.
8. How much of the volume of a book is white space?
9. What is drop?
10. Define frontmatter, backmatter.
11. What is casting off?
12. What is the significance of the number 32 in book design?
13. How is desktop publishing changing the way book designers work?
14. What book design principle came out of the Bauhaus?
15. Compare and contrast book and magazine design concepts.
16. Why is book use important to a designer?
17. What is a royalty?
18. When does a book have end notes as part of the backmatter?
19. What are the relationships between the various margins in a book?
20. What caused the revival of good book design in the mid 1950s?

Exercises

1. Design (full size) the following strategic pages for a non-fiction book on some subject of your choice. Use previously saved text as greek text for filling in body copy, but type out all titles, heads, subheads, etc.

> – Half Title and Title page
> – Copyright page
> – Table of Contents
> – Preface or Foreword
> – Chapter opener
> – A chapter facing page showing placement of a
>   graphic, a long quote, and subheads

2. Create a Specification Sheet for the above book, listing at least:

> – trim size
> – margins
> – size of copy area
> – typesizes, styles, and leading for all major areas
> – paragraph style
> – page number typesize, style, and placement
> – drop white space

3. Take an existing book (other than this text) and, using a "pica pole" or typographer's ruler, create an "after the fact" specification sheet for the book. List the dimensions and placement of as many elements of the book's design as you can distinguish.

Chapter 8: Design & Layout of Newsletters and Newspapers

All successful newspapers are ceaselessly querulous and bellicose. They never defend anyone or anything if they can help it; if the job is forced upon them, they tackle it by denouncing someone or something else.

-- H.L. Mencken

Newsletter: A self-covered periodical, normally 4 to16 pages long, that carries news aimed at a special set of audience interests, but generally no advertising; may issue in any frequency or irregularity. Newsletters may appeal to an audience of any size, with subscription lists ranging from a few hundred to hundreds of thousands, and with subscription prices ranging from a few dollars to thousands of dollars per year.

There are well over 100,000 newsletters published in the United States every year. They are published by everyone from grade school students to major corporations, and they cover practically every subject under the sun.

Newsletters are almost as specialized as magazines, but less meaty. They range from a single sheet of letter- or legal-sized paper printed on two sides up to a practical limit of about 24 pages. The average newsletter is 8.5" x 11" in size, has no advertisements except small classified ads, and never uses a glossy cover. It presents specialized information in summary style (2 to 6 short articles per page). Magazines (see Chapter 6) usually have glossy covers, are regularly over 24 pages long, accept advertisements from almost anyone, and present specialized information in a more expansive prose style of writing.

Newsletters are a prime area of opportunity for desktop publishing because the techniques of desktop publishing and laser printing produce a much higher quality newsletter without the expense and hassle of typesetting and mechanical layout. Newsletters are both fun and challenging to design. The fun is that each one is a separate project covering a new topic; the challenge is making each one different – not making every newsletter you create look like every other newsletter you create.

Newsletter Design

Here are the basic newsletter design elements. As the designer it is up to you which elements you will use, and how you will put them together. Don't create a hodgepodge of bits and pieces; design an integrated document from the page one nameplate to the back page mailer.

• **Logotype, Nameplate, or Flag.** This is the display font name of the newsletter along with any associated graphic. It can be placed along the top (the usual position), along the fold (or stitch side), even at the bottom of the page.

Coming up with a good name for a newsletter is really difficult and time consuming if you don't want to look or sound like all the rest of the newsletters in the world. Be creative but not cute when trying to come up with a name for the newsletter: NEWS, BULLETIN, REPORT, SPOTLIGHT ON…, are all over-used nouns. On the other hand, THE BEAVER VALLEY TAIL and THE SALEM WITCHFINDER are perhaps going a bit too far. Later in this chapter you will find an extensive list of newsletter- and newspaper-related names that can be used as inspiration.

Once you've named your newsletter, it shouldn't change its name; you may lose some readers. If a name change becomes absolutely necessary, do a complete makeover – change the layout as well, so the publication has a new, fresh look.

Fig. 8.1 Four variations on column numbers and widths.

• **Page Size.** The most common sizes are full 8.5" x 11" and full 8.5" x 14". Other possibilities are half-letter (8.5" x 11" folded to 8.5" x 5.5" pages) and half-legal (8.5" x 14" folded to 8.5" x 7" pages). Some newsletters use full tabloid (11" x 17"), but this isn't very common. A half-tabloid is really letter size with a fold rather than staples holding the sheets together.

• **Columns.** Once you've chosen the page size, you have to decide on how many columns each page will have. Wider columns mean less hyphenation, fewer lines and more consistent word spacing. Narrower columns mean that you will get more copy on a page, because narrow columns need smaller typefaces to have easily readable lines. On a letter-sized newsletter with 2 columns good choices for type sizes might be 9 or 10 point; with three columns the sizes can drop to 8 or 9 points for body copy. The basic idea is to keep the column width readable. **Readable** can be defined as seven to ten words per line.

One interesting technique is to vary column widths (but at regular increments, not randomly). Using a three column format, you can have three columns 1/3 of the page wide, or two columns, one of which is 2/3 of the page wide, the other 1/3 wide. The position of the wide column can be alternated on left and right pages to produce symmetrical two-page spreads. With a standard three-column format, you can also add interest by occasionally putting an article into two columns, each of which is 1.5 regular columns wide.

• **Justification.** Will the columns be ragged right, or justified both left and right? The advantages of ragged right columns of text are complete constancy of word spacing, less hyphenation, less chance readers will lose their place, and narrower column gutters (the raggedness makes the gutters appear wider than they actually are). Full-justified columns, on the other hand, give your newsletter a more formal, professional, less chatty look.

There is some belief that full-justified lines will contain more text than ragged right lines; this is probably true only when hyphenation is also employed. Full justification is usually accomplished by uniformly adding spaces between words until the line fills out. Short last lines often look very bad due to excessively wide word spacing. In many programs, adding an additional carriage return to the end of the short last line will alleviate the problem.

• **Color.** Are you going to go to the extra expense and work of using multiple colors on a regular basis? With a large enough distribution and/or big enough budget, then color becomes more viable. Usually, however, newsletters are kept black and white, but may vary paper color from issue to issue as a way of adding visual interest.

• **Rules and Borders.** Are you going to use them or not? If so, where? Top and bottom rules help set off the page boundaries; column gutter rules allow narrower gutters because the rule provides a mechanical break between columns. What thicknesses and styles? Very wide rules can overpower not only body copy but headlines as well, while hairlines may not make enough impact. Use rules and borders sparingly, for emphasis. Don't box or rule around things just because they're there. Experiment with styles and sizes to see which go best with the newsletter you are creating.

One good use of rules in a newsletter design is to place them in the column gutters. This works very well if you have three or four columns on 8.5" x 11" paper, and have the text set full-justified. The rules act as visual breaks so that the reader's eye returns to the left rather than accidentally carrying on into the next column.

- **Standing Elements.** The most common standing elements in a newsletter are:
    - Mailing address block if the newsletter will be folded into a self-mailer.
    - A descriptive phrase related to the Nameplate: "Serving Widget Dealers Everywhere!" This phrase can also be repeated as a running header or footer on each page.
    - A copyright notice.
    - A calendar of coming events.
    - Page numbers (also called **folios**). If you are going to use them, which of several styles will you use? The basic possibilities are: near the outside top or bottom corner; top or bottom at the inside gutter between pages; or centered left and right at the top or bottom of the page. The type style of folios should be different enough from the body copy type style that the folios don't get lost against the body.
    - A Masthead listing the editor(s), committee folk, addresses, phone numbers, and subscription information.
    - The issue information: date, volume, number, etc. This is another candidate for header/footer treatment.
    - Regular columns on particular subjects by continuing authors.

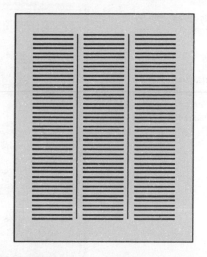

Fig. 8.2 Rules placed between columns of full justified text help the reader distinguish between columns.

Of course, not every newsletter needs all of these elements. However, if you include any of these elements, they should appear in the same location(s) on every page of every issue, so that readers don't get confused trying to find the calendar or the Question & Answer column.

- **Type Family and Faces.** What will you use for body copy, headlines or titles, subheads, bylines, and other text elements? See Chapter 2 for a full discussion of typographic possibilities. Basically, make sure that the type family suits the publication style.

Fig. 8.3 Masthead from the Journal of the American Chemical Society Division of Physical Chemistry Newsletter. Here, officers and committee members are more important than the editor, publisher, or other production personnel.

EXECUTIVE COMMITTEE
DIVISION OF PHYSICAL CHEMISTRY

F. Fleming Crim, Chairman
University of Wisconsin
Madison, WI 53706
(606) 263-7364

David Chandler, Chairman-Elect
University of California
Berkeley, CA 94720
(415) 643-6821

Daniel J. Auerbach, Vice-Chairman
IBM Almaden Res. Division
650 Harry Road
San Jose, CA 95120-6099
(408) 927-2432

Edward M. Eyring, Secretary-Treasurer
University of Utah
Salt Lake City, UT 84112
(801) 581-8658

Thomas F. George, Past Chairman
State University of New York at Buffalo

G. J. Small, Exec. Committee
Iowa State University

W. R. Gentry, Exec. Committee
University of Minnesota

Veronica Vaida, Exec. Committee
University of Colorado, Boulder

Ahmed Zewail, Exec. Committee
California Institute of Technology

Sylvia T. Ceyer, Exec. Committee
Mass. Institute of Technology

J. T. Hynes, Exec. Committee
University of Colorado, Boulder

Joyce Kaufman, Councilor
Johns Hopkins University

Donald W. Setser, Councilor
Kansas State University

Alvin L. Kwiram, Councilor
University of Washington

Terry A. Miller, Councilor
Ohio State University

Isaiah Shavitt, Alternate Councilor
Ohio State University

Louis E. Brus, Alternate Councilor
AT&T Bell Labs

Michael T. Bowers, Alternate Councilor
University of California, Santa Barbara

Paul L. Houston, Alternate Councilor
Cornell University

SUBDIVISION OF THEORETICAL
CHEMISTRY
William P. Reinhardt, Chairman
University of Pennsylvania
Philadelphia, PA 19104
(215) 898-4845

Bruce J. Berne, Chairman-Elect
Columbia University
New York, NY 10027
(212) 280-2186

Kenneth D. Jordan, Vice-Chairman
University of Pittsburgh
Pittsburg, PA 15260
(412) 624-8690

Donald G. Truhlar, Secretary
University of Minnesota
Minneapolis, MN 55455
(612) 624-7555

• **Will the Newsletter Accept Paid Advertisements?** If so, will you integrate the ads among the articles, or set them off on a page of their own?

There are many more ways to put these basic elements together than there are newsletter designers. Experiment, have fun, be creative!

Categories of Newsletters

There are four categories that newsletters fall into in presenting their specialized information.

Subscription newsletters are by far the most prevalent. They include investment and financial reports such as *Bull & Bear Tips*, business in-house newsletters like *Acme Widget Happenings*, and consumer publications on the order of *"The Seybold Report on..."* for large national audiences. Also in this category are club, group, or affinity newsletters such as *The Mame Bonsai Growers of America News*, and institutional publications such as *Anthroquest*, put out by the American Museum of Natural History.

Organizational newsletters are published by a variety of non-profit and governmental agencies. These publications are very comprehensive in their coverage of news for their constituents (fellow researchers, advocacy groups, etc.) or employees and volunteers.

Franchise newsletters, or **syndicated newsletters**, are found in some fields of interest. They are prepared generically, with the nameplate left blank, and the purchasing agency or group simply tacks on its own nameplate and ships the master off to a printer. An example of this is the *Good Health News* newsletter which is marketed to retail drugstore chains. The chain imprints its own logo on the masthead, and makes the newsletter available free of charge to customers in countertop stands by the pharmacy window.

Public relations newsletters are sales pitches in disguise. To give them credit, however, they usually give much more information than a brochure or flyer. Besides the product description there are normally several interesting articles, sometimes by nationally known experts, on subjects related to the particular product line. Adobe Systems, makers of several computer software products related to desktop publishing, uses this approach with great success in their *Font & Function* newsletter/type catalogue.

Fig. 8.4 Newsletter subjects cover many fields that may be too small or too specialized for larger publications. They also serve to augment information from more traditional news and information sources.

Newspapers

Newspaper: a periodical that carries both news and advertisements, usually on newsprint, self-covered and unbound in large sheets, and generally issued at least once a week.

The obvious success story of desktop publishing and newspapers is Knight-Ridder's *USA Today* daily, which jumped immediately into competition with major dailies across the country. A major reason for its success is that for the same amount of equipment money as a for conventional electronic newspaper, *USA Today* got many times the computing power and ease of use. Except for final printing, the entire newspaper is written, edited, and composed with desktop publishing equipment – Macintosh computers, QuarkXpress desktop publishing software, and a variety of graphics programs.

The real niche for desktop-published newspapers is in the district, regional, or rural weekly or monthly markets. There are hundreds, if not thousands, of possibilities for weekly newspapers which focus on the activities of part of a city, or the county surrounding a metropolitan area. Some examples include *The Triangle Review*, a weekly that competes strongly with the daily *Fort Collins Coloradoan*; and *Foothills People*, a monthly newspaper covering one of several named but politically unrecognized districts in Salt Lake City, Utah.

Horace Greeley (of "Go West, young man!" fame) wrote the following advice to another young man whom he understood was going to start a small country newspaper. For the most part his advice holds true for desktop publishers who are going to go out and start a district, rural, or regional newspaper today.

I. Begin with a clear conception that the subject of deepest interest to an average human being is himself; next to that, he is most concerned about his neighbors. Asia and the Tongo islands stand a long way after these in his regard. It does seem to me that most country journals are oblivious to these vital truths. ...Secure a wide awake judicious correspondent in each village and township of your county...who will promptly send you whatever of moment occurs in his vicinity, and will make up at least half your journal of local matter thus collected, nobody in the county can do long without it. ... In short, make your paper a perfect mirror of everything done in your county that its citizens ought to know... .

II. Take an earnest and active, if not a leading, part in the advancement of home industry. If anyone undertakes a new branch industry in the county, especially if it be a manufacturer, do not wait to be solicited, but hasten to give him a helping hand. ...Encourage and aid him to the best of your ability.

III. Don't let the politicians and aspirants of the county own you. They may be clever fellows, as they often are; but if you keep your eyes open, you will see something that they seem blind to, and must speak out accordingly. Do your best to keep...rates of taxation, other than for common schools, as low as may be. Remember that – in addition to the radical righteousness of the thing – the taxpayers take many more papers than the tax consumers.

Newspaper Design

From the standpoint of design and layout, newspapers don't differ too much from newsletters, except they have more pages. The same basic elements of design are used in both newsletters and newspapers (see above).

One major difference is that newspapers, because of their large page size, generally have more columns: four or five being the norm, rather than two or three. Five columns give more design flexibility than four columns; a story can be 1-5 columns wide, with potential mixes being stories 1& 4, 2&3, 2& 2, and a full 5 columns wide. A four-column layout only allows 1& 3, 2& 2 and full 4 columns wide.

Another difference is that newspapers survive on their advertising. The design and placement of ads are major factors in newspaper design. Ads are most often sold on a column inch basis: an ad will be one inch deep by one column wide (a one column inch ad), one inch deep by two columns wide (two column inches), two inches deep by two columns wide (four column inches), etc. Ad position is important to advertisers, so ads are often sold as "above the fold" or below it. Ads above the center fold are more easily seen, and thus that space is sold at a premium.

Many newspapers also sell ad space in advertising supplements – multiple page sections containing mostly ads. Some advertising supplements are created with themes: hunting season, spring gardening, home improvement, etc. These supplements may contain small articles relevant to the theme written by representatives of major advertisers or the newspaper staff.

Fig. 8.45 Possible layouts for four- and five-column newspapers.

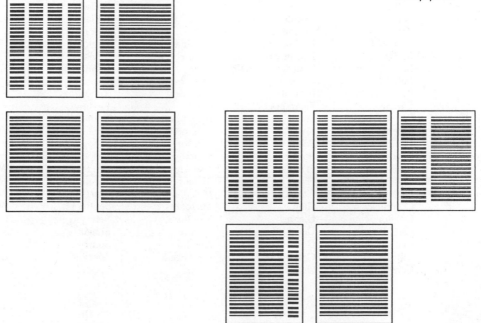

Names for Newsletters and Newspapers

Acent	Commentator	Guide	Newsgram	Spectrum
Advance	Commercial	Headlight	Newsweek	Spirit
Ad-Vantages	Compiler	Herald	Nugget	Spotlight
Advertiser	Courier	Hermes	Observer	Standard
Adviser	Crescent	Hub	Onlooker	Star
Advocate	Crier	Independent	Opinion	Suburbanite
Aegis	Crusader	Index	Oracle	Suburban Life
Agenda	Defender	Informer	Outlook	Success
Alert	Delphic	Inquirer	Pacesetter	Sundial
Almanac	Developer	Indicator	Packet	Tattler
Alternative	Dial	Intelligencer	Patriot	Telegram
Announcements	Digest	Investigator	Pendulum	Telegraph
Appeal	Directory	Javelin	People	Tempo
Argosy	Dispatch	Journal	Pflag	This Week
Argus	Doings	Junction	Pioneer	Tidings
Atlas	Drummer	Kaleidoscope	Plain Talk	Time Piece
Balloon	Easy Reader	Keynoter	Press	Times
Bandwagon	Eccentric	Kronicle	Progress(ive)	Today
Banner	Echo	Landmark	Prompter	Topic
Barb	Enquirer	Lantern	Quill	Tower
Beacon	Enterprise	Leader	Realm	Town Crier
Beat	Epigraph	Ledger	Record(er)	Townsman
Billboard	Essay	Leaf	Reflection	Town Talk
Booster	Events	Light	Reflex	Trader
Breeze	Examiner	Local	Reformer	Tribune
Broadside	Exchange	Luminary	Region	Traveler
Budgeteer	Exponent	Magnet	Register	Trumpet
Bugle	Express	Mail	Reminder	Truth Teller
Bulletin	Extra	Manifest	Reporter	Upbeat
Bystander	Favorite	Maverick	Repository	Vanguard
Cadence	Fishrapper	Media	Review	Vigil
Call	Flier	Megaphone	Roundup	Villager
Camera	Flyer	Memorial	Scene	Vista
Candle	Focus	Mentor	Scoop	Voice
Carrier	Forum	Mercury	Scope	Watchman
Challenge	Frontier	Messenger	Scribe	Wave
Champion	Free Lance	Meteor	Scrutinizer	Welcomat
Chanticleer	Gazette	Metropolitan	Searchlight	Window
Chronicle	Gem	Mirror	Sentinel	Witness
Citation	Gleam	Monitor	Sentry	World
Civic Press	Good Life	Needle	Signal	X-Ray
Clarion	Good News	Neighbor	Source	Yeoman
Clipper	Grapevine	New Era	Speaker	Zealot
Comet	Guardian	News	Special	

Review Questions

1. List at least six standing elements found in a newsletter or newspaper design.
2. Define the four categories of newsletters.
3. What are the differences between a newsletter and a newspaper?
4. Why are newsletters a good subject for desktop publishing?
5. Discuss at least five of the major design elements of a newsletter or newspaper.
6. What advantages and disadvantages are there to having a greater or lesser number of columns in a newsletter or newspaper design?
7. When would you want to use color in a newsletter design? In a newspaper design?
8. Why do you want standing elements to appear in the same location from issue to issue?
9. Why would you want to put rules in the column gutters of a newsletter?
10. Why should the type style of the folio be different than the type style of the body copy?
11. Define newspaper.
12. What is a column inch?
13. What does "above the fold" mean to an advertiser?
14. How many columns of text do newspapers generally have?
15. What is an advertising supplement?
16. What kinds of newspapers are best suited to desktop publishing?
17. What are two major differences between newspapers and newsletters?
18. How do newsletters differ in content from magazines?
19. List at least six good subjects for newsletters.
20. Name at least one newspaper that is produced using desktop publishing.

Exercise

1. Design and create a four page self-mailing newsletter with at least one continuing column. If you don't have enough electronic text from previous assignments, use greek text for the copy in articles.

Twelve Things to Look For in a Desktop Publishing Program

- Ability to compose complex text within the program (word processing rather than just text editing)
- Ability to import a wide variety of graphics formats
- Built-in spelling checkers and thesauri
- Kerning and letter spacing capabilities
- Availability of sophisticated drawing tools for creating lines, rules, boxes, and arbitrary shapes
- Ability not only to see, but to work across, facing page layouts
- Ease of creating and modifying Text and Graphics Blocks in the formats you most commonly use.
- Keyboard equivalents for most-used commands– the more, the better
- A user interface that uses system standard commands and methods of activating them
- Accurate screen display versus printed appearance from high-quality printers
- Ability to handle color separations and other color graphics manipulations
- "Canned" formats or stylesheets for various standard projects such as books and brochures.

In addition to those programs specifically identified as desktop publishing software, there are a great many word processing programs that are adding desktop publishing features to new revisions of old software. Notable among these are Microsoft Word and WordPerfect for both the Macintosh and the PC. These programs contain sophisticated ways of making multiple-column documents, embedding graphics in the text, at least partially wrapping text around graphics, and some controls over kerning and letter spacing as well as line spacing.

Even some of the drawing programs can be used for one and two-page desktop publishing projects. Programs like MacDraw II and PC Draw also accommodate multiple-column text.

What differentiates these other programs from desktop publishing today is the ease of precision placement of text and graphics elements on the page. Word processors still need more development in that regard, and drawing programs don't have really sophisticated typographic text controls.

Appendix A: Desktop Publishing Software

Reading computer manuals without hardware is as frustrating as reading sex manuals without software.

– Arthur C. Clarke

Since desktop publishing was coined as a term, the variety of software available has changed and continues to change dramatically. In the beginning there were only a couple of programs for the Macintosh. Today there are several programs for most, if not all, operating systems.

The most difficult task for the software purchaser is to decide which program, among all the offerings, to spend hard earned money on. The task isn't made any easier by the plethora of advertising hype about new and wonderful features. Here's a list of some of the things you should look for in desktop publishing software, regardless of which computer you use to run the program.

An aspect of publishing that no desktop publishing software addresses is the creation of signatures (sometimes called impositions), where several pages of text (usually 8, 16, or 32) are printed out on a single piece of paper, folded appropriately, and cut along one or more sides to form a booklet. Successive signatures are then bound together to make up the entire book. Because of the folding of the paper, some of the book pages are printed upside down relative to others on the single sheet. To date, only Ventura Publisher for the PC allows text or Text Block rotation. No program allows more than one page number on a sheet of paper, and there are no provisions for linking page numbers on a sheet so that printed pages are correctly sequentially numbered.

Another aspect that will keep desktop publishing programs ahead of the competition will be the inclusion of much more complete drawing tools. Springboard Publisher for the Macintosh does include a sort of clone of MacPaint. With this program you can create a Graphic Block and double click in it to bring up the paint program tools. The only drawback is that Springboard's drawing tools are bit-oriented, not object-oriented or PostScript tools.

Things to look for in the future

- More than one page number on a virtual page (the "page" where you create the layout on screen)
- The ability to create signatures for multipage documents such as books, magazines, booklets, etc.
- The ability to rotate Text and Graphic Blocks and their contents
- A "complete" drawing and/or post-digitizing graphic modification program as part of the desktop publishing program
- The ability to create virtual pages of nonstandard sizes that are visually of those proportions, not just inscribed within a larger standard size (a visual 7"x 9" page, not just a 7 x 9 area in a letter-size page)
- Better methods of recording information so that display on full page, double page, and high-resolution monitors is better (Display PostScript is one possibility just beginning to be explored as this book goes to press.)

Current Software Comparisons

The following tables compare the acknowledged industry leaders in desktop publishing software: PageMaker, ReadySetGo! and QuarkXpress on the Macintosh, and PageMaker, Ventura, and GEM for the PC.

As is readily apparent, with a few exceptions, all six programs have essentially the same features. The real test to determine which program is best for your needs is to sit down and try out the programs on a few of your most common project types. Unfortunately, this can be an expensive proposition, unless there is a user group or some other computer support group (such as a University Computer Center) which has several of these programs available for short-term loan so that you can become familiar with them.

In the following tables, a question mark indicates that the status of a particular feature could not be ascertained.

Mac PageMaker
Aldus Corp.

Hardware	512K RAM, hard disk
Operating System	Macintosh
Import ASCII Files	Y
Import Formatted Text	Y
Command Driven	Y
Icon/Mouse Driven	Y
Spelling Checker	N
Max Document	110,000 words
Snaking Columns	Y
Max # of Columns	?
Tables	N
Index/TOC Generation	N
Footnotes	N
Dictionary Hyphenation	Y
Discretionary Hyphenation	N
Type of Fonts	Any Macintosh compatible
Font Size Limit	4 to 127 point
Fonts per Page Limit	N
Kerning	Y
Leading	Y
Letterspacing	Y
Text Wraparound Graphics	Y
Drawing Tools	Y
Import Graphics	Y
Import Color Graphics	Y
Manipulate Color Graphics	Supports CYMK, RGB, HLS, and Pantone color spot, process and 4-color color separations of EPSF
Automatic Pagination	Y
Manual Pagination	Y
Stylesheets	?
Typesetters Supported	Linotronic 100, 300, others
Laser Printers Supported	Apple LaserWriter, LaserWriter Plus, Dataproducts LZ2665, and others

ReadySetGo!
Letraset USA

Hardware	512K RAM, hard disk
Operating System	Macintosh
Import ASCII Files	Y
Import Formatted Text	Y
Command Driven	Y
Icon/Mouse Driven	Y
Spelling Checker	Y
Max Document	Limited only by available memory
Snaking Columns	Y
Max # of Columns	Unlimited
Tables	Y
Index/TOC Generation	Y
Footnotes	N
Dictionary Hyphenation	Y
Discretionary Hyphenation	Y
Type of Fonts	Any Macintosh compatible
Font Size Limit	1 to 321 point
Fonts per Page Limit	N
Kerning	Y
Leading	Y
Letterspacing	Y
Text Wraparound Graphics	Y
Drawing Tools	Y
Import Graphics	Y
Import Color Graphics	Supports full Pantone and RGB
Manipulate Color Graphics	Spot and mechanical color separations
Automatic Pagination	Y
Manual Pagination	Y
Stylesheets	Y
Typesetters Supported	Linotronic 101/P, 300
Laser Printers Supported	Apple LaserWriter, Laser-Writer Plus

QuarkXpress
Quark, Inc.

Hardware	1Mb RAM, hard disk
Operating System	Macintosh
Import ASCII Files	Y
Import Formatted Text	Y
Command Driven	Y
Icon/Mouse Driven	Y
Spelling Checker	Y
Max Document	Limited by disk space
Snaking Columns	Y
Max # of Columns	?
Tables	Y
Index/TOC Generation	N
Footnotes	N
Dictionary Hyphenation	Y
Discretionary Hyphenation	Y
Type of Fonts	Any Macintosh compatible
Font Size Limit	2 to 500 point
Fonts per Page Limit	N
Kerning	Y
Leading	Y
Letterspacing	Y
Text Wraparound Graphics	Y
Drawing Tools	Y
Import Graphics	Y
Import Color Graphics	Supports Pantone, HSB, RGB, and 4-color
Manipulate Color Graphics	Spot and process color separations of imported EPSF
Automatic Pagination	Y
Manual Pagination	Y
Stylesheets	Y
Typesetters Supported	Linotronic 100, 300
Laser Printers Supported	Apple LaserWriter, LaserWriter Plus

PC PageMaker
Aldus Corp.

Hardware	PC/AT, XT, PS/2, 640K RAM, 20Mb hard disk
Operating System	DOS with Windows
WYSIWYG	Y
Displays	EGA, VGA, Hercules, others
Import ASCII Files	Y
Import Formatted Text	Y
Command Driven	Y
Icon/Mouse Driven	Y
Spelling Checker	N
Max Document	128 pages
Snaking Columns	Y
Max # of Columns	?
Tables	N
Index/TOC Generation	N
Footnotes	N
Dictionary Hyphenation	Y
Discretionary Hyphenation	Y
Type of Fonts	Bitstream soft fonts, conofonts, and others
Font Size Limit	4 to 128 point
Fonts per Page Limit	N
Kerning	Y
Leading	Y
Letterspacing	Y
Text Wraparound Graphics	Y
Drawing Tools	N
Import Graphics	Y
Import Color Graphics	Y
Manipulate Color Graphics	Supports CYMK, RGB, HLS, and Pantone color. Does spot, process, and 4-color separations of EPSF
Automatic Pagination	Y
Manual Pagination	Y
Stylesheets	Y
Typesetters Supported	Linotronic 100, 300
Laser Printers Supported	HP LaserJet Plus, IBM Page-printer 3812, PostScript compatibles

Ventura Publisher
Xerox Corp.

Hardware	PC/AT, XT, PS/2, 640K bytes RAM, hard disk
Operating System	DOS with Windows
WYSIWYG	Y
Displays	CGA, EGA, VGA, Hercules
Import ASCII Files	Y
Import Formatted Text	Y
Command Driven	N
Icon/Mouse Driven	Y
Spelling Checker	N
Max Document	9,999 pages
Snaking Columns	N
Max # of Columns	16 per page
Tables	Y
Index/TOC Generation	Y
Footnotes	Y
Dictionary Hyphenation	Y
Discretionary Hyphenation	Y
Type of Fonts	All PC-compatible fonts
Font Size Limit	1 to 255 point, 6 styles
Fonts per Page Limit	N
Kerning	Y
Leading	Y
Letterspacing	Y
Text Wraparound Graphics	Y
Drawing Tools	Y
Import Graphics	Y
Import Color Graphics	Y
Manipulate Color Graphics	Spot color separations
Automatic Pagination	Y
Manual Pagination	Y
Stylesheets	Y
Typesetters Supported	Linotronic 100, 300
Laser Printers Supported	HP LaserJet and LaserJet Plus, Xerox 4045, JLaser, PostScript compatibles

GEM Desktop Publisher
Digital Research, Inc.

Hardware	PC/AT, XT, PS/2, 640K RAM, Hard disk
Operating System	DOS
WYSIWYG	Y
Displays	EGA, VGA, Hercules, Wyse 700, Genius, others
Import ASCII Files	Y
Import Formatted Text	Y
Command Driven	Y
Icon/Mouse Driven	Y
Spelling Checker	N
Max Document	999 pages
Snaking Columns	N
Max # of Columns	?
Tables	N
Index/TOC Generation	N
Footnotes	N
Dictionary Hyphenation	Y
Discretionary Hyphenation	N
Type of Fonts	Compugraphic Intellifonts
Font Size Limit	4 to 72 point
Fonts per Page Limit	8
Kerning	Y
Leading	Y
Letterspacing	N
Text Wraparound Graphics	Y
Drawing Tools	Y
Import Graphics	Y
Import Color Graphics	N
Manipulate Color Graphics	N
Automatic Pagination	N
Manual Pagination	Y
Stylesheets	Y
Typesetters Supported	Linotronic 100, 300
Laser Printers Supported	HP LaserJet Plus, IBM Pageprinter 3812, PostScript compatibles

Interleaf Publisher
Interleaf, Inc.

This is the program of choice if you have a multi-system environment, with users on PCs, others on Macs, and still others using workstations/minicomputers. It is the only desktop publishing program with versions available for all three of these environments.

Hardware	386-based PS/2 PCs, Mac IIs, or workstations with 6Mb RAM and 40Mb hard disk
Operating System	Various
WYSIWYG	Y
Displays	Varied
Import ASCII Files	Y
Import Formatted Text	Y
Command Driven	Y
Icon/Mouse Driven	Y
Spelling Checker	Y
Max Document	999 pages
Snaking Columns	Y
Max # of Columns	Unlimited
Tables	Y
Index/TOC Generation	Y
Footnotes	Y
Dictionary Hyphenation	Y
Discretionary Hyphenation	Y
Type of Fonts	13 fonts included; does not support downloadable fonts
Font Size Limit	6 to 72 point
Fonts per Page Limit	8
Kerning	N
Leading	Y
Letterspacing	Y
Text Wraparound Graphics	Manual only
Drawing Tools	Very extensive
Import Graphics	Y
Import Color Graphics	N
Manipulate Color Graphics	N
Automatic Pagination	Y
Manual Pagination	Y
Stylesheets	Extensive
Typesetters Supported	Varied
Laser Printers Supported	Varied

The programs listed on the preceding pages are just the major entries in the desktop publishing program race; there are literally dozens of other programs available which will do some or all of the things these programs will. Which one is perceived as Number One varies from month to month, as the manufacturers introduce new versions with even more capabilities.

When it comes time to purchase your desktop publishing software, the only real test is to beg, borrow, or rent copies of the software you think you might like. Then give them a good trial with a complicated document. Which program is right for you? Only you can tell.

Appendix B: Desktop Publishing Hardware

If the automobile had followed the same development cycle as the computer, a Rolls-Royce would today cost $100, get a million miles per gallon, and explode once a year, killing everyone inside.

-- Robert X. Cringely

Although almost every computer system now has some form of desktop publishing available, the two systems most frequently used for producing documents are the Macintosh and IBM or compatible PCs. Thus, those are the two systems we will look at here. For specific recommendations, see page 244.

Macintosh

The advent of the Macintosh, with its graphically-oriented operating system and readily interchangeable and malleable fonts, caused the term "desktop publishing" to be coined.

The original Macintosh computers came with the monitor and floppy drive(s) in a single unit, detachable keyboard, a mouse, utility programs, and an operating system. The operating system is inherently graphic in nature (making working with graphics as well as text reasonably transparent to the user).

Early Macs

The first Mac introduced had 128K RAM (Random Access Memory). Next came the 512K Mac, which was four times faster. Both of these machines use 3.5" floppy disks that can store 400K of data or programs on a disk (about 200 pages of text). A great many 128K and 512K Macs still exist, but the more current, full-featured programs often don't run on them. If you own, or are looking to purchase secondhand, one of these machines with the intent to use it for desktop publishing, make sure that the program(s) and version(s) that you want to use will run on that level of machine.

Mac Plus

The Mac Plus is really the entry-level desktop publishing Macintosh. It has one megabyte (1024K) of RAM, making it approximately twice as fast as a 512K Mac. In addition, the Mac Plus is the first to utilize 3.5" floppy disks, which can store up to 800K of data or programs, and it uses a Hierarchical File Structure. The introduction of the SCSI (Small Computer Systems Interface) port allows expansion of the computer with up to seven peripheral devices, including additional disk drives, hard disks, tape backups, and scanners.

Fig. B.1 The Macintosh Plus is the first Macintosh suited for desktop publishing operation.

Courtesy of Apple Computer, Inc.

Mac Plus Specifications:

Processor: MC68000, 32-bit internal data bus, 7.83 MHz clock speed

Memory: 1Mb RAM, expandable to 4Mb in a socketed SIMMs (Single Inline Memory Module) configuration 128K ROM (Read Only Memory) standard

Disk Storage: One built-in double-sided drive, using 3.5" hard-case floppy disks, either single- (400K capacity) or double-sided (800K capacity)

Keyboard: 78 keys, including numeric keypad and cursor keys; detachable, software mapped

Mouse: Mechanical tracking, optical shaft encoded at 3.54 pulses per mm (90 pulses per inch) travel

Screen: 9 inch (diagonal), 512 x 342 pixel bitmapped display

Interfaces: Two RS-422 serial ports (230.4 Kb data transfer rate, up to 920 Kb if externally clocked); one SCSI parallel port (up to 256Kb/sec. depending on the application)

Sound Generator: Four-voice sound with 8-bit digital/analog conversion using 22 KHz sampling rate

Clock/Calendar: CMOS custom chip with 4.5V user-replaceable battery backup (includes 256 bytes of memory which holds system parameters even with machine powered off)

Electrical Requirements: 105-125VAC, 50-60Hz, maximum power 60 watts

Size & Weight: 9.7" x 10.9" x 13.5" high, weighs 16 lbs., 7 oz.

Mac SE

The SE combines the compact design of the Mac Plus with a variety of expansion options, making the SE much more versatile than the Mac Plus. First, there is an expansion slot, which allows hardware customization for things like accelerator cards to speed up the 68000 processor, or cards to drive secondary large screen monitors (important bonuses for power users like desktop publishers). There are also three storage configurations: a dual 800K floppy disk-drive version, a version with one 800K floppy drive and a 20Mb internal hard disk, or a single 800K floppy disk drive and a 40Mb internal hard disk. With the introduction of the SE, Apple Computers also included its first-generation multitasking operating system, Multifinder; and HyperCard, an information-management tool kit. The keyboard is packaged and sold separately, allowing the user to choose from a variety of Apple and third-party possibilities.

Any program that will operate on a Mac Plus will also operate on an SE, and vice versa.

Fig. B.2 The Macintosh SE computer features either dual floppy disk drives or a single floppy disk drive and a 20 Mb hard disk.

Courtesy of Apple Computer, Inc.

Mac SE Specifications:

Processor: MC68000, 32-bit internal data bus, 7.83 MHz clock speed

Memory: 1 or 2Mb RAM, expandable to 4Mb; 256K ROM standard, 256 bytes of parameter memory

Disk Storage: One built-in double-sided drive, using 3.5" hard-case floppy disks either single- (400K capacity) or double-sided (800K capacity); second drive is either an 800K floppy disk drive, a 20Mb, or 40Mb SCSI internal hard disk drive

Keyboard: Detachable, two Apple options: 81 keys, including numeric keypad and cursor keys; Extended keyboard with 105 keys including 15 function keys , separate cursor pad, 10 key numeric pad, and Desktop Bus connectors; software mapped

Mouse: Mechanical tracking, optical shaft encoded at 3.54 pulses per mm (90 pulses per inch) travel; connects through Desktop Bus

Screen: 9 inch (diagonal), 512 x 342 pixel bitmapped display

Interfaces: Two RS-232 serial ports (230.4 Kb maximum data transfer rate uses mini-8 connectors; external disk drive interface); Mac SE expansion slot uses 96-pin euro-DIN connector; SCSI interface uses a 50-pin internal connector and a DB-25 external connector; sound port for external audio amplifier (standard miniature)

Sound Generator: Four-voice sound with 8-bit digital/analog conversion using 22 KHz sampling rate

Clock/Calendar: CMOS custom chip with a seven-year lithium battery backup

Fan: 10CFM cross flow; 38 dB

Electrical Requirements: 90-140VAC or 170-270VAC, 47-63Hz, maximum power 100 watts

Size & Weight: 9.7" x 10.9" x 13.6" high, weighs 17 to 21 lbs.

SE/30

The SE/30 gives the maximum performance from the compact design of the original Macintosh. It provides up to four times the speed of an SE. This increase comes from the full 32-bit MC68030 microprocessor chip that runs at a clock speed twice that of the standard SE. It can also move twice the data at a time due to its double width external data bus. Included is a 68882 floating-point math coprocessor for faster handling of complex mathematical functions, up to 100 times faster than an SE.

The SE/30 also has a different floppy disk drive, the FDHD, which can handle 400K, 800K, or 1.4 Mb floppy disks for storage. This drive also lets users read from and write to MS-DOS, OS/2, and ProDOS formatted disks (from IBM PC and compatible computers), using the Apple File Exchange utility. This makes the SE the first Mac which can readily operate in places where both Macs and IBM-type PCs are in use. The SE/30 also has a 030 Direct Slot which can accept communications cards such as Ethernet and Token Ring cards, and high-performance video cards supporting large screen gray-scale and color monitors.

Like all Macs, the SE/30 comes with the MultiFinder operating system, utility programs, and the HyperCard information management toolkit.

Fig. B.3 The SE/30, with its 68030 processor, runs nearly as fast as a Macintosh II.

Courtesy of Apple Computer, Inc.

Mac SE/30 Specifications:

Processor: MC68030, 32-bit internal Harvard architecture, 15.667 MHz clock speed; built-in Paged Memory Management Unit (PMMU); 256 byte instruction and data caches

Coprocessor: MC68882 floating-point unit

Memory: 1 or 4Mb RAM, expandable to 8Mb or higher, 256K ROM standard, 256 bytes of user-settable parameter memory

Disk Storage: One built-in 1.4 Mb high-density floppy disk drive, external floppy disk drives optional; second drive is either a 40Mb or 80Mb SCSI internal hard disk drive, external hard disks optional

Keyboard: Detachable, two Apple options: 81 keys, including numeric keypad and cursor keys; Extended keyboard with 105 keys including 15 function keys , separate cursor pad, 10 key numeric pad, and Desktop Bus connectors; software mapped

Mouse: Mechanical tracking, optical shaft encoded at 3.54 pulses per mm (90 pulses per inch) travel; connects through Desktop Bus

Screen: 9 inch (diagonal), 512 x 342 pixel bitmapped display; color QuickDraw in ROM supports gray-scale and color video cards installed in the 030 Direct Slot

Interfaces: Two RS-232 serial ports (230.4 Kb maximum data transfer rate uses mini-8 connectors); external disk drive interface; two Apple Desktop Bus connectors for communication with keyboard, mouse, etc.; 030 Direct Slot supports full 32-bit address and data lines through 120-pin euro-DIN connector; SCSI interface uses a 50-pin internal connector and a DB-25 external connector; stereo sound port for external audio amplifier

Sound Generator: Apple Sound Chip including four-voice, wave table synthesis and stereo sampling generator capable of driving stereo mini-phone-jack headphones or other stereo equipment, mixed stereo/mono sound output through internal speaker

Clock/Calendar: CMOS custom chip with seven-year battery

Fan: 10CFM radial

Electrical Requirements: 120-240VAC, RMS automatically set, 48-62Hz single phase, maximum power 75 watts

Size & Weight: 9.6" x 10.9" x 13.6" high, weighs 21.5 lbs.

Mac II

The Mac II was the first of the "component Macs," similar to IBM-style PCs with separate monitor, drive box, and keyboard. The Mac II has a much larger "footprint" (occupies more desk space) than a standard Mac. Like PCs, the Mac II is fully expandable, with the capability of adding a variety of cards for increased capability, and includes a standard 800K internal floppy disk drive. Unlike PCs, the Mac II comes standard with the MultiFinder Operating System, utility programs, and the HyperCard information management toolkit. In spite of its different architecture, the Mac II is compatible with virtually all Macintosh programs (although more sophisticated programs requiring color or special sounds may run only on the Mac II).

Fig. B.4 The Macintosh II was the first Macintosh computer to have the drive unit and monitor separate.

Courtesy of Apple Computer, Inc.

Mac II Specifications:

Processor: MC68020, 32-bit internal Harvard architecture; 15.7 MHz clock speed

Coprocessor: MC68881 floating-point coprocessor; 15.7MHz clock speed

Optional 68851 PMMU: 15.7MHz clock speed, required for running A/UX (Unix)

Interfaces: Two min-8 serial (RS-232/422) ports; SCSI interface with 50-pin internal and DB-25 external connectors; two Desktop Bus ports allow daisy-chaining of peripherals; six NuBus internal slots support full 32-bit address and data buses; sound jack for stereo output

Mouse: Mechanical tracking, optical shaft encoded at 3.94 ± .39 pulses per mm (100 ± pulses per inch) travel

Sound Generator: Custom digital sound chip, 8-bit stereo sampling at 44.1KHz, includes 4-voice wave-table synthesis

Electrical Requirements: 90-140VAC, 170-270VAC, automatically configured, 48-62Hz, maximum power 230 watts not including monitor power

Size & Weight: 18.7" wide x 14.4" deep x 5.5" high main unit; weighs 24 lbs.

Mac IIX

More advanced than the Mac II, the IIX comes with the MC68030 processor, MC68882 coprocessor, and the FDHD 1.4 Mb internal floppy disk drive. The monitor and keyboard must be purchased separately. Comes with operating system and other software.

Fig. B.5 The Mac IIX is a more advanced version of the original Mac II.

Courtesy of Apple Computer, Inc.

Mac IIX Specifications:

Processor: MC68030, 32-bit internal Harvard architecture; 15.667 MHz clock speed

Coprocessor: MC68882 floating-point coprocessor (IEEE standard 80 bits precision); 15.667MHz clock speed

Interfaces: Two min-8 serial (RS-232/422) ports; SCSI interface with 50-pin internal and DB-25 external connectors; two Desktop Bus ports; six NuBus internal slots support full 32-bit address and data buses; stereo sound jack

Mouse: Mechanical tracking, optical shaft encoded at $3.94 \pm .39$ pulses per mm ($100 \pm$ pulses per inch) travel

Sound Generator: Custom digital sound chip, 8-bit stereo sampling at 44.1KHz, includes 4-voice wave-table synthesis

Electrical Requirements: 90-140VAC, 170-270VAC, automatically configured, 48-62Hz, maximum power 230 watts

Size & Weight: 18.7" wide x 14.4" deep x 5.5" high main unit; weighs 24 lbs.

Mac II CX

Essentially the same as the Mac IIX, except that the physical size has been changed and the weight reduced considerably. There are also a number of port and size changes in the following specifications.

Courtesy of Apple Computer, Inc.

Fig. B.6 The Mac IICX has the same power as the Mac IIX but a smaller footprint on your desktop.

Mac IICX Specifications:

Processor: MC68030, 32-bit internal Harvard architecture; 15.667 MHz clock speed

Coprocessor: MC68882 floating-point coprocessor (IEEE standard 80 bits precision); 15.667MHz clock speed

Interfaces: Two mini-8 serial (RS-232/422) ports; SCSI interface with 50-pin internal and DB-25 external connectors; one DB-19 serial port for connecting external floppy disk drives; two Desktop Bus ports allow daisy-chaining of peripherals; three NuBus internal slots support full 32-bit address and data buses; sound jack for stereo output

Mouse: Mechanical tracking, optical shaft encoded at 3.94 ± .39 pulses per mm (100 ± pulses per inch) travel

Sound Generator: Custom digital sound chip, 8-bit stereo sampling at 44.1KHz, includes 4-voice wave-table synthesis

Electrical Requirements: 90-140VAC, 170-270VAC, automatically configured, 50-60Hz single phase , maximum power 90 watts not including monitor power

Size & Weight: 11.9" wide x 14.4" deep x 5.5" high main unit; weighs 14 lbs.

IBM and Compatible PCs

A major problem when attempting to desktop publish with one of these computers is that, in general, the DOS or disk operating systems are not graphically oriented. Separate programs must be run concurrently with the desktop publishing software, to provide the "window" capability of viewing things graphically that is standard with the Macintosh operating system. This additional software costs more and slows down machine performance. The two most common windowing programs are Windows and GEM. Make sure which of these programs will run with the software and hardware you intend to use.

IBM has created its own operating system, called OS/2, which has a windowing program and some built-in graphics capabilities. Although new at the time of this writing, OS/2 will probably be the preferred IBM operating system for desktop publishing operations because of its more graphic nature. The first desktop publishing program to operate under OS/2 will probably be IBM Interleaf Publisher (an IBM-licensed version of Interleaf Publisher).

Remember that the operating system is not necessarily included in the purchase price of the PC, but may be an extra cost option.

Another difficulty of PC publishing is making sure you have the right kind of graphics monitor and graphics card for your PC and the desktop publishing program. Make sure you check the monitor requirements before purchasing any software; otherwise it may not work correctly with your hardware.

Fonts on the Macintosh are handled primarily by the system. Secondly, fonts are controlled by the printer (in the case of the Laser-Writer and other smart printers using downloadable fonts). On PCs, the fonts can be controlled by the application, by the windowing program, or by the printer via downloadable or cassette loaded fonts. Make sure which kinds and styles of fonts the hardware, software, and printer work with before you purchase them.

PCs, ATs, XTs and Their Compatibles

The original PC was an 8088 microprocessor-based computer. At the speed of that processor, by the time Windows and a desktop publishing program are running, the computer is slowed down so much that many operations are frustrating. For serious desktop publishing, at least an AT (80286 processor) grade machine is recommended, with 80386 processor-based machines preferred.

In the PC world, the machines created by IBM Corporation have become defacto standards. All other PCs that mimic the capabilities, and run (more or less) the same programs, but which are not built by IBM, are called compatibles. Thus Zenith, Tandy, Toshiba, and a host of other companies that make PC-type computers offer machines essentially similar to, but at widely diverse price ranges from, the IBM originals. Comparison shopping among the many clones and IBM machines is usually a good way to find an adequate computer for the tasks you need to do at a reasonable price. Because there are so many compatibles, this chapter will not try to discuss them. Instead, the current IBM products are described.

Model 25

This is the entry-level machine of the PS/2 (Personal System/2) generation of IBM PCs. It can be purchased with either the Space Saving Keyboard or PS/2 Enhanced Keyboard, has built-in enhanced graphics and color (256 colors plus 64 shades of gray) and has either 512K or 640K RAM memory. The drive unit and monitor are an integrated unit.

Fig. B.7 The IBM Model 25 is the entry-levl PC for desktop publishing operations.

Courtesy of IBM Corporation

Model 25 Specifications:

Processor: 8086, 8MHz, 0 wait states, 16-bit memory data bus

Coprocessor: Optional 8087 math coprocessor, 8MHz

RAM: 512K standard, 640K maximum

Integrated Functions: 64K ROM MultiColor Graphics Array and display port, serial port, parallel port, pointing device port, keyboard port, audio earphone connector

System Expansion: one full size slot, and one 8" expansion slot

Operating System: DOS 3.3 or 4.0

Storage: One 720K, 3.5" floppy drive standard, two maximum; optional 20Mb hard disk, 5.25" floppy disk drive, or IBM Optical disk

Text/Graphics Support: MCGA supports existing color modes, up to 256 colors (from a 256,000 color palette) and 64 shades of gray

Display Modes: All CGA modes, plus 320x200 pels x 256 colors, 640 x 480 x 2 colors, 16 color - 8x16 character box text

Displays: 12 inch (diagonal) monochrome or color

Supported Printers: IBM Proprinter family, IBM Quietwriter family, IBM Color Jetprinter, IBM Quickwriter

Communications Support: IBM Token-ring Network, IBM PC Network, IBM PC Network Baseband, 3278/79 and 5250 emulation

Power Supply: 90 or 115 watt, 50-60Hz

Size: 15" high x 12.6" wide x 14.8" deep

Model 30

The Model 30 is the first of IBM's separate monitor and drive unit machines. It comes in several varieties for different environments. The Model 30 a slightly more powerful and useful machine than the Model 25. The real difference is that the Model 30 has the drive and monitor unit separated, allowing for third-party monitors.

Model 30 Specifications:

Processor: Intel 8086, 8MHz, 0 wait states

Coprocessor: Optional 8087 math coprocessor, 8MHz

RAM: 640K standard, 640K maximum

Integrated Functions: 64K permanent memory (ROM) MultiColor Graphics Array and display port, serial port, parallel port, pointing device port, keyboard port, diskette controller, clock/calendar

System Expansion: Three 8-bit expansion slots

Operating System: DOS 3.3 or 4.0

Storage: One 720K, 3.5" floppy disk drive standard, two maximum; optional 20Mb hard disk, 5.25" disk drive, or IBM Optical disk

Text/Graphics Support: MCGA supports existing color modes, up to 256 colors (from a 256,000 color palette) and 64 shades of gray

Display Modes: All CGA modes, plus 320x200 pels x 256 colors, 640 x 480 x 2 colors, 16 color - 8x16 character box text

Supported Displays: all IBM PS/2 monitors

Supported Printers: IBM Proprinter family, IBM Quietwriter family, IBM Pageprinter family, IBM Quickwriter

Communications Support: IBM Token-ring Network PC Adapter, IBM PC Network Adapter II, IBM PC Network Baseband Adapter, 3270 Emulation Adapter, 5250 Emulation Adapter

Power Supply: 70 watt worldwide with switch voltage selection

Size: 4" high x 16" wide x 15.6" deep (without monitor)

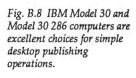

Fig. B.8 IBM Model 30 and Model 30 286 computers are excellent choices for simple desktop publishing operations.

Courtesy of IBM Corporation

Model 30 286

This is the first of IBM's 80286-based machines, and the first that will run the new OS/2 operating system. Otherwise, this model is very similar to the standard Model 30. The VGA graphics, of all the available graphics modes, offers the closest to WYSIWYG (What You See Is What You Get) text display. Other graphics modes may show text drastically larger or smaller than the true size due to the way these modes map the letters to the varying sizes and numbers of pixels on the screen.

Model 30 286 Specifications:

Processor: Intel 80286, 10MHz, 1 wait state

Coprocessor: Optional 80287 math coprocessor, 10MHz

RAM: 512K to 4Mb, maximum 16Mb

Integrated Functions: 128K permanent memory (ROM), VGA graphics and display port, serial port, parallel port, pointing device port, keyboard port, diskette controller, clock/calendar

System Expansion: Three 16-bit expansion slots

Operating System: DOS 3.3 or 4.0, or OS/2

Storage: One 1.44Mb, 3.5" floppy disk drive and 20Mb hard disk standard; optional 20Mb hard disk, 5.25" floppy disk drive, IBM Streaming Tape drive or IBM Optical disk

Text/Graphics Support: VGA supports CGA, EGA, and MCGA, up to 256 colors (from a 256,000 color palette) and 64 shades of gray

Display Modes: All CGA and EGA modes, plus 320x200 pels x 256 colors, 640 x 480 x 2 colors, 16 color - 9x16 character box text

Supported Displays: all IBM PS/2 monitors

Supported Printers: IBM Proprinter family, IBM Quietwriter family, IBM Pageprinter family, IBM Quickwriter, IBM Color Jetprinter

Communications Support: IBM Token-ring Network PC Adapter, IBM PC Network Adapter II, IBM PC Network Baseband Adapter, 3270 Emulation Adapter, 5250 Emulation Adapter

Power Supply: 90 watt worldwide with switch voltage selection

Size: 4" high x 16" wide x 15.6" deep (without monitor)

Model 50

The Model 50 isthe workhorse of the IBM line, probably the best all around PS/2 computer, slightly more powerful than the Model 30 286.

Model 50 Specifications:

Processor: Intel 80286, 10MHz, 0 wait states

Coprocessor: Optional 80287 math coprocessor, 10MHz

RAM: 1Mb standard, maximum 16Mb

Integrated Functions: 128K permanent memory (ROM), VGA graphics and display port, serial port, parallel port, pointing device port, keyboard port, diskette controller, clock/calendar

System Expansion: Three 16-bit expansion slots

Operating System: DOS 3.3 or 4.0, OS/2, or AIX PS/2

Storage: One 1.44Mb, 3.5" floppy disk drive and 30-60Mb hard disk standard; optional 5.25" disk drive or IBM Optical disk

Text/Graphics Support: VGA supports CGA, EGA, and MCGA, up to 256 colors (from a 256,000 color palette) and 64 shades of gray

Display Modes: All CGA and EGA modes, plus 320x200 pels x 256 colors, 640 x 480 x 2 colors, 16 color - 9x16 character box text

Supported Displays: all IBM PS/2 monitors

Supported Printers: IBM Proprinter family, IBM Quietwriter family, IBM Pageprinter family, IBM Quickwriter, IBM Color Jetprinter

Communications support: IBM Token-ring Network PC Adapter, IBM PC Network Adapter II, IBM PC Network Baseband Adapter, 3270 Emulation Adapter, 5250 Emulation Adapter

Power supply: 90 watt worldwide with switch voltage selection

Size: 4" high x 16" wide x 15.6" deep (without monitor)

*Fig. B.9 The IBM
Model 50 and Model 55
computers will handle any
desktop publishing task.*

Model 55 SX

This is IBM's entry-level 80386 machine, roughly 20% faster than
an 80286-based computer. It also comes with 2Mb of RAM as the
standard memory. This is an impressive machine for the price.

Model 55 SX Specifications:

Processor: 80386SX, 16MHz, 0-2 wait states

Coprocessor: Optional 80387SX math coprocessor, 16MHz

RAM: 2Mb standard, maximum 16Mb

Integrated Functions: 128K permanent memory (ROM), VGA graphics and display port, serial port, parallel port, pointing device port, keyboard port, diskette controller, clock/calendar

System Expansion: Three 16-bit expansion slots

Operating System: DOS 3.3 or 4.0, or OS/2 Standard and Extended Editions, AIX PS/2

Storage: One 1.44Mb, 3.5" floppy disk drive and 30Mb hard disk standard; optional 5.25" floppy disk drive, IBM Streaming Tape drive or IBM Optical disk

Text/Graphics Support: VGA supports CGA, EGA, and MCGA, plus 640x480 graphics, up to 256 colors (from a 256,000 color palette) and 64 shades of gray

Display Modes: All CGA and EGA modes, plus 320 x 200 pels x 256 colors, 640 x 480 x 2 colors, 16 color - 9x16 character box text

Supported Displays: all IBM PS/2 color and monochrome monitors

Supported Printers: IBM Proprinter family, IBM Quietwriter family, IBM Personal Page Printer II, IBM Quickwriter

Communications Support: IBM Token-ring Network Adapter/A and 16/4 Adapter /A, IBM PC Network Adapter II/A, IBM PC Network Baseband Adapter/A, 3270 connection, System 36/38 Workstation Emulation Adapter/A, IBM Dual Async Adapter/A, IBM Multi-Protocol Adapter/A, IBM 300/1200 Internal Modem/A, IBM Realtime Interface Coprocessor Multiport/2

Power Supply: 90 watt worldwide with switch voltage selection

Size: 4" high x 16" wide x 15.6" deep (without monitor)

Model 60

In a sense the Model 60 is an overgrown Model 50. It has the Model 50's 286 processor, but the drive unit is what IBM calls its "tower" style – intended to be floor-standing on end, rather than set on the desktop.

Model 60 Specifications:

Processor: Intel 80286, 10MHz, 1 wait state

Coprocessor: Optional 80287 math coprocessor, 10MHz

RAM: 512K to 4Mb, maximum 16Mb

Integrated Functions: 128K permanent memory (ROM), VGA graphics and display port, serial port, parallel port, pointing device port, keyboard port, diskette controller, clock/calendar

System Expansion: Three 16-bit expansion slots

Operating System: DOS 3.3 or 4.0, or OS/2

Storage: One 1.44Mb, 3.5" floppy disk drive and 20Mb hard disk standard; optional 20Mb hard disk, 5.25" floppy disk drive, IBM Streaming Tape drive or IBM Optical disk

Text/Graphics Support: VGA supports CGA, EGA, and MCGA, up to 256 colors (from a 256,000 color palette) and 64 shades of gray

Display Modes: All CGA and EGA modes, plus 320 x 200 pels x 256 colors, 640 x 480 x 2 colors, 16 color - 9x16 character box text

Supported Displays: all IBM PS/2 monitors

Supported Printers: IBM Proprinter family, IBM Quietwriter family, IBM Pageprinter family, IBM Quickwriter, IBM Color Jetprinter

Communications Support: IBM Token-ring Network PC Adapter, IBM PC Network Adapter II, IBM PC Network Baseband Adapter, 3270 Emulation Adapter, 5250 Emulation Adapter

Power Supply: 90 watt worldwide with switch voltage selection

Size: 23.5" high x 6.5" wide x 19" deep (without monitor)

Model 70 386

This is the top of the line PS/2 machine available in three versions. The max version runs at 25MHz with a 64K memory cache to really speed up operations. This machine has power to spare for even the most high-powered user!

Model 70 386 Specifications:

Processor: 80386, 16-25MHz, 0-2 wait states or 64K memory cache

Coprocessor: Optional 80387 math coprocessor, 16-25MHz

RAM: 1Mb standard, maximum 16Mb

Integrated Functions: VGA graphics and display port, serial port, parallel port, pointing device port, keyboard port, diskette controller, clock/calendar

System Expansion: Three slots, two 32-bit, one 16-bit

Operating System: DOS 3.3 or 4.0, OS/2, or AIX PS/2

Storage: One 1.44Mb, 3.5" disk drive and 60-120Mb hard disk standard; optional 1.44Mb 3.5" or 5.25" disk drive or PS/2 Internal Tape Backup Unit, IBM Streaming Tape drive or IBM Optical disk

Text/Graphics Support: VGA supports CGA, EGA and MCGA, up to 256 colors (from a 256,000 color palette) and 64 shades of gray

Display Modes: All CGA and EGA modes, plus 320 x 200 pels x 256 colors, 640 x 480 x 2 colors, 16 color - 9x16 character box text

Supported Displays: all IBM PS/2 monitors

Supported Printers: IBM Proprinter family, IBM Quietwriter family, IBM Pageprinter family, IBM Quickwriter, IBM Color Jetprinter

Communications Support: IBM Token-ring Network PC Adapter, IBM PC Network Adapter II, IBM PC Network Baseband Adapter, 3270 Emulation Adapter, 5250 Emulation Adapter

Power Supply: 132 watt autosensing and autoswitching

Size: 5.5" high x 14.2" wide x 16.5" deep (without monitor)

Model 80 386

Like the Model 50/60, the Model 70 386 and 80 386 are the desktop and large-storage versions of each other, with other minor differences (notably the number of expansion slots). The 80 386 is the tower version of the 70 386.

Model 80 386 Specifications:

Processor: Intel 80386, 16-20MHz, 0-2 wait states

Coprocessor: Optional 80387 math coprocessor, 16-20MHz

RAM: 1-2Mb standard, maximum 16Mb

Integrated Functions: 128K ROM memory, VGA graphics and display port, serial port, parallel port, pointing device port, keyboard port, diskette controller, clock/calendar

System Expansion: Seven slots, three 32-bit, four 16-bit

Operating System: DOS 3.3 or 4.0, OS/2, or AIX PS/2

Storage: One 1.44Mb, 3.5" disk drive and 44-314Mb hard disk standard; optional 1.44Mb 3.5" or 5.25" disk drive or PS/2 Internal Tape Backup Unit, IBM Streaming Tape drive or IBM Optical disk

Text/Graphics Support: VGA supports CGA, EGA, and MCGA, up to 256 colors (from a 256,000 color palette) and 64 shades of gray

Display Modes: All CGA and EGA modes, plus 320 x 200 pels x 256 colors, 640 x 480 x 2 colors, 16 color - 9x16 character box text

Supported Displays: all IBM PS/2 color monitors

Supported Printers: IBM Proprinter family, IBM Quietwriter family, IBM Pageprinter family, IBM Quickwriter, IBM Color Jetprinter

Communications Support: IBM Token-ring Network PC Adapter, IBM PC Network Adapter II, IBM PC Network Baseband Adapter, 3270 Emulation Adapter, 5250 Emulation Adapter

Power Supply: 225 watt autosensing and autoswitching

Size: 23.5" high x 6.5" wide x 19" deep (without monitor)

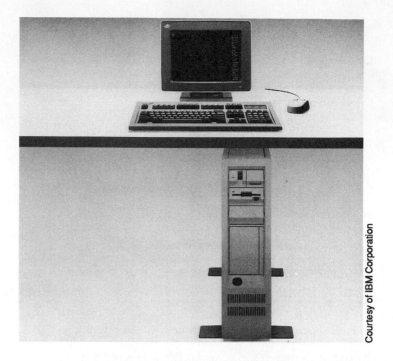

Fig. B.10 The IBM Model 70 and Model 80 are the top-of-the-line PCs for desktop publishing.

Courtesy of IBM Corporation

As you can see from the wealth of just Macintosh and IBM computers, there are a great many choices to be made when you are ready to purchase a computer for desktop publishing. Neither the author, nor anyone else, can tell you which is the best computer for what you want to do. All we can do is make recommendations.

My personal recommendation is, when you think you are ready to buy, haunt every computer shop in your area. Collect all the PR hype and brochures and study them with care. Listen to your friends as they discuss the merits of the various computers. However, the ultimate proof of the usefulness of any computer is how well you and it "get along," and whether or not it does the jobs as easily and quickly as you'd like. How can you really tell? Spend a hundred or so dollars to rent for a week the couple of machines (and software) that seem like they might do what you want. Put them to the test. Will they or won't they work with you? Only you can tell.

Appendix C: Printers

Babbage's original idea was to connect his Analytical Engine to an automatic typsetting machine so that his calculations (output) could be used wherever necessary, without errors in copying. Today's computer printers produce the equivalent of the proofs of more traditional presses. Here we see, in black and white (rather than green phosphor), the culmination of our writing, designing, and desktop publishing process. When the reproduction masters look good, we gather them up and send them off to the pressman for duplication, binding, etc. For desktop publishers, activating the Print function for the last time is their final step in the process.

What kind of printer do you need? First, let's do away with the notion that any sort of dot matrix or daisy-wheel printer labelled "letter quality" has a place in the desktop publishing field. When it comes to publishing, letter quality isn't good enough by half! Some folks try to use these printers to produce draft copy to check the look of their design or the content of their text. Using a printer like this to check spelling (but why don't you trust your spelling checker program?) or sentence structure/grammar is acceptable. The words will stay the same no matter what printer you use. The problem comes when trying to use a dot matrix/daisy-wheel printer to proof the design or layout.

Such printers simply do not give accurate representations of where on the page a given word may be. Is it at the end of this line, or at the start of the next? Only a printer that is smart enough to handle PostScript will accurately position the words on the page. Even then, there can be some discrepancy between where the word shows on the computer screen and where the printer places it, particularly if the program being used does not have a good algorithm for displaying PostScript fonts as bitmaps at the screen resolution you are using. So, all in all, it's best to forget about any printer that is not at least a laser printer or capable of at least 300 dots per inch output.

For many desktop publishers, the laser printer with its 300-400 dots per inch resolution is more than adequate. For the very finest resolution, however, some desktop publishers send their output to a modern typesetting printer such as a Linotronic 300, which produces up to 2450 dpi resolution, or others which print at 1600 or 1800 dpi.

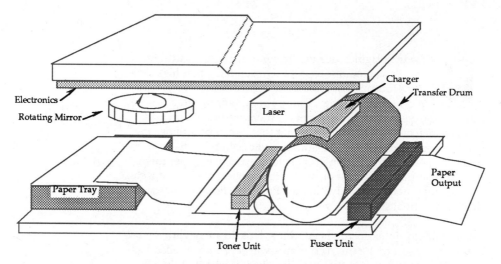

Fig. C .1 The basic parts of a laser printer.

As with other kinds of hardware, the brand name of printer you choose isn't as important as whether or not it does the job you want, as quickly as you need it to, at a cost you can afford. With the right kinds of cable and the appropriate printer driver software, almost any printer can be made to work with any computer.

Apple LaserWriter/LaserWriter Plus

This was the printer that made desktop publishing possible. Hewlett-Packard and other companies had been producing laser printers for years that had the capability of printing several type families. The problem with those machines, however, was that they were not very smart. The type family existed on a tape cartridge version of a metal type family. There was Times Roman 12, distinct from Times Roman Bold 12 , distinct from Times Italic 12, and so on. Only a couple of families could reside on a given cartridge, which was OK if you didn't mind sticking to those faces and families, but if you wanted more than a couple different sizes or styles or families of type, you couldn't get them without swapping cartridges. If you needed an oddball size or style, you were stuck.

Apple Computers contracted with Adobe Systems to produce a laser printer that carried the descriptions of type families on ROM chips in the printer rather than tapes. The characters were mathematically described using the Adobe page description language PostScript. Because the descriptions were in ROM, the computer and its programs could read those descriptions, modify them, and send them back to the printer to produce a much wider range of effects than was previously possible. A whole new world of typography had opened up!

The original LaserWriter was limited to four type families in ROM: Times, Helvetica, Courier, and Symbol. The LaserWriter Plus expanded that to 11 families by adding Avant Garde, Bookman, Palatino, New Century Schoolbook, New Helvetica Narrow, Chancery, and Dingbats. Each of these families produced Roman, Roman Bold, Italic, Bold Italic, Roman Outline, Roman Shadow, *and any conceivable combination of those styles*. Type sizes were limited only by the programs – originally most ranged in whole number sizes from 4 pt. to 127 pt. More modern programs are capable of creating 1 pt. to 999 pt. in 1/10th or 1/100th of a point increments. Gutenberg would be green with envy of such typesetting capabilities!

Although Apple Computers no longer manufactures the LaserWriter or LaserWriter Plus, a great many of them are to be found in businesses and on college campuses around the world.

Fig. C.2 The Apple LaserWriter and LaserWriter Plus printers made desktop publishing possible.

Apple LaserWriter/LaserWriter Plus Specifications:

Marking Engine: Canon LBP-CX laser xerographic
Processor: 68000, 12MHz
Memory: LaserWriter = 512K ROM, 1.5Mb RAM; LaserWriter Plus = 1Mb ROM, 1.5Mb RAM
Interfaces: AppleTalk and RS-232-C
Print Quality: Text and graphics at 300 x 300 dpi, full page
Speed: 8 pages per minute maximum throughput
Printing Protocols: PostScript and a subset of the Diablo 630 command set
Print Materials: Letter, legal, A4, and B5 sizes in 16-20 pound photocopy bond, 8-34 pound letterhead and color stock or transparency overhead film; envelopes and labels by manual feed
Printable Surface: Letter = 8 x 10.9", legal = 6.75 x 13", A4 = 7.41 x 10.86", B5 = 7.69 x 10.16"
Power Requirements: 115 volts AC, 60Hz
Size: 11.5" high, 18.5" wide, 16.2" deep

Apple LaserWriter II SC

To replace the original LaserWriter and LaserWriter Plus, the Laser-Writer II SC was created as the new entry level laser printer. The LaserWriter II SC is intended as a single-user printer, and is not net-workable. The fonts Times, Helvetica, Courier, and Symbol are stored in ROM. The II SC is not a PostScript printer.

Fig. C.3 The LaserWriter II SC is not a PostScript printer. It uses QuickDraw, Apple's drawing protocol, instead.

Courtesy of Apple Computer, Inc.

LaserWriter II SC Specifications:

Marking Engine: Canon LBP-SX laser xerographic
Processor: 68000, 7.54MHz
Memory: 16K ROM, 1Mb RAM
Interfaces: SCSI and Apple Desktop Bus ports
Print Quality: Text and graphics at 300 x 300 dpi, full page
Speed: 8 pages per minute maximum throughput
Built-in Font Families: Times, Helvetica, Courier, Symbol
Printing Protocols: PostScript and a subset of the Diablo 630 command set
Print Materials: Letter, legal, A4, and B5 sizes in 16-20 pound photocopy bond, 8-34 pound letterhead and color stock or transparency overhead film; envelopes and labels by manual feed
Print Capacity: 200 sheets of 20# paper; envelope cassette holds 15 envelopes
Printable Surface: Letter = 8 x 10.5", legal = 8.0 x 13.0", A4 = 7.41 x 10.86", B5 = 7.69 x 10.16"
Power Requirements: 90-126 volts AC, 50-60Hz
Size: 8.6" high, 20" wide, 18.5" deep

Apple LaserWriter II NT

The LaserWriter II NT is Apple's mainstream networkable or single-user laser printer. Physically similar to the II SC printer, it contains more font families in ROM and more RAM memory as well as other differences. May be used with MS-DOS or OS/2 PCs running a LocalTalk PC card or RS-232-C cable and appropriate software.

Fig. C.4 The LaserWriter II NT is a general-purpose laser printer

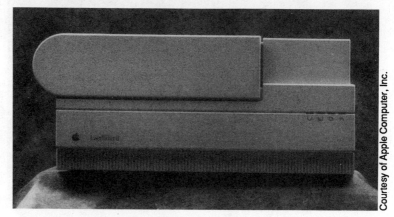

Courtesy of Apple Computer, Inc.

LaserWriter II NT Specifications:

Marking Engine: Canon LBP-SX laser xerographic
Processor: 68000, 12MHz
Memory: 1Mb ROM, 2Mb RAM
Interfaces: SCSI and Apple Desktop Bus and RS-232-C ports
Print Quality: Text and graphics at 300 x 300 dpi, full page
Speed: 8 pages per minute maximum throughput
Built-in Font Families: Times, Helvetica, Courier, Symbol, Avant Garde, Bookman, New Century Schoolbook, New Helvetica Narrow, Palatino, Chancery, and Dingbats
Printing Protocols: PostScript and a subset of the Diablo 630 command set
Print Materials: Letter, legal, A4, and B5 sizes in 16-20 pound photocopy bond, 8-34 pound letterhead and color stock or transparency overhead film; envelopes and labels by manual feed
Print Capacity: 200 sheets of 20# paper; 15 envelopes
Printable Surface: Letter = 8 x 10.5", legal = 8.0 x 13.0", A4 = 7.41 x 10.86", B5 = 7.69 x 10.16"
Power Requirements: 90-126 volts AC, 50-60Hz
Size: 8.6" high, 20" wide, 18.5" deep

Apple LaserWriter II NTX

The "X" in NTX stands for expandable. This is Apple's top-of-the-line laser printer, with the ability to expand ROM and RAM, and add a hard disk on which to store downloadable fonts. It's also faster than the other Apple laser printers. May also be used with MS-DOS or OS/2 PCs running a LocalTalk PC card or RS-232-C cable and appropriate software.

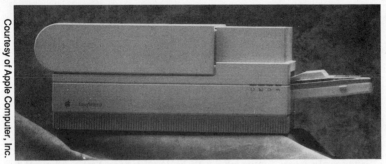

Courtesy of Apple Computer, Inc.

Fig. C.5 The LaserWriter II NTX has expandable RAM and ROM for use with downloadable fonts.

LaserWriter II NTX Specifications:

Marking Engine: Canon LBP-SX laser xerographic
Processor: 68000, 16.67MHz
Memory: 1Mb ROM, 2Mb RAM
Interfaces: SCSI and Apple Desktop Bus and RS-232-C ports
Print Quality: Text and graphics at 300 x 300 dpi, full page
Speed: 8 pages per minute maximum throughput
Built-in Font Families: Times, Helvetica, Courier, Symbol, Avant Garde, Bookman, New Century Schoolbook, New Helvetica Narrow, Palatino, Chancery, and Dingbats
Printing Protocols: PostScript and a subset of the Diablo 630 command set
Print Materials: Letter, legal, A4, and B5 sizes in 16-20 pound photocopy bond, 8-34 pound letterhead and color stock or transparency overhead film; envelopes and labels by manual feed
Print Capacity: 200 sheets of 20# paper; 15 envelopes
Printable Surface: Letter = 8 x 10.5", legal = 8.0 x 13.0", A4 = 7.41 x 10.86", B5 = 7.69 x 10.16"
Power Requirements: 90-126 volts AC, 50-60Hz
Size: 8.6" high, 20" wide, 18.5" deep
Expansion Capabilities: ROM expansion via font-expansion slot, RAM expansion up to 12Mb, external SCSI port for hard disk font storage

HP DeskWriter

This is the exception to the "use laser printers for desktop publishing" rule given above. Although not a laser printer, it does deliver 300 x 300 dpi resolution for text and graphics. The DeskWriter doesn't use PostScript, but does use Apple's QuickDraw graphics routines for high-quality art output. In addition to the built-in fonts, various other fonts are available on cartridge.

DeskWriter Specifications:

Print Method: Plain paper drop-on-demand thermal inkjet
Print Speed: 2 pages per minute
Print Resolution: "Best" mode = 300 x 300 dpi; "Faster" mode = 150 x 150 dpi
Paper Handling: Letter, legal, A4, and #10 envelope from 16 to 24#; built-in sheet feeder holds up to 100 sheets, manual envelope feed
Imageable Area: Letter = 8.0 x 10.13, legal = 8.0 x 13.15, A$ = 8.0 x 10.83
Built-in Fonts: Times, Courier, Symbol, Triumvirate; scaleable up to 250 pt.
Screen Fonts: Times, Helvetica, Courier, Symbol
I/O Interface: RS-422-A serial, 57.6K baud
Memory Buffer: 12K receive buffer
Power Requirements: 100-240 volts AC, 50-60Hz
Size: 8.0" high, 17.3" wide, 14.8" deep
Reliability: 60,000 page life; MTBF 20,000 hours, 2000 hrs. power on and 12,000 pages per year

HP LaserJet II

The Hewlett-Packard laser printers are very nice for high-volume use with their two paper trays. They can be used with built-in fonts, cartridge-based fonts, or disc-based (soft) fonts to produce a multitude of styles and sizes of type.

HP LaserJet II Specifications:

Print Speed: up to 8 pages per minute
Text Resolution: 300 x 300 dpi full page
Graphics Resolution: standard 300 x 300 dpi half page
Printing Format: single-sided, portrait, or landscape modes
Paper Handling: One tray holding 200 sheets, manual feed for envelopes, 16 to 35 # paper
Paper Sizes: Letter, legal, A4, Executive (7.5" x 10.5")
Printable Surface: letter = 8.0 x 10.6, legal = 8.0 x 13.6, A4 = 7.8 x 11.3, Executive = 6.75 x 10.1
Font Orientations: depend on font, not printer
Internal Fonts: 6 = Courier Medium, Bold, and Italic 10 pt, and Courier Medium, Bold, and Italic 12 pt.
Number of Fonts per Page: Maximum of 16 or memory space limit
Standard Memory: 512K ROM, 395K RAM
Additional Memory Available: 1-4Mb
Hardware Interfaces: Centronics parallel, RS-232-C, RS-422-A
Video Interface: Yes
Extended I/O Slot: Yes
Power Requirements: 100-115 or 220-240 volts AC, 50-60Hz
Size: 12.3" high, 18.0" wide, 25.0" deep

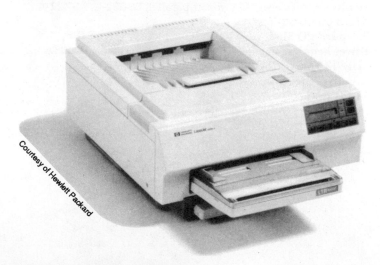

Fig. C.6 The LaserJet II is good for high-volume printing.

Courtesy of Hewlett Packard

HP LaserJet IID

This is HP's high-end laser printer, with twin paper trays and selectable single- or double-sided printing capabilities. Also has more internal fonts, printer controlled font rotation, and other useful features.

HP LaserJet II Specifications:

Print Speed: up to 8 pages per minute single-sided on 8 sheets of paper, 7.4 ppm double-sided on 4 sheets of paper

Text Resolution: 300 x 300 dpi full page

Graphics Resolution: standard 300 x 300 dpi half page

Printing Format: single or double-sided selectable, portrait or landscape modes

Paper Handling: Two trays holding 200 sheets each, manual feed for envelopes, 16 to 35# paper

Paper Sizes: Letter, legal, A4, Executive (7.5" x 10.5")

Printable Surface: letter = 8.0 x 10.6, legal = 8.0 x 13.6, A4 = 7.8 x 11.3, Executive = 6.75 x 10.1

Font Orientations: printer rotatable to either portrait or landscape

Internal Fonts: 14 = Courier Medium, Bold, and Italic 10 pt, and Courier Medium, Bold, and Italic 12 pt plus eight others

Additional Fonts: both cartridge and downloadable fonts may be used; comes standard with S2 cartridge (Times and Helvetica Medium, Bold, and Italic in 8, 12, and 14 pt)

Number of Fonts per Page: Limited only by available memory

Standard Memory: 640K ROM, 395K RAM

Additional Memory Available: 1-4Mb

Hardware Interfaces: Centronics parallel, RS-232-C, RS-422-A

Video interface: Yes

Extended I/O Slot: Yes

Power Requirements: 100-115 or 220-240 volts AC, 50-60Hz

Size: 12.3" high, 18.0" wide, 25.0" deep

NEC Silentwriter LC 890

Designed specifically for the desktop publishing market, this laser printer features a PostScript interpreter plus HP LaserJet Plus and Diablo 630 emulation, so it can be used with both Macs and PCs.

LC 890 Specifications:

Microprocessor: 80186
Print Speed: 8 pages per minute
Print Resolution: 300 x 300 dpi
Paper Handling: two 250-sheet hoppers, uses 16-24# paper
Paper Sizes: Letter, legal, A4, B5
Printable Area: unlisted
Memory: 3Mb RAM
Resident Fonts: 35 typefaces
Additional Fonts: Uses any Apple or Adobe downloadable font or cartridge-based fonts
Interfaces: AppleTalk, Centronics parallel, RS-232, RS-422
Power Requirements: 115-230 volts AC, 50-60Hz
Size: 10.9" high, 18.5" wide, 20.7" deep

QMS PS 800 II

The QMS Model PS 2200 laser printer is one of the few that will handle tabloid sized paper (11" x 17"). It has 13 resident fonts, accepts computer-resident downloadable fonts, three 600-sheet paper bins, emulates Diablo 630 and HPGL printers, and has same range of interfaces as the PS 800 II. It is a single-user or networkable laser printer for both Macs and PCs with large capacity paper trays, a host of scaleable resident fonts, and proprietary software for handling PostScript.

PS 800 II Specifications:

Processor: 68000, 16MHz
Print Speed: 8 ppm
Print Resolution: 300 x 300 dpi full page
Graphics Handling: full legal page bitmapped or PostScript generated graphics
Paper handling: two 250-sheet trays, faceup or facedown output collation selectable, 16-24# stock, manual or tray envelope feed
Paper Sizes: Letter, legal, and A4
Memory: 2Mb RAM standard, 3Mb optional; 1Mb ROM
Printer Emulations: HP LaserJet Plus, HP 7475 pen plotter, Diablo 630, PostScript
Resident Fonts: 35 typefaces including the Apple LaserWriter II NT typefaces scaleable from 4 pt. upwards
Additional Fonts: Accepts computer-resident downloadable fonts
Interfaces: AppleTalk, Centronics parallel, RS-232, RS-422; user selectable serial baud up to 56K
Software: Utilities for handling basic and advanced printing functions such as text rotation , filling, etc.
Power Requirements: 110-120 or 220-240 volts AC, 50Hz
Size: 18.1" high, 18.7" high, 19.5" deep

QMS ColorScript 100

If you really want to print your own color print masters or need color output for presentations, this is is the printer to have. It's not fast, but it certainly does print vibrant color at 300 dpi! It is however much more expensive per page than black and white printing.

ColorScript 100 Specifications:

Processor: 68020, 16.67MHz
Memory: 8Mb RAM, 1Mb ROM, 20Mb hard disk
Printer Language: PostScript
Graphics Handling: full (legal) page PostScript
Print Method: Thermal transfer heat-fusible ink film
Colors: 4-color = yellow, magenta, cyan, black; 3-color = yellow, magenta, cyan; monochrome = black
Paper Sizes: Letter, legal, A4, A3 (11.7" x 16.6")
Print Resolution: 300 x 300 dpi
Print Speed: 1 ppm (Letter), .75 ppm (Legal)
Resident Fonts: 35 typefaces, including the Apple LaserWriter NT set, scalable from 1 pt. upwards
Additional Fonts: Any Apple or Adobe style downloadables
Interfaces: AppleTalk, Centronics parallel, RS-232, RS-422
Power Requirements: 90-130 or 180-250 volts AC user-selectable
Size: Printer: 9.6" high, 20.9" wide, 19.7" deep; controller: 4.6" high, 20.7" wide, 18.9" deep

These are just a few of the many printers available that are suitable for desktop publishing. Major characteristics to look for when purchasing a printer are: ability to handle a wide variety of fonts, at least 300 dpi printing resolution, ability to manipulate PostScript, and, of course, cost. When it comes time to purchase your desktop publishing printer, don't buy it without trying it. Any reputable dealer will plug a printer in and let you print a page or two of a test document so you can compare output quality.

Appendix D: Potpourri

pot·pourri (po poo-ré) *n.*, *pl.* **-ris** **1.** A combination of various incongruous elements. **2.** A miscellaneous anthology or collection. **3.** A mixture of dried flower petals and spices kept in a jar and used to scent the air. [Fr. *pot pourri*, trans. of Sp. *olla podrida.*]

A jar of flower petals this chapter isn't. But it does contain a miscellaneous collection of goodies that can help make your desktop publishing excursions more pleasant. In keeping with the miscellaneous nature of this chapter, things are arranged in no particular order, for no particular reason. Serendipity rears its head. Have fun.

A Mouse by any other name...

The Macintosh comes standard with a mouse, and other computers can be fitted with one. With the advent of the Mac, users began to realize the usefulness of nonkeyboard ways of locating and moving cursors on the computer's screen. And efficient they are, even in nongraphics programs like word processors. At the University of Utah Computer Center, some informal tests (contests really) between hardcore keyboard/cursor arrow users and mouse users have been conducted. They show time and again that, even in word processing, it's faster to take your hands off the keyboard, grab the mouse, position the cursor, and return to the keyboard, than it is to wait out the lag time from when you press a cursor key(s) and the cursor finally arrives at its destination.

As soon as the mouse became popular, there were folks complaining about it, and other folks doing things about the complaints. Granted, trying to create finely detailed, complicated graphics with a mouse is like trying to draw with a deck of cards in your hand.

One of the first mouse replacements was the track ball, a 6" x 6" x 3" or so block of plastic with a large diameter ball mounted on the surface between a pair of buttons. Moving the large ball works just like moving the one in the mouse – the cursor moves on screen. The advantage is that because of the larger diameter, a track ball moves much less distance for an equivalent move on screen than does a mouse. Some people love track balls, others hate 'em. Try one for a couple of weeks if you're thinking of buying one.

Then there are the digitizer-type tablets that are connected to the computer. These devices have a flat surface that senses the location of a pen-shaped stylus which is connected to the tablet. The pen shape seems much more natural, because for several hundred years humans have been learning from childhood to hold a pencil, pen, or brush to write with. Modern tablets, such as the KAT from Koala Technologies, are touch sensitive, allowing either a non-electronic stylus or the user's finger to move the cursor on screen. There are even a few devices on the market that will do at least limited handwriting recognition. Write Cat on the tablet, and the computer screen shows CAT!

Other interesting and useful interfaces are being worked out for the future. Imagine being able to lie back in your easy chair, and by *looking* at a menu, cause it to open and by winking, select a function. How about wearing a face plate or set of strange glasses and being able to see the screen and keyboard superimposed on whatever else you're looking at. Type on this transparent, invisible keyboard and the words appear on the real screen as well as the one you're looking at!

Buck Rogers technology? No. Such systems are being developed by the military, where pilots use a "virtual" cockpit. All the buttons, switches, etc., show up on the transparent faceplate of their helmet, no matter which way they are looking. Interfaces developed for the handicapped already use eye motion and muscle contractions to choose and select computer menus. Maybe one of these days we'll have the ultimate interface, a direct implant to the brain. Close your eyes and visualize the screen. Think words and they are recorded; visualize a drawing and it is rendered.

Backup

With users having more and more storage space, making backups of all this data has become important. We all recognize that Murphy's Law works in the real world, and that at best, Murphy was an optimist. The paper you just finished, the report due in a couple of hours... if you store it on electronic media, it may not be accessible when you need it. The unwritten law of computer operation is that if something is even marginally useful, make a backup copy of it and store the backup copy somewhere other than at your normal work site.

If your computer has a 20Mb to 200Mb hard disk attached, you quickly learn the frustrations of backing up this mass of data onto floppies which can hold, at best, 1-2Mb of information. Mass backup units are available with either removable hard disks or cassette tape storage facilities, which make backing up a hard disk if not pleasant, at least easy and fast enough not to be boring. A backup tape containing a common system version, utilitiesand programs, is an excellent way to quickly restore a crashed system.

Scanners and Optical Character Recognition

A **digitizer** is a device that you hold over a drawing, center cross-hairs on some intersection of lines or points along a line, and click to record those locations – "connect the dots" in reverse. CalComp Corporation is one maker of a very wide variety of digitizers, from their 12" x 12" DrawingBoard to table size.

A **scanner** works more like a photocopier – only instead of a paper copy, the image of the object under the cover is recorded electronically. These graphics can then be used in your desktop publishing program just as if they were drawn in a graphics program. The best scanners allow recording of the image at resolutions from that of the computer screen (roughly 70 x 70 dpi) to laser printer or better (300 x 300 dpi +). They also allow the scanned image to be saved in a number of different formats, so the picture can be used by the widest variety of programs. Common storage formats include Paint (bitmapped), proprietary graphic formats such as QuickDraw, and so-called "universal" image formats such as RIFF,

TIFF, and GIF.   The Apple Scanner, from Apple Computers, Inc., is fairly representative of the better grade of scanner; take a look at its specifications.

Apple Scanner Specifications:

Type: Flatbed
Maximum Document Size: 8.5" x 14"
Interface: SCSI
Scanning Speed: 20.4 secs. for a 300 dpi scan measuring 8.5" x 11"
Scan Modes: line art, gray scale, halftone
Gray Scale: 16 levels (4 bits per pixel)
Scaling Capabilities: from 25% to 400% depending on output resolution
Output Resolutions: 75, 100, 150, 200, and 300 dpi
Contrast Levels: Up to 8 user specified
Brightness Levels: Up to 16 user specified
Gray-map Settings: more light detail, normal, more dark detail
Halftone Techniques: spiral, bayer, 2x2, line, user-definable patterns, adaptive dithering
Size: 4.4" high, 13.6" wide, 21.8" deep

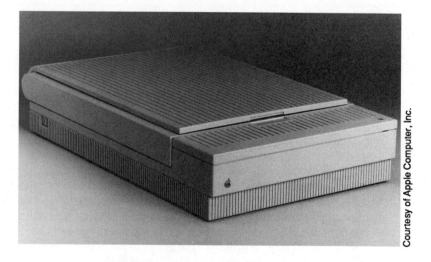

Courtesy of Apple Computer, Inc.

Fig. D.1 The Apple Scanner offers many features for desktop publishers who need to convert ordinary artwork to electronic art.

A short list of other scanner manufacturers would include Abaton, Agfa, Canon, Dest, Hewlett-Packard, Microtek, Ricoh, and UMAX. Some scanners will even accept documents up to tabloid size (11" x 17"). The scanners to avoid are those that record only in a single format (usually bit mapped) and at low (screen-level) resolution. They're fine if the artwork is going to stay at screen resolution, but do not make very good pictures when printing at desktop publishing resolutions.

The one problem with a scanner is that if you scan text, it isn't "text" in the word processing sense, it's a graphic. You can't go in and edit the text in a normal manner.

Have you ever discovered, just after you printed and then deleted a file, that you suddenly need the file again but all you've got is a hard copy? It's not too big a deal if it's only a page or two, but what about a sixty-page report? Ever wish you could do an extensive quote of some document you have in hand (a book or report for example) but really dread the hassle of typing in all that text? If so, what you need is optical character recognition (OCR) software and a high-quality scanner.

OCR software "reads" a document as it is being scanned and assembles the words in correct order *as a text file, not a graphic*. This text file can then be read by a variety of word processing programs and reformatted to match the original or your own requirements. The accuracy level of OCR software is usually better than 99%, but it can vary depending on the kind of characters and font that is being scanned. OmniPage, by CÆRE Corporation, is representative of OCR software. They make versions that will run on both PC and Mac scanners. Here are their specifications.

Courtesy of Thunderware Inc.

Fig. D.2 *The ThunderScan scanner is a low resolution device that replaces the print head of the Apple ImageWriter printer. An image on paper is automatically pulled through the printer and the software records the image one-pixel-at a-time.*

OmniPage Specifications:

Font Handling: Reads all nonstylized fonts from 8 pt. to 72 pt.; reads typeset, proportionally-spaced, and kerned characters; reads and outputs underlined, italicized, and bold characters; recognizes 10 European character sets

Document Handling: Scans portrait or landscape documents; differentiates columns automatically, differentiates text from graphics automatically, user controlled columns; full or partial page selection; reads a multi-page document into a single file; cut, copy, and paste text or graphics; find, search, and replace text; zoom in and out screen images

Speed: Average 40-character-per-second recognition, peak speed 115 cps

Output: Several standard word processing, database, and spreadsheet formats

System Requirements: 286 or 386 PC with Windows, or Mac SE, SE30, Mac II family computer; 1-4Mb RAM available, 4-8Mb hard disk space available, coprocessor board for PCs, MS-DOS 3.1 or later, or Mac System 4.2 or later, a compatible scanner

Post-Scan Image-Enhancement Programs

Quite often, the picture that you scan will be close to what you want as a final product, but not perfect. There may be a telephone pole in the background that looks ugly, or the model may have an unsightly blemish. What you would really like to be able to do is manipulate the image after you've saved it. Scanner software usually offers only marginal abilities to do this, and then usually only if the image is bitmapped. If the image is scanned as line art or grayscale, scanner software normally won't let you manipulate it, and neither will most ordinary graphics programs. Enter image enhancement software. Image enhancement software offers tools for doing all sorts of creative things to your scanned image – edit gray scales, separate backgrounds from foregrounds, select areas and change shading and halftone methods, and much more. ImageStudio by Letraset USA is a good representative of this kind of software.

ImageStudio Specifications:

User Interface: Standard Mac window and interface tools and features, keyboard shortcuts, magnify from 6.25% to 1600%

Tools: All tools can be user customized. In addition to standard paint and drawing tools there are an Air Brush, Water Drop, Charcoal, FingerTip and other tools to mimic those art forms electronically

Graymap Editor: adjust graymap levels, adjust contrast, posterize all or part of an image, solarize all or part of an image, and create a negative image

Effects: Filters that allow the user to blur, sharpen, or otherwise change a selection, trace edges to convert halftones to line art, separate background from foreground, rotate image up to 90°, and preview dithering for bitmaps

Halftone Operations: Create a much wider variety of halftone screens than is possible with conventional camera technology, set density ranges for highlights and shadows to control dot density, customize dot shapes

System Configuration: Minimum Mac Plus or SE, recommended Mac II with 2Mb RAM and a gray level monitor; supports 4-bit video display but gives improved images with 8-bit video card and 256 grayscale monitor

Printer Support: Prints halftones on PostScript compatible printers; dithered bitmaps to nonlaser printers

Custom Display Lettering

New at the time of this writing are programs that will allow manipulation of fonts to create custom effects for display typography. At present, there are two products: LetraStudio, by Letraset USA, and TypeStyler by Brøderbund. LetraStudio works only with fonts from Letraset USA's Electronic Type Library, while TypeStyler will work with Brøderbund's proprietary fonts as well as allow the conversion of any non-Adobe downloadable font into TypeStyler's format.

Basically, these programs take the PostScript description of the characters and present the user with various ways of stretching, shrinking, and arranging the relative sizes of the letters. The author was a beta tester for the Brøderbund product, and the following description is based on the beta version available at the time of this writing.

TypeStyler presents the user with a blank page and a toolbox. Selecting the "A" tool and clicking on the page opens the text specification window. Here the user enters the text to be manipulated. One of the dozen or so Brøderbund fonts that come with the program can be selected, or a conversion made on any Apple or downloadable fonts in the system. The user then makes a choice of text shape from the 35 possible selections including circular, wedge, fish, several kinds of perspectives and slants. Next, one of 35 different type styles is chosen, including numerous drop shadows, fills, borders, etc. Custom fills can also be created, selected, and applied. Pressing a button opens a dialog box from which line, letter, and word spacing can be selected, and other font attributes assigned such as preview and actual display size. Closing the specification window causes the text to be drawn at the selected spot on the page. Once there, the text can be further manipulated. PostScript-style drawing tools can be used to further shrink, stretch, rotate, and twist the lettering. Graphics solids can be drawn and added to the composition, and graphics from other programs can be imported for creating logos, letterheads, etc. Compositions can be exported in a variety of formats for use by other programs.

These are very impressive, very powerful program tools. They aren't the sort of tools one will use on a daily basis, but when that special look needs to be created, one of these text manipulators will be able to make it look right. For desktop publishers working in advertising agencies and the like, one of these programs should be on your "must buy" list.

Large-Screen Displays

Large-screen monitors aren't absolutely necessary for desktop publishing, but they certainly are a godsend, especially for the Macintosh with its small screen. On the small Macs, the large screen is run in addition to the built-in screen, while on the Mac II family and PCs, the large screens are run in lieu of another monitor. In early large screens, one problem for the user was screen curvature. Because of the curved face of the CRT, the image near the edge often suffered barrel distortion – parallel lines weren't parallel, straight vertical lines curved. When the page was printed, everything was as it should be, but the curvature gave layout folks ulcers because the image on the screen didn't *look* right! Newer generations of screens with flatter CRTs have minimized these display problems.

At the time of writing, the following three large-screen monitors are very popular items in this field.

Apple Portrait Display

This is a 15-inch high-resolution monochrome monitor that will show an entire letter-size page on screen at once. The very flat screen and fast screen refresh rate help minimize eyestrain. This monitor works only with the Mac II family of computers, not with the Mac Plus/SE/SE30 series.

Apple Portrait Display Specifications:

CRT: 15 inch (diagonal), square, flat screen; phosphor EIA Type P4 (white; high contrast antiglare surface)
Screen Resolution: 640 pixels horizontal X 870 pixels vertical (at 80 dpi)
Active Video Display Area: 8" horizontal X 10.87" vertical
Connectors: 3 Apple Desktop Bus
Input Signal: Video = analog RS-343 standard; Sync. = separate sync, negative going, TTL
Raster Rates: Vertical = 75Hz; Horizontal = 68.85KHz
Power Requirements: 90-270 volts AC self configuring, 47-63Hz
Size: 13.1" high, 11.5" wide, 14.9" deep

Courtesy of Apple Computer, Inc.

Fig. D.3 The Apple Portrait Display works only with the Mac II, not with original Macs.

Apple Two-Page Monitor

A high resolution 21-inch monochrome monitor that is ideal for multi-window work, desktop publishing, etc. The Apple Two-Page monitor displays two letter-sized pages (portrait) side by side. It comes with a built-in tilt and swivel stand.

Apple Two-Page Monitor Specifications:

CRT: 21- inch (diagonal), square, flat screen; phosphor EIA Type P4 (white; high-contrast antiglare surface)
Screen Resolution: 1152 pixels horizontal X 870 pixels vertical (at 80 dpi)
Active Video Display Area: 15" horizontal X 11.3" vertical
Connectors: 3 Apple Desktop Bus
Input Signal: Video = analog RS-343 standard; Sync. = separate sync, negative going, TTL
Raster Rates: Vertical = 75Hz; Horizontal = 68.7KHz
Dot Clock: 100MHz
Power requirements: 90-270 volts AC self configuring, 47-63Hz
Size: 13.1" high, 11.5" wide, 14.9" deep

Fig. D.4 The Apple Two-Page monitor is a real boom to desktop publishers.

Fig. D.5 For PC desktop publishers, the IBM Model 7554 gives both a two-page display and color.

IBM Model 7554 19" Color Display

The Model 7554 is everything you ever wanted in a color monitor for your PC and more – brilliant color, high resolution, and a two-page display.

IBM Model 7554 Specifications:

CRT: 19 inch diagonal, 16 to 256 colors displayed simultaneously from a palette of 262,144 colors
Screen Resolution: 1640 x 480 pixels in VGA mode, 1024 x 768 pixels in IBM Advanced Function Display mode
Raster Rate: Vertical = 55-85Hz
Dot Pitch: .31mm
Power Requirements: 110-240 volts AC self configuring, 50-60Hz
Size: 15.75" high, 17.75" wide, 18.75" deep

File Transfer

A problem that many desktop publishers run into is that clients or co-workers bring them files from a computer system other than the one they are using for desktop publishing. How can you convert a Mac document to one readable by Ventura Publisher on a PC, or include a MacPaint graphic in your PC PageMaker-generated newsletter?

The easiest way to accomplish cross-system transfers is to have the various machines operating on a common network. Then, files placed on the network server machine are transparent to the various computers connected to the net. In this situation, text files should probably be saved as "text only" to avoid problems with different word processors getting confused with the formatting information embedded in the files. "Text only" mode reduces the contents of the file to the ASCII (international) characters which are recognized by nearly every computer in the world. Special characters that may be available in some computers or programs will appear as "garbage" characters once the transfer takes place, and will have to be replaced as needed. Only in the desktop publishing program computer, where everything comes together, should formatting be added. Likewise, with graphics it is most convenient to save graphics in one of the so-called universal formats such as TIFF, RIFF, or GIF.

For text transfer between non-compatible standalone computers, there are some "magic black box" converters on the market, notably those from Dayna Communications, Inc., which makes a device called the FT100, that attaches to the Macintosh. The box contains a standard 5.25" PC floppy disk drive. Running the FT100 software allows a user to see the contents of both the Mac disk and the PC disk and by selecting a file and clicking a Copy button, transfer from Mac to PC or PC to Mac. The DaynaFile device also plugs into a Mac. It has both a 360K 5.25" PC drive, and a drive for the newer 720K 3.25" floppy disks. With the DaynaFile, a PC disk inserted in it shows up on the Mac desktop as if it were any other floppy disk. Double click to open the disk icon and drag from PC to Mac or Mac to PC disk icon to make the copy. The DaynaFile software also allows some manipulation of PC file extensions and Mac Creator and Type so that transferred files can be formatted for certain applications such as spreadsheets and databases. With both of the Dayna file transfer devices, the safest bet is to save text files in text-only mode, and re-create the formatting once the transfer has been made.

This has been just a small sample of the literally thousands of miscellaneous products related to desktop publishing that are available for the Macintosh and PC computers. The 1989 *Publish!* magazine's second annual Buyers Guide listed over 1500 products. Which ones do you need? Which ones are the best for your desktop publishing setup? Only experience can tell. Ask around. Talk to others who are using desktop publishing in advertising agencies, quick-print shops, printers, etc. Find out what they are using, and whether they think it will be useful for what you want to do.

References & Readings

Alice's Adventures Underground Facimile Edition
by Lewis Carroll
Holt, Reinhart and Winston
Forward & Introduction © 1985
Edition © 1985 Pavilion Books Limited

Art of Desktop Publishing, The
Tony Bove, Cheryl Rhodes, Wes Thomas
© 1986 by Tony Bove, Cheryl Rhodes, Wes Thomas
Bantam Books, New York

Book, The
Douglas C. McMurtrie
© 1943 by Douglas C. McMurtrie
Oxford University Press, London

Book Design: Systematic Aspects
Stanley Rice
© 1978 R.R. Bowker Company

Book Design: Text Format Models
Stanley Rice
© 1978 R.R. Bowker Company

*Chicago Guide to Preparing Electronic Manuscripts
for authors and publishers*
©1987 The University of Chicago Press

Chronology of Printing, A
Colin Clair
© 1969 by Colin Clair
Frederick A. Praeger Publishers, New York

Connections
James Burke
© 1978 by James Burke
Little, Brown and Company, Boston

Designing...For Magazines
Jan V. White
© 1976 R.R. Bowker Company

Desktop Publishing
Frederick E. Davis, John Barry, Michael Wiesenberg
© 1986 Dow Jones-Irwin

Desktop Publishing
Ken Ritvo & Greg Kearsley
© 1986 Park Row Press, La Jolla, CA

Desktop Publishing: Applications & Exercises
Arnold Rosen
© 1989 Harcourt Brace Jovanovich

Desktop Publishing Bible
ed. by James Stockford
© 1987 Howard W. Sams & Co., Indianapolis, IN

Desktop Publishing with your IBM PC & Compatible:
The Complete Guide
Jerry Willis
©1987 Knight-Ridder Press

Desktop Publishing Type & Graphics
A Comprehensive Handbook
Deke McClelland & Craig Danuloff
Publishing Resources Inc.
© 1987 Harcourt Brace Jovanovich

Desktop Publishing with WordPerfect
Roger C. Parker
© 1988 by Roger C. Parker
Ventana Press, Chapel Hill, NC

Dictionary of Publishing, The
David M. Brownstone, Irene M. Franck
© 1982 Van Nostrand Reinhold Co.

Editing by Design
Jan White
© 1979 by Xerox Corp.
R.R. Bowker Company

From Printout to Published
Michael Seidman
© 1988 by Michael Seidman
Sandia Publishing Corporation, Albequerque, NM

From Quill to Computer
Robert F. Karolevitz
© 1985 National Newspaper Foundation
privately printed

Grid Book, The
Jan V. White
© 1987 LetraSet USA

Hackers
Steven Levy
© 1984 Anchor Press, Anchor Press/Doubleday, NY

Highlights in the History of the American Press
edited by Edwin H. Ford and Edwin Emery
© 1954 The University of Minnesota
University of Minnesota Press

History of Computing, The
Marguerite Zientara
© 1981 CW Communications, Inc., Framingham, MA

History of European Printing, A
Colin Clair
© 1976 Colin Clair
Academic Press, Inc., NY & London

How To Do Leaflets, Newsletters and Newspapers
Nancy Brigham with Ann Raszmann & Dick Cluster
© 1982 Nancy Brigham
PEP Publishers, Boston; distributed by Hastings House Publishers

How To Produce a Small Newspaper
by the Editors of the Harvard Post
© 1978 The Harvard Common Press

Illustrated Handbook of Desktop Publishing,The
Michael L. Kleper
© 1987 TAB Professional and Reference Books, Inc.

Layout: The Design of the Printed Page
Allen Hurlburt
© 1977 Allen Hurlburt
Watson-Guptill Publications, NY

Layout and Graphic Design
Raymond A. Ballinger
© 1970 Van Nostrand Reinhold Company

Looking Good in Print: A Guide to Basic Design for Desktop Publishing
Roger C. Parker
© 1988 Ventana Press, Chapel Hill, NC.

Newsletter Publishing with PageMaker; IBM Edition
John A. Barry and Frederic E. Davis, with Todd Egan
© 1988 John A. Barry and Frederic E. Davis
Dow Jones-Irwin Publishers

Observations on the Mystery of Print and the Work of Johann Gutenberg
Hendrik Willem van Loon
© 1937 The Book Manufacturers' Institute
Published at the 1937 Book Manufacturing Exhibit of the Book Manufacturers' Institute, New York

Printing
Clifford Burke
© 1972 Clifford Burke
Wingbow Press, Berkeley, CA

Publication Design
© 1971 & 1976 Allen Hurlburt
Van Nostrand Reinhold Company

Publication Design
Roy Paul Nelson
© 1972, 1978 Wm. C. Brown Company

Publishing Newsletters
Howard Penn Hudson
© 1982 Howard Penn Hudson
Charles Scribner's Sons

Short History of the Printed Word, A
Warren Chappell
© 1970 The New York Times
Alfred A. Knopf, Inc.

So Far: The First Ten Years of a Vision
Rob Price
© 1987 Apple Computer, Inc.
Printed by George Rice & Sons

Writer's Home Companion, The
James Charlton & Lisbeth Mark
© 1987 Franklin Watts Publishers

Glossary

30 Bug: A dingbat that signifies the end of a department or section of a publication.

Above the Fold: The upper half of a newspaper page.

Acknowledgements Page: A page of frontmatter where the author acknowledges those who helped with the book.

Actual Page: The page or piece of paper as it is printed.

Advertisement Page: A page of frontmatter where the publisher lists other titles by the author and publisher.

Antique Book Paper: Heavy, tough, anti-glare stock used in printing books.

Apex: The highest point of characters such as A.

Appendix: A section of a book that contains information related to the subject but not of primary concern. Also used to present reference materials related to the book.

Artwork: A generic term for illustrations of any kind.

Ascenders: Parts of characters that extend above the x-height.

ASCII Format: a "universal" text format that contains only characters and symbols.

Asymmetrical Design: A basic design emphasizing "balanced unbalance."

Backmatter: Also called endmatter; elements of a book after the last chapter.

Baseline: The imaginary line on which rest the bottoms of capitals and the bodies of lowercase letters of a typeface.

Bible Stock: Special thin opaque paper used for printing bibles and other massive books.

Bibliography: A section of backmatter listing books and other publications relevant to the book.

Bitmap: A method of computer graphics creation where the computer stores the state, location, and size of pixels.

Body Type: The type used for the main portions of text in a publication.

Booklet: A bound volume of less than 50 pages.

Border Structure: A basic design style with the elements enclosed in a frame or border.

Broadside: A kind of giant folder (q.v.) or poster-sized publication.

Brochure: An alternative name for a booklet.

Byline: The name of an author as listed in a publication.

Camera-Ready Pasteup: The final form of a publication prior to printing.

Cap-Height: The distance above the baseline to which uppercase characters are drawn.

Capital, Embedded: Initial letter of a paragraph that displaces two or more subsequent lines of body text.

Capital, Illuminated: Initial letter of a paragraph that is surrounded by artistic embellishments.

Capital, Raised: Initial letter of a paragraph that extends above the cap height of the body text.

Caption: Explanatory text for an illustration.

Card: Also called an ad or advertisement; an arrangement of text and graphics intended to sell a product or service.

Carryover: Text that continues beyond its initial column or page.

Casting Off: Calculating or counting the number of words or characters in a manuscript in order to estimate its typeset length.

Chapter Opener: The first page of each chapter in a book; usually designed separately from other chapter pages.

Cicero: The secondary unit of measure in the Didot System of type measurement.

Clip Art: Previously drawn art which can be placed in a publication.

Close Set Type: Also called solid set type; type which has the same leading value as its point size – 12/12, etc.

Coated Stock: A smooth-surfaced paper used in books with high-quality illustrations.

Colophon: A short description in the backmatter of a book describing the typography and other technical details of the book's production.

Color Reversal: A technique for making text stand out by printing the text in one color and its background in another color.

Color Separation: The primary method of printing multicolor illustrations in a publication.

Columns: Vertical arrangements of text on a page.

Come To The Meeting Leaflet: A leaflet inviting the reader to a function.

Condensed Type: Type whose letters are set closer together than normal.

Contoured Text: Text whose letters have been raised, lowered, flipped, or otherwise manipulated to present some overall graphic impression.

Copy Area: The nominally rectangular area of a book page that contains the body of the text.

Copyfitting: The process of turning a manuscript into a rough book format to see how long the finished book will be.

Copyright Notice: The notification of who owns the rights to a particular written work.

Copyright Page: The page in the frontmatter of a book that contains the copyright notice.

Counters: Enclosed or hollow parts of characters.

Cover Lines: Teaser statements related to articles in a magazine intended to draw the browser into buying and reading the publication.

Cropping: Choosing which portion of a piece of art to print.

Dedication Page: The frontmatter page of a book on which the author dedicates his work.

Descenders: Parts of characters that extend below the baseline.

Desktop Publishing: The term, coined by Paul Brainerd, used to distinguish pre-press publishing operations with small (desktop) computers from the same operations performed by large, dedicated typesetting and page composition computers.

Didot: The base unit of measure in the Didot or French Point System of type measure.

Didot System: A system of measuring type size based on the French inch.

Digitizer: A computer input device for electronically recording a drawing or other art.

Display Type: Large type (usually greater than 14 pt) used for headlines or titles.

Double Space Type: Type set with one blank line of space between each two lines of type.

Drop: Also called drop white space; the distance from a title to the first line of copy.

Dummy: A typeset copy of a pasted-up publication made to check copyfit.

Editorial: A functional page design of magazines where the editor speaks to the readers.

Educational Leaflet: A leaflet whose chief purpose is to teach the reader something.

Electronic Page Composition: The electronic equivalent of layout.

Endmatter: The pages of a book after the last chapter and before the back cover.

End Notes: A style of footnoting where all reference notes are gather together at the end of the book.

English Finish Stock: A smoother surfacedversion of Antique Stock with a hard finish.

Facing Pages: Verso and recto pages that face each other across the gutter of a publication when it is opened.

Feature Opener: The initial page (or spread) of a magazine feature article.

Flag: The display type name of a newsletter or newspaper.

Flyer: Also called a leaflet; a single-page, single-sided publication.

Folder: A small publication created from a single piece of paper printed on two sides folded in one of several ways to produce a number of pages or panels.

Font: A complete alphabet and symbol set of one size of one typeface.

Footer: A piece of text or a graphic which appears at the bottom of every page of a publication.

Foreword: Pages of frontmatter explaining or praising a book; written by someone other than the author.

Form: On a hand-press, the adjustable frame into which individual lines of type are locked to create a page of text.

Format: To produce computer material in a specified form.

Four-Color Printing: A process of producing multicolor printed pages by over-printing each page four times (once each for magenta, cyan, yellow, and black).

Franchise Newsletter: A generic newsletter to which the purchaser attaches a flag before printing and distributing to subscribers or patrons.

French Point System: See Didot System.

Frontmatter: Also called preliminaries; the elements of a book which precede the first page of the first chapter.

Full Bleed: A graphic that extends to the edge of the trimmed page.

Full-Justified: Copy aligned on both the left and right margins.

Get On The Bandwagon Leaflet: A leaflet which exhorts its readers to join a cause.

Glossary: A section of backmatter where terms used in a book are defined.

Graphic Block: In a desktop publishing program, an area in which a graphic can be placed.

Graphic Element: A generic term for art in a layout.

Graphic Font: Also called an ornamental or novelty font; a font consisting of pictures rather than alphabetic characters.

Gray Pages: Pages in a publication that are all body copy and visually uninteresting.

Gray Scale: A process of recording an image as continuous graduations of shade from white to black.

Grid Design: A basic design structure where elements are fit into imaginary rectangular areas on the page.

Gutter: The white space between copy areas at the binding of a publication or between columns on a page.

Hairline: A very fine rule used as a decorative element in a design.

Half-Letter Booklet: A booklet made by creating signatures that use one half of a letter-size piece of paper as a page.

Half-Title Page: A single page of frontmatter that contains the title of the book.

Halftone: A picture in which graduations of shade are obtained by the relative density of small dots produced by photographing or recording the art through a fine screen.

Hand Press: A totally mechanical printing press capable of printing one or both sides of a single sheet of paper at a one time.

Head: A nickname for a headline; also the top of a page.

Heading: In a book or magazine, the display type copy which introduces chapters or sections.

Headers: Text or graphic elements which appear at the top of every page of a publication.

Headline: The title of a newspaper or newsletter story.

Illustration: The primary graphic element of a publication; also a synonym for non-photographic artwork.

Imported Text: Text created in a word processing program that is electronically transferred into a desktop publishing program.

Imposition: Also called a signature; an arrangement of pages printed on a large sheet of paper, so that, when folded, the pages will fall in the proper order.

Index: A section of backmatter listing the page locations of specific subjects in a book.

Infographics: Charts and graphs that graphically portray information.

Intaglio Printing: A printing technique where the design to be printed is recessed into a surface and the hollows are filled with ink.

Integrated Circuit: An electronic component that takes the place of transistors.

Interneg: The negative made when taking a photograph of a positive print so that print can be reproduced.

Introduction: A section of frontmatter that, like a foreword or preface, helps set the stage for the reader of a book.

Invisible Book Design: A style of design where the typography and other design elements are not intrusive on the reader.

Justification: The alignment of lines of copy.

Kerning: The process of adjusting type so that characters fit closely together in a word.

Layout: The process of arranging both text and graphics as they will appear on the printed page. All publications must be laid either out mechanically or electronically.

Layout Master: Also called an electronic blueline; the background on which typographic and graphic elements are arranged to produce a layout.

Laser Font: A computerized type family specifically designed for use with a laser printer.

Leading: The amount of space between lines of type.

Leaflet: See Flyer.

Left Opener: A magazine article or book chapter which begins on a verso page.

Legal Size: Paper that is 8.5" X 14" in size.

Letter Size: Paper that is 8.5" X 11" in size.

Ligatures: Common character pairs that are permanently kerned and are typed with a single keystroke.

Link: An electronic process that causes text to flow from one Text Block to another.

Lithography: An early printing process in which drawings were carved into the surface of a smooth stone block.

Logo: A graphic used to identify an organization or publication.

Logo Font: A font which contains a company logo that can be displayed by tapping appropriate keys.

Logotype: The distinctive style of lettering used with a logo.

Lowercase Letters: Non-capital letters of a typeface.

Mailing Information Block: Also called a mailer; the area on a publication containing the return address of the publication, postage or the postage meter number, and the mailing label of the subscriber.

Margin: The white space between a copy area and the trimmed edges of a publication.

Masthead: A block of text in a publication which lists the editors and other staff, subscription information, addresses, and other information.

Matrix: In handmade type, the piece of metal stamped with a character which is placed in a mold that casts the letters.

Mechanical: The physical equivalent of a Layout Master (q.v.).

Microprocessor: A special kind of integrated circuit (IC) that contains all of the functionality of a large computer's central processing unit.

Mood Book Design: A style of design where the typography and other elements are intended to "set the reader up" as to the content and style of the text.

Mouse: A computer input device used extensively when doing electronic drawing.

Multicolor Print: A publication printed in colors other than black and white.

Nameplate: Another name for a newsletter Flag (q.v.).

Newsletter: A coverless periodical that generally contains no advertising.

Non-Laser Font: A type family created by bitmap graphics, not intended for use with a laser printer.

Non-Proportional Type: A style of type where all characters, regardless of their actual width, occupy the same amount of line space.

Object-Oriented Graphics: A method of computer drawing where the computer essentially records a mathematical equation describing the shapes of objects and their locations on the virtual page.

OCR: An achronym for Optical Character Recognition. A process of electronically recording printed text and making it manipulatable by a word processing program.

Offset Printing: A common method of printing where the image is transferred from the printing plate to an intermediary roller (offset) before it is transferred to the paper.

Offset Stock: Special paper used for offset printing.

One Shot: A publication with a single, limited purpose.

Opener: The first page(s) of a magazine feature. May be a left page, right page, or two-page spread.

Organizational Newsletter: A newsletter produced by and for the members of an organization rather than a more general public.

Orphan: A short line of copy standing alone at the top of a column or page.

Page: One side of one piece of paper bound in a publication.

Panel: A portion of a folder treated as a page of text.

Pantographic Engraving: A process for reproducing a piece of art or type to any desired scale, simultaneously engraving it on some medium.

Parchment: An early writing medium created from the skins of animals.

Photoengraving: A process of engraving by transferring a photographic image to a surface and then etching it in relief.

Phototypesetting: A process of typesetting wherein images of the characters are projected onto photographic film which is then used to make the printing plates.

Pica: The secondary unit of measurement in the American Point System.

Pictogram: Another term for an ornamental or graphic font (q.v.).

Picture Block: See Graphic Block.

Pitch: A typewriter unit of character measure; the number of charcters per inch of line length.

Pixel: An achronym for picture element; the indivisible unit of a computer screen, graphic, or printer output.

Plate Stock: See English Finish Stock.

Point: The basic unit of measure in the American Point System of type measurement.

Poster: Another term for a Leaflet (q.v.).

PostScript: A page description computer language used extensively with microcomputers.

Preface: A section of frontmatter, written by the author, used to describe and content of a book and promote its purchase.

Preferred Position: In magazine parlance, advertising space either near a major feature or inside the covers.

Preliminaries: See Frontmatter.

Printed Resolution: The quality or clarity of a computer graphic as output by a particular type of printer.

Proportional Type: a style of type where each character occupies a unique width of a line of type.

Pseudo Flash Form: A device used by magazines to separate news from features. It does not contain truly late-breaking news, but rather short news items grouped together under a single heading.

Public Domain: Works of art which may be freely copied and used with permission.

Public Relations Newsletter: A newsletter used to promote products as well as provide information for product users.

Pull Quote: Also known as a call out or pull out; important, interesting, or provocative phrases from the body copy that are enlarged and set off from the body and heads.

Ragged Left: Copy whose lines are aligned on the right margin but not the left.

Ragged Right: Copy whose lines are aligned on the left margin but not the right.

Recto: Right-facing pages.

Registration Marks: Tiny crossed lines used to align items in multi-color printing.

Reversal: Text set white against a black background, or black against a gray or colored background, or colored text set against a black or colored background.

Reversed Out: Text set as a reversal.

Right Opener: The initial page of a chapter or article beginning on a recto page.

Rotated Text: Text that has been turned about one or more axes.

Royalty: Payments made to an author by a publisher for books which have been sold; based on a percentage of the cover or wholesale price of the book.

Rule: A decorative line; also a nickname for a ruler.

Runaround: Text that is set around the top, bottom, and sides of a graphic.

Saddle Stitch: A method of binding a publication by sewing or stapling through the central fold of an imposition.

Sans Serif: A style of type where the characters have no extensions at the ends of the strokes.

Scaling: The process of shrinking or enlarging a graphic to fit the required space in a publication.

Scanner: A device for electronically recording artwork.

Screen Resolution: The number of pixels per inch on a computer screen.

Secondary illustration: Any illustration other than the main illustration.

Self-Mailer: A publication that has the Mailing Information Block on its cover so that it does not need to be enclosed in an envelope to be mailed.

Serif: Lines or strokes which project beyond the main strokes of a character.

Side: A printing surface of a piece of paper. Each piece of paper has two sides.

Sidebar: A technique for enclosing related information within the body of a publication.

Side Stitch: A method of binding a publication by sewing through the side of an imposition near the central fold.

Signature: Another name for an imposition (q.v.); also a synonym for a logotype (q.v.).

Specification Sheet: A technical description of the tyopography, design, and layout of a book.

Spillover: Text that exceeds the boundaries of a Text Block.

Spread: Also called a two-page spread or facing-page spread; consecutively numbered recto and verso pages which can be viewed simultaneously, and treated as a single unit for design purposes.

Stand-Off: The distance between runaround text and the graphic it is running around.

Standing Elements: Elements that appear in every issue of a publication.

Stock: Another name for paper.

Strokes: The major lines that make up a character.

Subhead: A title for a subdivision of a publication that is of lesser importance than the head.

Subscription Newsletters: Newsletters that are available only by subscribing to the publication or joining the group that publishes the newsletter.

Subscript: Characters that drop partially or totally below the baseline of the text.

Superscript: Characters raised partially or totally above the cap-height of the text.

Swash: Decorative flourishes on characters.

Symmetrical Design: A basic design structure where all elements are centered on a page.

Syndicated Newsletters: See Franchise Newsletter.

Tabloid Size: Paper that is 11" X 17" in size.

Terminals: The ends of character strokes.

Text: Also called body; the major portion of most publications.

Text Blocks: In a desktop publishing program, an area in which typing can be done.

Thumbnails: Miniature sketches of layouts used to help establish continuity.

TIFF: An achronym for a Tagged Image Format File; one of several "universal" file formats for electronic graphics.

Tiling: The electronic division of larger-than-paper-sized virtual pages into paper-sized units for printing.

Title Page: The page or pages of frontmatter where the title of a book is displayed.

Toolbox: A collection of virtual computer tools for drawing, writing, or layout.

Trademark: Also called a logo; a registered graphic or text and graphic element that identifies a company or product.

Transistor: An electronic component.

Trim Size: The dimensions to which typeset book pages will be cut.

Tympan: In a hand press, the pressure distribution plate which goes between the type form and the platen.

Type: Carved or cast characters of an alphabet used for printing, and their electronic equivalents.

Typeface: A particular design of an alphabet.

Type Family: A group of all related sizes and styles derived from a master typeface.

Typeset: The process of putting a manuscript in the typeface, leading, etc. for publication.

Typestyle: A 17th century division of typefaces into five basic groups.

Typewriter: An electromechanical device that took much of the drudgery out of creating clean, easy-to-read manuscripts.

Typography: The art and craft of planning, selecting, and setting of type for a printed work.

Uppercase Letters: Capital letters of an alphabet.

Vellum: A high-quality parchment (q.v.).

Verso: Left-facing pages.

Vertex: The low point of a character such as V.

Virtual Page: The page as created by the computer before it is printed.

White Space: The space around or between text or graphics.

Widow: A short line of copy standing alone at the bottom of a column or page.

Woodblock Printing: A kind of printing where a design is raised above the surface of a block of wood.

WYSIWYG: An achronym for What You See Is What You Get; computer jargon meaning that the image of the document seen on the computer screen is the same as what will come out when the document is printed.

X-Height: The height of the body of most lowercase characters in a typeface.

Index